PATTERNS

PATTERNS

FOUR TELEVISION PLAYS WITH THE AUTHOR'S PERSONAL COMMENTARIES

Rod Serling

With a
Foreword
by
Mark
Dawidziak

Copyright ©1955, 1956, 1957 by Rod Serling. Renewed copyright © 1983, 1984, 1985 by Carol K. Serling, Anne C. Serling, and Jodi S. Serling. All rights reserved.

Introduction copyright © Mark Dawidziak

Cover copyright © Sam Serling-Sutton

ISBN 13: 9781505707465

For my wife, Carol

Publication of these original books is done in tribute to Rod Serling, whose concern for the well-being of humanity still resonates with all who are exposed to his work.

CONTENTS

Foreword	IX
About Writing for Television	XXIII
Patterns	1
Act One	3
Act Two	25
Act Three	39
Author's Commentary On Patterns	49
The Rack	57
Act One	59
Act Two	74
Act Three	97
Author's Commentary On The Rack	108
Old Macdonald Had A Curve	115
Act One	117
Act Two	131
Act Three	142
Author's Commentary On Old Macdonald Had A Curve	154
Requiem For A Heavyweight	157
Act One	158
Act Two	188

Act Three 210
Author's Commentary On Requiem For A Heavyweight 223

About The Author 228

FOREWORD

By Mark Dawidziak

Rod Serling was the most recognized writer on the planet. During the 1960s and '70s, people who couldn't pick Norman Mailer or Saul Bellow out of a police lineup knew Rod Serling. They knew the voice, the face, the mannerisms.

The Twilight Zone did that. It turned a well-known and acclaimed writer into that awful and bewilderingly amorphous American creation – a celebrity. It's a status that few writers attain. Mark Twain pulled if off before Rod Serling. There aren't many in their league.

And, let's face it, if you recognize the name Rod Serling, and there's every good chance you do, it's undoubtedly because you have spent some quality time in that "wondrous land whose boundaries are that of imagination." At some point, you crossed over into *The Twilight Zone*. It is, without question, his towering contribution to American culture and American literature (yes, make no mistake, literature). Serling was the beloved anthology show's creator, iconic host, and principal writer (penning a staggering ninety-two of the 156 episodes).

But keep in mind that Serling, if not yet a mega-watt celebrity, was a well-known and acclaimed writer before he opened *The Twilight Zone* for business on October 2, 1959. Keep it in mind because that's what the book in your hand is all about.

Many are fond of quoting F. Scott Fitzgerald's line about there being no second acts in American lives. They're probably misusing the line, since there's evidence that Fitzgerald didn't believe it. Anyone with doubts about the line can happily point to Serling's career, which more than refutes this oft-cited sentiment. It obliterates the whole notion of no second acts. That's because *The Twilight Zone* WAS the second act.

The illustrious first act, of course, was Serling's mighty contributions to television's golden age of the drama anthology. Serling lived such a crowded life, he even managed a post-*Twilight Zone* third act before his death at fifty on June 28, 1975. It featured honored TV movies, screenplays, and his contributions to the NBC horror anthology *Night Gallery*. None of this would have happened, however, without the landmark work for the live dramas of the 1950s. First published in July 1957, well before anyone had ever heard of *The Twilight Zone*, this book is representative of that work. It not only contains his two greatest "golden age" scripts, *Patterns* and *Requiem for a Heavyweight*, it features Serling's remarkably candid commentary on his writing, on writing for television, and on being a writer.

Patterns and *Requiem for a Heavyweight* make this volume valuable. Serling's engaging introduction and four wonderfully frank commentaries make it invaluable. Anyone interested in knowing what made Rod Serling tick should read these sections, word by illuminating word. Anyone interested in the history of television should read them. Everyone interested in the writing process should read them.

Here is an in-the-trenches view of what it was like in those heady days of live television – the challenges, the compromises, the adrenalin rushes, the limitations, the arguments, the rewards. Here is a writer proud of what he accomplished, yet unsparing in his appraisal of where scripts came up short. Here is a young artist challenging himself and the infant medium where he has found a home. Here is a man who sees the possibilities, fully realizing how incredibly difficult they are to attain. Here is a man pushing himself to meet his own high standards, knowing those standards are not measured by how many Emmy awards they hand you. Here is the path that leads to *The Twilight Zone*.

Two years before the frustrations of dealing with sponsors and network censorship drove him into "a dimension as vast as space and timeless as infinity," Serling cautioned that television drama could get stuck in "its own creative rut by not fighting for something a little bit better, and not looking for something that is new." This is a call to arms for the television industry, for the audience, for the critics, and for himself. After the publication of this book, Serling will go on fighting for something better, and he will do it by finding something fantastically new.

"I don't know where I'm going and I'm not sure where I am," he wrote in this book.

Submitted for your approval: picture of a writer who has made all of his dreams come true. He is championed by the critics. He has a loving wife and two lovely daughters. He has a wide circle of devoted friends. He is about to win his third Emmy. He doesn't know it, but he's at a crossroads. That's the signpost up ahead. His next stop – *The Twilight Zone*.

Before he got there, though, Serling was lionized as one of the writers responsible for putting the gleam on television's so-called Golden Age. At the height of those heady times, he often was called the medium's "angry young man." Yet he doesn't sound angry in these essays or these television plays. He sounds like the Rod Serling we'll get to know in *The Twilight Zone*, in interviews, in *Night Gallery*. He sounds confident, but that confidence is tempered by the ready admission of nagging doubts and insecurities. He is candid, but that straightforward nature is laced with a sense of irony and a self-deprecating sense of humor. He is dubious, yet underlying his concerns is a strong dose of optimism. You almost can picture Rod grinning at you from behind a hand holding a lit cigarette. That's the absolute joy of his debut book. You get to spend time with Rod and with four of the plays that put him on the map as a writer.

Stepping back and looking at the career of an artist, you often can spot that moment of arrival. For Rod Serling, that moment was January 12, 1955. This was the night that NBC's *Kraft Television Theater* aired the live production of *Patterns*, Serling's riveting play about a young executive hired by the hard-driving, hard-hearted president of a major corporation. A record of what happened that night survives thanks to kinescope, the filming of a television program by setting up a camera in front of a video monitor. The picture quality, as you might imagine, is not the sharpest, but you can plainly see why this drama inspired *New York Times* critic Jack Gould to write: "Nothing in months has excited the television industry as much as the *Kraft Television Theatre*'s production of *Patterns*, an original play by Rod Serling. The enthusiasm is justified. In writing, acting and direction, *Patterns* will stand as one of the high points in the TV medium's evolution." It was an amazingly prophetic evaluation on Mr. Gould's part. The *Times* reviewer added that, "For sheer power of narrative, forcefulness of characterization and brilliant climax, Mr. Serling's work is a creative triumph."

Serling's assessment: ". . . it was good, perhaps better than good."

Indeed, it was. The cast was superb, led by Richard Kiley as idealistic Manhattan newcomer Fred Staples, Ed Begley as aging and vulnerable Andy Sloane, and Everett Sloane as ruthless boss Walter Ramsey. Fiedler Cook was the talented director for this 463rd presentation of *Kraft Television Theatre* (which started its illustrious run on May 7, 1947, when Serling was twenty-two, attending Antioch College in Ohio, and dating education and psychology major Carolyn Louise Kramer). But it was Serling's writing that truly caused a sensation.

For Serling, this was one of those overnight successes that took years of struggle and patient attention to craft. He had written seventy-one television scripts before hitting this prime-time home run. He was thirty years old.

Intriguing autobiographical touches can be spotted here and there in *Patterns*. Consciously or not, Rod Serling gave his lead character a name that followed the, uh, pattern of his own: same number of syllables, first name ending in a 'd', last name starting with an 'S.' Like Fred Staples, Rod Serling had moved from Cincinnati, where he was pegged as a talented young man with great potential. Like Staples, Serling had a wife supportive of his career choices. Like Staples, he was living in Connecticut. Like Staples, he was doing everything in his power to do good work in a competitive business that often challenged principles and demanded compromise.

If Serling's experiences in television didn't shape the plot and themes of *Patterns*, they certainly informed it.

Early in the drama, a secretary played by twenty-one-year-old Elizabeth Montgomery says, "You never know when you're going to hit a nerve." *Patterns* hit a nerve, all right, rocketing Serling to the head of television's star class of writers. The two writers who most came to symbolize the Golden Age were Serling and Paddy Chayefsky, whose tale of a lonely Bronx butcher, *Marty*, aired to great acclaim in May 1953. Small wonder they were the first two writers specializing in drama inducted into the Academy of Television Arts & Sciences' Hall of Fame.

To fully appreciate how and why Rod Serling became a star in the 1950s, you must start with the realization that TV very much needed stars in the 1950s. With this upstart medium sweeping the nation, the major film studios went to war. Television was keeping Americans home with free entertainment, and the studio bosses were fighting to protect their endangered territory. Film stars were told in no uncertain terms that they should not consort with the enemy. Television had little leverage and less money to compete for talent back then, so programmers' answer was to make their own stars. This included writers, and the outgoing, articulate Serling had charisma, drive, and talent to spare.

"I have never ceased liking publicity," Serling admits in this book. "This isn't ego for its own sake, because I don't drop names and I don't purposely seek it. But I still get a kick when I see my name in the paper, and I probably always will."

Rod and Paddy were in good company. Also contributing distinguished scripts to live dramas were Gore Vidal, Horton Foote, J.P. Miller, Tad Mosel, William Gibson, Helene Hanff, Robert Alan Aurthur, Reginald Rose, Ernest Kinoy, and Ira Levin.

Plays by these writers "were stamped with that particular quality that forced recognition," Serling commented. Their stories were compelling reasons for Americans to stay home, anxious to see what this new medium had to offer.

"The medium began to show a cognizance of its own particular fortes," Serling observed. "It had the immediacy of the living theater, some of the flexibility of the motion pictures, and the coverage of radio. It utilized all three in developing and improving what was actually a new art form. As indicated previously by the plays on *Kraft, Studio One* and *Celanese Theatre*, one could see that the television play was beginning to show depth and a preoccupation with character. Its plots and its people were becoming meaningful. Its stories had something to say."

Patterns had a great deal to say about ambition, competition, talent, success, decency, ethics, power, and the misuse of power. Like Arthur Miller's *Death of a Salesman*, it spoke eloquently about the value and dignity of each human life, and the need for that dignity to be recognized. It indicted a culture – any culture – that views age and experience as disposable items to be pushed toward the scrap heap. It cautioned the individual to beware of those moments that tempt what Serling called a "minimum set of ethics." The dilemma: "When he refuses to compromise those ethics, his career must suffer; when he does compromise them, his conscience does the suffering." It's symbolically perfect that this play and this book are titled *Patterns*, because they established patterns Serling would follow for the rest of his career. These are themes he would revisit again and again, examining them through an ever-changing prism altered by age and experience.

Fred Staples is climbing the corporate ladder in *Patterns*. Andy Sloane is on his way down. Four years later, in one of Serling's best *Twilight Zone* episodes, thirty-six-year-old business executive Martin Sloan (Gig Young) is wearying of the rat race and yearning for a simpler time in "Walking Distance." Martin Sloan is looking backwards, but if he could see himself a few years in the future, he might be looking at Andy Sloane.

Already farther down that road is Gart Williams (James Daly), the main character in another of Serling's exceptional *Twilight Zone* excursions, "A Stop at Willoughby." Hounded by a Ramsey-like "what-have-you-done-for-me-lately" boss, Gart Williams already knows the demons haunting Andy Sloane. And, as Marc Scott Zicree points out in his excellent book *The Twilight Zone Companion*, Serling's finest script for *Night Gallery*, "They're Tearing Down Tim Riley's Bar," is pretty much a companion piece to *Patterns* and "Walking Distance" (although I'd add the stop at "Willoughby" to this ongoing journey). At forty-five, Serling told the story of Randy Lane (William Windom), a tired, disillusioned business executive desperately trying to hold on to the ladder rungs, but losing his grip, nonetheless, and slipping down and down. Zicree rightly notes that this *Night Gallery* story "represents Serling at his best, writing with an insight and power the equal of anything he had done before."

Patterns, "Walking Distance," and "They're Tearing Down Tim Riley's Bar" "offer a progression of what is essentially the same character at different points in his life," say Scott Skelton and Jim Benson in their comprehensive book, *Rod Serling's Night Gallery: An*

After-Hours Tour. "All three characters hold up a mirror to Serling as he responds to the fortunes of his career."

Unquestionably true, but the other characters and other pieces, like "A Stop at Willoughby," add significant threads to the tapestry. You can follow the path that leads from Fred Staples to Martin Sloan to Randy Lane. You also can trace the thread that takes you from Andy Sloane to Gart Williams to Randy Lane. It's not as clean or direct, perhaps, yet it is no less fascinating.

You can just dwell on how the choice of names seem to echo each other: Sloane to Sloan, Andy to Randy . . . patterns, indeed.

These are merely some of the themes you see established in the four plays selected by Serling for his first book. There are more – much more, so you can view this volume as both the astonishing fulfillment of a dynamic young talent and the promise of searing works to come.

When we first meet Fred Staples in *Patterns*, he is about to board the elevator that will take him up to the executive offices and into television history.

"You've arrived, Mr. Staples," his wife, Fran, tells him.

It could have been Carol Serling telling her husband, "You've arrived, Mr. Serling."

Yes, he had, and the sensation caused by *Patterns* cleared the way for a presentation of Serling's *The Rack* on *The U.S. Steel Hour*. Aired three months later, on April 12, 1955, and also chosen by Serling for this volume, *The Rack* was a provocative drama about a mentally tortured American POW accused of collaborating with his North Korean captors. A former Army paratrooper scarred physically and emotionally during World War II, Serling wasn't about to make it easy on himself or his audience. He delved into many sides of a thorny issue, managing to make all the viewpoints sympathetic.

While impressed, some critics griped that *The Rack* wasn't another *Patterns*. It was a complaint that Serling would grow tired of hearing during this typically prolific phase of his career. "By and large I think *The Rack* is one of the most honest things I have ever written," Serling said in the commentary following the second television play in this book.

The third play in the collection, *Old MacDonald Had a Curve*, actually was aired by *Kraft Television Theatre* before *Patterns* – on August 5, 1953. It tells of an ex-major league pitcher, irascible Maxwell "Firebrand Lefty" MacDonald (Olin Howlin), who frequently exaggerates his record while charging down memory lane at the Carterville Home for the Aged. A freak accident leaves Lefty with an unhittable curve ball. Although sixty-seven, he decides to try out for his old team, the Brooklyn Nationals, who are languishing in last place. The Nationals need a miracle. Lefty needs a new lease on life.

Not all of Serling's comedies sailed out of the strike zone, so to speak. Such delightful *Twilight Zone* episodes as "Night of the Meek" and "Mr. Garrity and the Graves" are whimsical proof of that. But he had a surer hand with drama, and *Old MacDonald Had a Curve* is the slightest of the four works in this book. That's not say it's a bad script. It is, in fact, a charming, life-affirming tale that happily foreshadows the fantasy flourishes of *The Twilight Zone*. Looking for more patterns? Again indulging his great love of baseball, Serling reworked this idea for "The Mighty Casey," a first-season episode of *The Twilight Zone*. This time, a robot seemingly was the answer to a miserable team's prayers, but, in both, the long-suffering manager is named Mouth McGarry. Jack Warden is featured in both.

"I think it did show, even at this relatively early date, something of my later preoccupation with the age-youth problem, so obvious in *Patterns*," Serling wrote in the commentary for *Old MacDonald Had a Curve*. We already know it would continue to be a preoccupation.

Still, any teleplay would suffer in comparison to the other three in this volume. Serling almost certainly included it as something of a change-up pitch for the collection, and, as such, it works very well. It fully justifies his own judgment: "*Old MacDonald* was fun to write. And I think it was fun to watch." It's also fun to read.

If 1955 was the year of arrival for Rod Serling, the following year was what confirmed his stature as an important new writer. There were film versions of *Patterns* (with Sloane, Begley, and Van Heflin replacing Kiley as Fred) and *The Rack* (with Paul Newman in the role played by Marshall Thompson on television). On March 17, 1956, Serling won the first of his six Emmys (it was, of course, for *Patterns*). And on October 11, 1956, *Playhouse 90* premiered one of the most triumphant dramas ever written (or ever will be written) for television, *Requiem for a Heavyweight*.

This is Serling summoning all of his considerable powers and delivering the knockout blow. He worried that his career would always be defined by *Patterns* – measured by it. While *The Rack* was greatly admired by many critics, Serling still was that guy who wrote *Patterns*. *Requiem for a Heavyweight* was stirring proof that the writer could reach back and throw an even more devastating dramatic punch. It was proof, as Serling said, that *Patterns* "was not a happy accident."

During his Army days, Serling had climbed into the ring for eighteen bouts (winning seventeen of them). He earned an appreciation of the Sweet Science (and a broken nose). *Requiem for a Heavyweight* is the story of Harlan "Mountain" McClintock, a one-time contender on his way to Punchy Land. The doctor says his fighting days are done, but he only knows boxing. Meanwhile, his manager, Maish, is deep in debt. Absorbing horrific punishment in his last fight, Mountain managed to stay on his feet until the seventh round. Maish bet that his aging fighter wouldn't last three rounds.

Now a desperate Maish is pushing the proud Mountain to become a wrestler. Mountain's loyal handler, an ex-boxer named Army, knows this will hurt more than any punch. As battered as he is, Mountain is holding on to the dignity of a bruiser who never threw a fight and always gave Maish and fight fans everything he had. Now Maish wants to strip away whatever dignity is left.

"You're not a winner anymore, Mountain," Maish tells the washed-up fighter who has left so much of himself behind in smoke-filled arenas. "And that means there's only one thing left – make a little off the losing."

Everything fell into place for this three-act *Playhouse 90* drama. Jack Palance, stunningly convincing as a thick-voiced pug, didn't make a wrong move as Mountain. "There are times in a career of a writer when a single performance in a play can add such a fantastic dimension and moving quality that the role appears to have been molded into the actor's shape," Serling wrote of Palance's portrayal.

Keenan Wynn, so memorable as defense attorney Steve Wasnik in *The Rack*, found all the many levels Serling envisioned in the deeply conflicted Maish. Wynn's father, comedian Ed Wynn, overcame a shaky rehearsal period to deliver a moving performance as the sympathetic Army. And Kim Hunter made the most of every moment on screen as Grace, the social worker trying to help Mountain. While the characteristically self-critical Serling thought Grace could have been better drawn, she couldn't have been better played.

The sets, Ralph Nelson's direction, the pacing – it all clicked. Towering above all, however, was Serling's writing, properly recognized with the Emmy for best teleplay on March 16, 1957. *Requiem for a Heavyweight* also won the Emmys for program of the year, best single performance by an actor (Palance), and best direction. A film version appeared in 1962, with Anthony Quinn, Jackie Gleason, Mickey Rooney, and Julie Harris. Like the film adaptation of *Patterns*, it was good, but not as good as what aired on television. So the scripts for *Patterns* and *Requiem for a Heavyweight* are the tent poles at either end of this collection, representing Serling at the very top of his game as a writer pushing a new medium toward the possibilities of becoming a true art form. In 1958, Serling won his third consecutive writing Emmy, this one for *The Comedian*, his *Playhouse 90* adaptation of Ernest Lehman's novella about a bullying, egomaniacal television comedian (played by Rooney). Edmond O'Brien, Kim Hunter, and Mel Torme also were in the cast.

Just as Serling would return to the baseball diamond for "The Mighty Casey," he would revisit the boxing ring for "The Big Tall Wish," another first-season episode of *The Twilight Zone*. A fifth-season episode by Richard Matheson, "Steel," has a futuristic *Requiem* ring to it (although here, the manager is the one put through the ringer).

Looking forward to *The Twilight Zone* and *Night Gallery*, you can see dozens of specific casting connections, as well as those many thematic threads. Warden, who also starred in Serling's outstanding first-season *Twilight Zone* episode "The Lonely," wouldn't be the only actor from one of these four plays to appear in future Serling projects. *Patterns* star Everett Sloane had top billing in Serling's "The Fever," a first-season episode of *The Twilight Zone*. Richard Kiley starred in "Escape Route," one of the three Serling stories in the 1969 *Night Gallery* movie. Elizabeth Montgomery was featured in writer-director Montgomery Pittman's "Two," which opened the third season of *The Twilight Zone*. Ed Wynn starred in two *Twilight Zone* installments: Serling's "One for the Angels" and Richard DeRoy's reworking of a GeorgeClayton Johnson story, "Ninety Years Without Slumbering." And Keenan Wynn had the lead in the episode that ended the first season of *The Twilight Zone*, Matheson's comedy "A World of His Own."

Looking for themes that will recur in Serling's work, you'll be able to identify many of what he might have called preoccupations: the fundamentally decent person tossed into the middle of a morally ambiguous situation; the worn-out professional coping with dissatisfaction, obsolescence, or just being forgotten; the aging warrior striving to keep on his feet as the ground is being cut out from under him; the worth of the individual; the yearning for simpler times; the enduring spirit battling to survive under the merciless assault of forces beyond one beleaguered person's control.

Again and again, Serling will be drawn to the individual faced with a moral crisis, a midlife crisis, a crisis of quiet desperation. We've all been there, or will be there, and it's this recognition that makes Serling's writing so incredibly timely and timeless.

That's the continuing magic of Serling's stories. Some writers' work seems as fresh and as relevant as the day it first appeared. Their writing transcends eras and fashions. This is yet another comparison point between Rod Serling and Mark Twain, two distinctly American writers who enjoyed spending summers with their families at beloved upstate New York retreats (Twain at his sister-in-law's Quarry Farm in Elmira, Serling at the Lake Cayuga cottage near Ithaca). Serling's work, as this collection so forcefully demonstrates, was incredibly relevant when it was first produced. It remains incredibly relevant today. And it will be relevant 500 years from now when *The Twilight Zone* is being shown on some distant planet where humans have taken a slight step into the galaxy.

Serling was very much a man of his time, becoming a part of an emerging medium at a fortunate moment when he could fully explore his passions and exploit his abilities. Fortunate for him. Fortunate for us. It was the ideal place and time for Serling, who recognized the possibilities and seized them. But the best of his writing, from *Patterns* to "They're Tearing Down Tim Riley's Bar," has a quality best described by those three words Serling penned for a *Twilight Zone* introduction – "timeless as infinity."

I've been a television critic for more than thirty years, and, during that time, I've interviewed dozens upon dozens of writers and producers responsible for hours and hours of superlative television. The writer most named as an inspiration, a profound influence, and a hero is Rod Serling. These are not just writers specializing in science-fiction, horror, and fantasy. These are writers of all kinds. They responded to their hero's declaration, "For us the heartening thing is that there are still things to strive for." They are the artists who heard Serling's challenge to fight "for something a little bit better."

And like the hero of *Requiem for a Heavyweight*, Rod kept fighting, kept swinging. He had the boxer's mentality. You don't stop swinging. You keep throwing leather until the man rings the bell, ending the fight . . . or the man counts ten. There is something deeply heroic about how he kept fighting. The whirlwind energy and social conscience that powered script after script reminds one of President Benjamin Harrison's description of a young Theodore Roosevelt: "He wanted to put an end to all the evil in the world between sunrise and sunset."

Serling knew he couldn't put an end to evil, injustice, ignorance, prejudice, greed, and cruelty, but he could blast away at them with every weapon in his writer's arsenal, every storytelling tool at his disposal.

One more Mark Twain parallel. In 2009, Hal Holbrook addressed a group of Twain scholars assembled at Elmira College. "We need someone to tell us the truth," he said. "Not twist it, not make it their own territory, but to tell us the truth."

That's also why we still need Rod Serling, sixty years after the airing of *Patterns*. It's why we'll continue to need him.

ABOUT WRITING FOR TELEVISION

THERE IS probably no single "absolute" anyone can use as a yardstick to describe the nature of the television writer, his background, his fortes, or the nature of his advent into the realm of television writing—save for the simple statement that there are no absolutes.

The TV writer is never trained to be a TV writer. There are no courses, however specialized and applied, that will catapult him into the profession. And it was especially true back in the twilight days of radio that coincided with the primitive beginnings of television that the television playwrights evolved—and were never born. In my case the decision to become a television writer arose from no professional master plan. I was on the writing staff of a radio station in the Midwest. Staff writing is a particularly dreamless occupation characterized by assembly-line writing almost around the clock. It is a highly variable occupation—everything from commercials and fifteen-second public-service announcements to half-hour documentary dramas. In a writing sense, it serves its purpose. It teaches a writer discipline, a time sense for any kind of mass-media writing, and a technique. But it also dries up his creativity, frustrates him, and tires him out.

It's axiomatic that the beginning free-lance writer must have some sort of economic base from which he operates. Usually it is a job with at least a subsistence wage to give him rent money and three square meals a day while he begins the treacherous and highly unsure first months of writing on his own. The most desirable situation encompasses an undemanding job that draws little out of the writer's mind during the working day so that his nocturnal writing will be fresh, inspired and undiverted. In my case this was a wish but never a reality.

I used to come home at seven o'clock in the evening, gulp down a dinner and set up my antique portable typewriter on the kitchen table. The first hour would then be spent closing all the mental gates and blacking out all the impressions of a previous eight hours of writing. You have to have a pretty selective brain for this sort of operation. There has to be the innate ability to single-track the creative processes. And after a year or so of this kind of problem, you have rent receipts, fuel for the furnace and a record of regular eating; but you have also denied yourself, as I did, a basic "must" for every writer. And this is simple solitude—physical and mental.

The process of writing cannot be juggled with another occupation. The job of creating cannot be compartmentalized with certain hours devoted to one kind of creation and other hours set aside for still another. Writing is a demanding profession and a selfish one. And because it is selfish and demanding, because it is compulsive and exacting, I didn't embrace it. I succumbed to it.

I can pinpoint the day and almost the hour that it happened for me. After two years of double-shift writing, I had made approximately six sales to network television programs. These weren't bad scripts. There was usually a kind of strength to them that showed in dialogue and a sense of character. But they were stamped with the lack of professional polish. They showed in many ways that they were done on a kitchen table during the eleventh and twelfth and thirteenth hours of a working day. They were always sharpened, but never to their finest points.

So, on a midwinter day, I gave in to free-lance writing. This was not the overtly courageous plunge that some writers make. In my case I had just finished a three-week assignment as a staff radio writer, planning a documentary series designed to honor certain towns and cities in the listening area. (In regional radio, adjoining localities are forever being honored. This is designed to make for excellent public relations, but it is only on rare occasions that it makes for even a modicum of good listening. In most cases, the towns I was assigned to honor had little to distinguish them save antiquity. Any dramatization beyond the fact that they existed physically, usually had one major industry, a population and a founding date was more fabrication than documentation.)

I had just turned in a sample script to the program director that was essentially above and beyond the call of duty, and well beyond the call of truth. My script called for a narrator and a 30-piece live orchestra, and contained the kind of prose that made Green Hills, Ohio, look like the Alamo!

When I was called into the P.D.'s office my script was lying face down on his desk, like a thumb in a Roman arena. He leaned back in his swivel chair and studied me pensively, as if searching for some velvet-glove language that could be utilized to castigate me without breaking my spirit.

"Serling," he said, "it's this way. Your stuff's too stilted. You seem to be missing the common touch. We're looking for grass roots here. We want to be close to the people. We're obliged to use the 'folksy' approach. In short, we want our people to get their teeth into the soil."

As he was talking I knew exactly what he meant. The "folksy approach" did not include a 30-piece orchestra, or prose out of Norman Corwin's *On a Note of Triumph*. It needed only two elements: a hayseed M.C. who strummed a guitar and said, "Shucks, friends"; and a girl yodeler whose falsetto could break a beer mug at twenty paces. This was getting the teeth into the soil. And the little thought journeyed through my brain that what these guys wanted was not a writer but a plow!

During the next couple of hours two things occurred to form and then cement a resolve of mine. The staff writer, in addition to writing, acts also as a kind of roving "idea man" for several current and varied types of programs. One of my duties was to supply "gimmicks" for an afternoon ladies' show. That afternoon I stopped by the studio to watch the tail end of one of its performances. The master of ceremonies was a semi-literate, ex-tent revivalist with curly hair and an absolutely devastating smile. He was winding up his show with a three-minute sermon on the boys in Korea and how we should pray for them. The ladies in the audience were totally captivated. There wasn't a dry eye in the studio. The program went off the air and the M.C., his eyes half closed, walked softly out of the studio, past the sighs and fluttering eyelashes of the good ladies who had come to see him and who now stared worshipfully and respectfully up at him. He nodded to me and we both got on the elevator. It went down one floor and a girl got off. The wavy head went up, the look of soulful ecstasy left the broad and dimpled face. He winked at me, nudged my elbow and said, "I wonder if she lays?"

(This same fat-faced, sanctimonious slob had told me earlier that he used to travel with his father, who was also an itinerant evangelist. But at the time, he said, his father did the preaching and he was the one who made the money: he had the "Bible concession.")

Two hours later I got my next assignment: to dream up an audition show for a patent medicine currently the rage. It had about 12 per cent alcohol by volume and, if the testimonials were to be believed, could cure everything from arthritis to a fractured pelvis. I spent two minutes studying the agency's work sheet, which stated the general purpose of the program. I read as far as the second paragraph: "This will be a program for the people. We'd like to see a real grass-roots approach that is popular and close to the soil." The pattern of whatever future I had was very much in evidence. I was either going to write dramatic shows for television, even at the risk of economics and common sense, or I was going to succumb to the double-faced sanctimony of commercial radio, rotating words as if they were crops, and utilizing one of the approaches so characteristic to radio—writing and thinking downward at the lowest possible common denominator of an audience. That afternoon I quit the radio station.

I sat that night with my wife, Carol, at a Howard Johnson's restaurant and after a few false starts—"You know, honey, a man could make a lot of money free-lancing"—I talked out my hope. Free-lance writing would no longer be a kind of errant hope to augment our economy, to be done around the midnight hour on a kitchen table. Free-lance writing would now be our bread, our butter, and the now-or-never of our whole existence. My wife was twenty-one, three months pregnant, and a most adept reader of the score. She knew all about free-lance writing. She'd lived with it with me through college and the two years afterward. She knew that in my best year I had netted exactly $790. She was well aware that it was a hit-or-miss profession where the lush days are followed by the lean. She knew it was seasonal, and there was no definition of the seasons. She knew that it was a frustrating, insecure, bleeding business at best, and the guy she was married to could get his pride, his composure and his confidence eaten away with the acid of disappointment. All this she knew sitting at a table in Howard Johnson's in 1951. And as it turned out, this was a scene with no dialogue at all. All she did was to take my hand. Then she winked at me and picked up a menu and studied it. And at that given moment, the vision of medicine bottles, girl yodelers, and guitar-strumming M.C.s faded away into happy obscurity. For lush or lean, good or bad, Sardi's or malnutrition, I'd launched a career. I'll grant you the perhaps inordinate amount of sentiment attached to all the above, but if this were a novel, patent medicines, Howard Johnson, and my wife, Carol, would all be part of an obligatory first chapter.

This was the nature of television in 1951. The medium had progressed somewhat past the primitive stage. There was still a sense of bewilderment on the part of everyone connected with the shows. And it was still more the rule than the exception to find the opening camera shot of almost every television play trained on the behind of one of the cameramen. But by this time there were six half-hour "live" shows that came out of New York, and two or three one-hour shows. On the Coast there were a dozen or more filmed half-hour anthologies. The television writer's claim to the title "playwright" had been made, but as yet was not universally accepted. The TV play, once called by Paddy Chayefsky "the most perishable item known to man," enjoyed no longevity through the good offices of the legitimate stage and the motion pictures. The motion-picture industry looked down at its newborn cousin somewhat as the president of a gourmet club might examine an aborigine gnawing a slab of raw meat. The movie people had no way of knowing at the time that this bumbling, inexpert baby medium would one day compete with them and come dangerously close to destroying them. For at that time the television play went on and off the air with few cheers and with no one to mourn its passing. The video diet was a lean mixture of wrestling and occasional football. These were the days of the 10-inch screen, the 1931 movies, and Gorgeous George. The television dramas extant were still in the process of feeling their way around, trying to find some kind of level of performance, some reason for being, and some set of techniques. At the time there existed no species referred to exclusively as "television writers." There were radio writers who were extending themselves a bit, realists who knew that the golden days of radio drama were dimming into twilight. There were screen writers doing television films as a stop-gap between picture assignments. There were also some embryonic playwrights who used the new medium as a kind of finger exercise for what they hoped would turn into legitimate writing later on. But neither the industry nor the public was prone to make any association between writing of real quality and the sort of thing done for television.

My first television script had been sold in early 1950 to an NBC film series on the Coast called *Stars Over Hollywood*. It was brave and adventuresome. Beyond this, the production and conception of the program were symptomatic of absolutely the worst features of Class-B moviemaking. The plots were an ABC mishmash, with the depth and levels of an adobe hut. The performances were rarely ever able to overcome the scripts. The piece I sold them was called "Grady Everett for the People." It starred Burt Freed, who turned in a pretty fair performance, considering everything. I don't recall too clearly the essence of the story or the way it was done, but I have a vivid recollection of the payment involved. It was exactly $100 for all television rights. I never met anyone connected with this production, nor did I set foot in the studio. But as of this writing it has been on at least twenty-four times at odd hours and on odd channels. I will claim immodestly that it surpassed wrestling; beyond that, I'll make no value judgment whatsoever.

The singularly distinguishing feature of television drama in those early days was a paucity of payment, sets, and theme. And to go along with this was a bleak desert which represented the area of identity of the television writer. He was practically anonymous; he had an ill-defined respect for his talents and no protection at all for his work. He had few prerogatives in terms of its production and only the barest of recognition for his contribution.

The *Kraft Television Theatre*, the oldest of the one-hour dramatic shows, wouldn't permit a writer at rehearsal until the day of the show. His presence at that late hour was probably a guarantee against intrusion. For by then the lines had already been changed, the interpretations made, the blocking and camera arranged. The writer could protest, but only as a gesture. The show was a *fait accompli* prior to his arrival. In the kindred areas of rewriting, casting, music, *et al*, the writer had even less to say. I cite the *Kraft Theatre* as an example not to single it out for a necessarily unique mistreatment of authors but because it was one of the few dramatic programs existent at the time. It aimed for quality and often achieved it. This was the show that did things like Molière's *A Doctor in Spite of Himself;*

Ibsen's *A Doll's House;* Galsworthy's *Justice* and *Loyalties.* It also produced plays like *Valley Forge, Berkeley Square, Comedy of Errors and Macbeth*—and some of these shows were produced as early as 1947. The reader can pretty much gather what the policies of the lesser programs were with regard to their conception and treatment of the men and women who wrote the material.

These first four and five years of television were the cradle days of a baby whose birth may not have been accidental but whose process of maturing was far from being planned. But thanks to programs like *Kraft* and some others, television was expanding its technique and coverage. And along with it came an expansion in quality. Besides *Kraft* there was *Studio One.* Tony Miner, a pioneer without coonskin, was producing the plays on *Studio One,* whose expanse was becoming as much horizontal as vertical. One of his productions took place on a submarine. He used actual water and a mock-up submarine, and he did it on a nickel-and-dime budget that today wouldn't pay for a cast on a half-hour show. It evolved as a striking and powerfully realistic illusion, and it pointed the way to a new horizon in live television.

Celanese Theatre went on the air and did things like Maxwell Anderson's *Winterset,* and it did them well and effectively. *Celanese* was directed by a man named Alex Segal, who became one of the early "names" in television. He was later to direct some television plays by Rod Serling, who at the time of Alex's arrival on the television scene was still writing prayer messages for an ex-tent revivalist in Ohio. But at this moment in the evolution of television drama there were even a few intellectual diehards who began to see the potential of it, and began to realize that a television play could come close to the legitimate theater, and even surpass it sometimes in terms of flexibility. Along with television's expansion and progress came the birth of a new school of television actors and actresses, men and women associated with the medium and known because of it. Like Hollywood and Broadway before it, television began to produce its own stars, and also like Hollywood and Broadway the writer was the last of the company to achieve an identity. To his everlasting credit, he did it on his own. The networks financed no campaign to make Chayefsky a known and associable quantity. Several million viewers began to make that association on their own. Plays by Paddy Chayefsky, Horton Foote, Bob Arthur, David Swift and David Shaw were stamped with that particular quality that forced recognition. The programs and networks helped, of course. The medium was improving to a point where it allowed them to help. They began to supply the financial and technical aid to enlarge the scope of the television drama. Now a writer could conceive of a story that played on more than two sets with more than four actors. He could write with an eye toward the fluidity of movement that came with three cameras. His sets and costumes were no longer slapped together as incidental accouterments to a one-shot performance. They were given thought, preparation and time.

But the major advance in the television play was a thematic one. The medium began to show a cognizance of its own particular fortes. It had the immediacy of the living theater, some of the flexibility of the motion picture, and the coverage of radio. It utilized all three in developing and improving what was actually a new art form. As indicated previously by the plays on *Kraft, Studio One* and *Celanese Theatre*, one could see that the television play was beginning to show depth and a preoccupation with character. Its plots and its people were becoming meaningful. Its stories had something to say. There was a flavor to it well beyond the early Hollywood half-hour film which shoved a product out that was obviously molded at an early age and became moldy at a late one. This product was sprinkled with a kiss, a gunshot, a dab of sex, a final curtain clinch, and it was called drama. Parenthetically it might be stated here that Hollywood did little to help in the evolution and improvement of television as a medium, at least in terms of drama. What accolades are deserved here should go to Chicago and New York.

In terms of technique, the "close-up" that had served as such a boon to the motion pictures was further refined and used to even greater advantage in television. The key to TV drama was intimacy, and the facial study on a small screen carried with it a meaning and power far beyond its usage in the motion pictures. I can't forget, for example, the endearing passage in Paddy Chayefsky's *Marty* between Marty and the girl in the little all-night beanery. This scene was a close-up of the two through the entire playing. And the wonderfully fabulous thing of two lonely people finding each other was played on the two faces. I am also reminded of one of my own things—a totally different piece from *Marty* but one which utilized the same kind of television technique that was so uniquely television. This was *The Strike*, produced on *Studio One* in June 1954. There was a moment in the play when Major Gaylord (extremely well played by James Daly) was recounting an experience during World War II when he was obliged to fire on an American soldier in the dead of night on a Pacific island. The camera stayed tight on his face for almost three solid minutes, and we had a moving, poignant and almost heart-rending picture of the fatigue and fear that go hand in hand in the province of wartime combat.

The physical and the fates conspired to force the maturing of the television drama. It was no longer a novelty; it had become a fixture. As such it competed with every other kind of entertainment; consequently it was forced to become better, to become different, and to aim higher. It was a medium that in a one-hour time period could play to an audience greater than a Broadway play reached in one solid year of SRO crowds. With this kind of potential and with this kind of impetus, however young, however groping, television was something to be reckoned with.

Television today remains a study in imperfection. Some of its basic weaknesses and mediocrity are still with us. There is still wrestling, soap opera, overlong commercials and some incredibly bad writing. There is really no defense for any of this, but there is an explanation. You need only look at a calendar to remember that only seven or eight years have gone by and the medium remains a young one and a groping one. There still remain new techniques to learn, new fields to examine and a myriad set of roadblocks to progress that still have to be breached. But there is still time and there are still ways. Radio was around for twenty-odd years before it really found its niche and ultimately wrote out a finis to its potential. Television hasn't exhausted its potential or altogether found its niche. And in the area of drama it has already far surpassed that of its sister medium.

Like any mass medium, it might still die from internal strangulation. But for those of us who professionally cast our lot with it in its early days, we haven't yet given up. For us the heartening thing is that there are still things to strive for.

A Few Recollections

A WRITER—at least this writer—measures his career not so much in terms of years as in individual moments. They are the good moments: the big sale, the well-received show, the award at the end of the year. The television playwright must savor his success and his good moments very hurriedly, because they're temporal at best. But the bad moments—his failures, the script rejections, the incisively bad reviews—cling to him with much more tenacity and for longer periods than the moderate successes.

Between late 1951 and 1954 I lived in Ohio, commuting back and forth to New York to take part in story conferences and the rehearsals of my shows. This was expensive and time-consuming, but was a concession to my own peculiar hesitancy about all things big, massive and imposing. New York television and its people were such an entity. For some totally unexplainable reason, every time I walked into a network or agency office I had the strange and persistent feeling that I was wearing overalls and Li'l Abner shoes.

I remember one incident during those early days when I had flown into New York to discuss a rewrite on a script called *You Be the Bad Guy*, which starred MacDonald Carey. The script editor, Dick McDonagh, asked if I'd like to meet the star of the show. I was ushered into a small office where the cast was assembled for the reading, and there was introduced to Mr. Carey, who turned out to be an extremely pleasant, affable guy, who stood up and shook my hand and complimented me on the script. I remember standing in the center of the room wondering what the hell I could do next, and deciding that I had outworn my welcome and my purpose and should at this time beat a retreat. I looked busily and professionally at my watch, nodded tersely to all assembled, mumbled something about it being a pleasure to see them all but that I had to catch a plane going west, and then turned and crashed into the wall, missing the door by two feet. Then, in backing out of the room, I ran into an oncoming secretary and dropped my briefcase, exposing not only scripts and writing material, but a couple of pairs of socks, some handkerchiefs and some underwear. (I traveled light in those days.) My exit from the J. Walter Thompson offices that day could not have been more pointed and obvious had it been staged by Max Leibman. But as a postscript to the story, I remember Dick McDonagh gripping my hand before I left the building and saying, "Look, little friend, these people don't give a good healthy damn what you carry in your briefcase, or how you leave a room. All they care about is what's in there!" He pointed at my head. Then he slapped me on the back and wished me well, and I headed back to the airport and Ohio.

On a writer's way up, he meets and does business with a lot of people. And in some rare cases there's a person along the way who happens to be around just when he's needed—perhaps just a moment of professional advice, a brief compliment to boost the ego when it's been bent, cracked and pushed into the ground, a pat on the back and eight words of encouragement, when a writer's self-doubts are so persistent, so deep-rooted and so destructive that they affect his writing. Dick McDonagh gave me many moments and several words of encouragement and enough pats on the back to keep me propelled forward. He once told me that there might be a day when he'd be reading some of my plays in a book anthology. He may know very well by now how prophetic were his words. But I wonder if he also realizes how instrumental he was in having it happen.

The writer in any field, and particularly the television writer, runs into "dry periods"—weeks or months when it seems that everything he writes goes the rounds and ultimately gets nowhere. This is not only a bad moment but an endless one. I remember a five-month period late in 1952 when my diet consisted chiefly of black coffee and fingernails. I'd written six half-hour television plays and each one had been rejected at least five times. What this kind of thing does to a family budget is obvious; and what it does to the personality of the writer is even worse. The typewriter on my desk was no longer a helpmate; it took on the guise of an opponent. The keys seemed stiff and unyielding. The carriage seemed bulky and sluggish, and the wastepaper basket would get crammed by the hour with discarded pages—a testimonial to my unsureness as to what to write and how to write it. Toward the end of this, I got a letter from Mr. Worthington Miner. I've mentioned Tony Miner earlier. Then as now he was a major-league, top-drawer television producer. And to get a letter from him, particularly a letter asking to see scripts, was like a third-string pony-league pitcher getting a telegram from John McGraw telling him to come up and pitch for the Giants. I flew into New York to see him, my briefcase bulging with manuscripts. (There wasn't even room for socks.) Tony read them, and during our second meeting informed me that he'd like to buy at least six of them. He was putting together a new show to be sponsored by an auto company, and my work impressed him. The feeling I got in that given moment was something akin to what a person feels when he is notified that he's just won the Irish sweepstakes. The knees begin to give out and there's a roar that begins some place down deep in the gut and starts to travel toward the throat. Fifteen minutes later I was on the telephone calling my wife and guzzling a Scotch on the rocks I ordered from room service (tipping the bellboy a whole buck), and adding up in my mind how much are six times six or seven hundred dollars. One week later, back in Ohio, I got another letter from Tony Miner apologizing and explaining that the show he was putting together had been shunted off to another agency and he would not be producing it. The guy who had won the Irish sweepstakes couldn't find his ticket stub. It was that kind of feeling. For some perverse reason I saved Tony's second letter; my wife put it into a scrapbook. And sometimes I take a look at it as a piece of memorabilia to document a bad moment that on the scale of a career's ups and downs represents the bottom of the barrel. A writer's career is studded with the near sales, the close hits, the almost-but-never-wases. And afterward, when he becomes accustomed to eating a little higher off the hawg, the bad moments get remembered. And no matter what you eat, it tastes like pheasant under glass.

Besides the good and bad moments in a career of writing, there is also an indefinable hard-to-peg turning point, a crossing of the Rubicon when suddenly you find your name somewhat known in the agencies and on the networks. You announce it at the reception desk and the girl nods knowingly and doesn't ask you to repeat it or query you as to its spelling. Exactly when this happens and how, you're never quite sure. But it does happen. Afterward the process of writing is never any simpler, the ideas are never easier to come by, and your craft and technique don't seem appreciably altered. But there is a difference, as if the long grind upward levels out a little bit and the going becomes a little easier. In my case it happened because of a single show that emanated live out of New York City. This was the *Lux Video Theatre*.

Over a two-year period they bought twelve of my shows and produced eleven of them. Since that time, *Lux* has gone the way of so many dramatic shows. They moved West, went into an hour form, and in this case began to use old movie properties instead of originals. But in its New York half-hour days, the *Lux Video Theatre* proved itself symptomatic of the basic difference between what was Hollywood television and what was then New York City television. It was a show that consistently aimed high. Its whole conception in terms of dialogue and production was adult, never hackneyed, and almost always honest. It touched upon themes like dope and marital infidelity. It did things like adaptations of short stories by Faulkner and Benét; it encouraged the submission of original scripts by any writer who knew how to write, regardless of what his credits were. The definitive characteristic of this show was that it never got rutted into a "type" program. It was never a till-death-us-do-part marriage between the policy of the program and the type of story and ending. The most meaningful and probably the most valuable thing that I can say about the *Lux Video Theatre* is applicable to all of television. On the basis of individual shows, it was as often unsuccessful as it was successful. But it always tried. And though its sights were sometimes aimed higher than its capabilities, it was rarely dull. If this could be said of the entire medium, flags could be raised on all the antennae.

The Problem Areas

DEFENSIVENESS in a television writer is a kind of occupational disease. His newfound stature has been somewhat therapeutic in combating it, but it remains in varying degrees. A writer is still thought of in some circles as a hack, plain and simple. His work is still regarded by some as merely an appendage to a sales message. And the medium he writes for is still maligned as being principally a display case and not an art form.

The TV writer falls prey to some of his criticism because he deserves it. A sizable bulk of television writing still must be dismissed as inconsequential or simply bad stuff, but there also exist reasons for this. And if they don't stack up as reasons all the time, they are at least in a sense explanatory of a condition. The mass-medium writer has two major problem areas in which he must write. These two areas represent roughly the nature of the medium and the writer's identity.

The Nature of the Medium

BUILT into television drama are innate and homegrown problems that do not exist in any other art form. Television, while unique in its potentials, is further unique in its limitations. In playwriting this is particularly true. For example, in no other writing form is the author so fettered by the clock. The half-hour program will sustain a story for only 23-odd minutes. The hour program calls for a 48- to 50-minute play. It is unheard of that a legitimate playwright must write within so rigid and inflexible a time frame. But the TV writer must. It is further arbitrary that his play must "break" twice in a half-hour show and three times in an hour show to allow time for the commercial messages. Obviously, there are some plays that will not in any circumstances lend themselves to such an artificial stoppage. The "break" will hurt the flow, the continuity and the build, but the "break" must come. And what do you do about it?

This time problem extends over into another area: production. The average hour television show rehearses for eight or nine days. This means a little over a week allotted to reading, staging, blocking, line learning, camera, dress rehearsals and, finally, production. Contrast this with a Broadway play that rehearses on an average of one month to stage a production that runs only twice as long as its television counterpart.

Very recently, when *Playhouse* 90 began telecasting on a weekly basis with a 90-minute play each week, it was thought that here at last was the time frame long and flexible enough to aid the writer in handling plot, character and pacing. I for one gratefully accepted the assignments for the first two plays of this new series, thinking, as did most others, that with about 70 minutes allotted the play, it would be moving out of an igloo into a mansion. But once again television's own peculiar limitations cropped up and, instead of aiding the playwright, the new time frame within this program did nothing but hurt him. For instead of a regular three-act arrangement, *Playhouse* 90 took a host of sponsors, each demanding at least two commercials. The result was that during the ninety minutes the show had to be divided into twelve- and thirteen-minute segments, each separated by a commercial, so that the over-all effect was that of a chopped-up collection of short dramatic segments torn apart and intruded upon by constantly recurring commercials. Scenes had to be automatically "curtained" at a high emotional pitch to accommodate the stoppage of action, the commercial, and then pick up the thread of story line. It is obvious that a succession of phony curtains or emotional high points will eventually dilute the effect of any play. An audience can get used to and almost oblivious to bomb blasts if they occur often enough.

The physical limitations of the television drama are part and parcel of the innate problems of the writer. Four or five basic sets represent the maximum stretching of both facilities and imagination. I might parenthetically state here that television's "intimacy," so often its strength, is an outgrowth of this weakness. We had to be intimate. We didn't have room to be anything else. In New York, the mecca of live television drama, the set problems are the greatest and show the least possibility of improvement. Most of the shows are berthed in old movie houses, buildings that are the victims of the young medium which now utilizes them. They are segmentized, overextended, and asked to serve in a capacity they were not designed for. This lack of space is often reflected in the techniques of television playwriting. The author must often probe vertically because there just aren't enough inches to let him spread out horizontally.

But while time and space present hurdles, the basic, the most important limitation of the television dramatist is not totally physical. In a sense it is more philosophical. And this happens to be the simple and fundamental fact that our economy is geared to advertising. For good or for bad, the television play must ride piggyback on the commercial product. It serves primarily as the sugar to sweeten the usually unpalatable sales pitch. It's the excuse to wangle and hold an audience. The play is forced to become a kissing cousin to an entity totally foreign to it. The audience, during a one-hour viewing of a drama, is forcibly deprived of that drama and in its place is exposed to three minutes of Madison Avenue dynamics. The audience must then make its own mental and emotional realignment to "get back with" the sole object of its intentions. That it can do it at all is a tribute to mass intelligence and selectivity.

I don't really believe there exists a "good" form of commercial. There are some that are less distasteful than others, but at best they're intrusive. And even in the most absolutely palatable form, they thrust a cleaver into the over-all effect of a television drama—and they do it three times during its all too brief playing, and even more during the 90-minute shows.

I make reference to this by way of pointing out a basic weakness of the medium. I do not presume to suggest any antidotes or alternatives. At the moment none seems possible. A sponsor invests heavily in television as an organ of dissemination. That organ would wither away without his capital and without his support. In many ways he hinders its development and its refinement, but by his presence he guarantees its survival.

Still, I don't think it is possible to generalize about the sponsor or the agency or the networks themselves. They vary as to the intensity of their dogmas, the legitimacy of their concerns, and the extent of their interference in a given television play. But, at their very worst, their interference is an often stultifying, often destructive and inexcusable by-product of our mass-media system. It extends into an area of dramatic creation that should by rights lie well outside their bailiwick and well beyond their scope of prerogative. I think it is a basic truth that no dramatic art form should be dictated and controlled by men whose training, interest and instincts are cut of entirely different cloth. The fact remains that these gentlemen sell consumer goods, not an art form.

A few years ago on a program called *Appointment with Adventure* I was called in to make alterations in some of the dialogue. I was asked not to use the words "American" or "lucky." Instead, the words were to be changed to "United States" and "fortunate." The explanation was that this particular program was sponsored by a cigarette company and that "American" and "lucky" connoted a rival brand of cigarettes. After establishing beyond any doubt that my leg wasn't being pulled and that this wasn't some cheap, overstated gag, I did the only thing a writer can do in television in the way of a protest. I asked that my name be withheld from the script. It was not that the alteration of the language in this case was of particular consequence or to any large degree changed the story. But in the matter of principle I felt that this was ludicrous interference, and I didn't want to be part of it. I'll never forget the man from Talent Associates, the outfit that produced the show, explaining to me that this was not the happiest state of affairs, but that writers, as well as any creative people connected with the show, should keep in mind that it's altogether proper for a sponsor to utilize certain prerogatives since he's paying for what goes on. Extending this kind of logic, we might assume that it is altogether proper for a beer-company executive to have a hand in managing a baseball club whose games are televised under his sponsorship.

Exactly where is the line of demarcation between the play and the commercial? No one seems to know. Ideally, the sponsor should have no more right of interference than an advertiser in a magazine. Theoretically, at least, this advertiser has no say over the policy of the magazine he buys space in, nor should he have even to a minute degree. But in television today, the writer is hamstrung and closeted in by myriad of taboos, regulations and imposed dogma that dictate to him what he can write about and what he can't.

In the television seasons of 1952 and 1953, almost every television play I sold to the major networks was "non-controversial." This is to say that in terms of their themes they were socially inoffensive, and dealt with no current human problem in which battle lines might be drawn. After the production of *Patterns*, when my things were considerably easier to sell, in a mad and impetuous moment I had the temerity to tackle a theme that was definitely two-sided in its implications. I think this story is worth repeating.

The script was called *Noon on Doomsday*. It was produced by the Theatre Guild on the *United States Steel Hour* in April 1956. The play, in its original form, followed very closely the Till case in Mississippi, where a young Negro boy was kidnaped and killed by two white men who went to trial and were exonerated on both counts. The righteous and continuing wrath of the Northern press opened no eyes and touched no consciences in the little town in Mississippi where the two men were tried. It was like a cold wind that made them huddle together for protection against an outside force which they could equate with an adversary. It struck me at the time that the entire trial and its aftermath was simply "They're bastards, but they're our bastards." So I wrote a play in which my antagonist was not just a killer but a regional idea. It was the story of a little town banding together to protect its own against outside condemnation. At no point in the conception of my story was there a black-white issue. The victim was an old Jew who ran a pawnshop. The killer was a neurotic malcontent who lashed out at something or someone who might be materially and physically the scapegoat for his own unhappy, purposeless, miserable existence. Philosophically

I felt that I was on sound ground. I felt that I was dealing with a sociological phenomenon—the need of human beings to have a scapegoat to rationalize their own shortcomings.

Noon on Doomsday finally went on the air several months later, but in a welter of publicity that came from some fifteen thousand letters and wires from White Citizens Councils and the like protesting the production of the play. In news stories, the play had been erroneously described as "The story of the Till case." At one point earlier, during an interview on the Coast, I told a reporter from one of the news services the story of *Noon on Doomsday*. He said, "Sounds like the Till case." I shrugged it off, answering, "If the shoe fits . . ." This is all it took. From that moment on *Noon on Doomsday* was the dramatization of the Till case. And no matter how the Theatre Guild or the agency representing U.S. Steel denied it, the impression persisted.

The offices of the Theatre Guild, on West 53rd Street in New York City, took on all the aspects of a football field ten seconds after the final whistle blew. Crowds converged, and if there had been a goal post to tear down, they would have done so. The White Citizens Councils threatened boycott and the agency people somberly told me that this was no idle threat. They had accomplished effective boycotts down South against the Ford Motor Company and the makers of Philip Morris cigarettes.

In the former case, it seemed that Negro workers had been permitted to work on assembly lines alongside whites; and in the case of Philip Morris, there had been a beauty contest in Chicago where one of the winners was a Negro girl. This was all it took for a wrathful wind to come up from the South. I asked the agency men at the time how the problem of boycott applied to the United States Steel Company. Did this mean that from then on that all construction from Tennessee on down would be done with aluminum? Their answer was that the concern of the sponsor was not so much an economic boycott as the resultant strain in public relations.

These, therefore, were the fears, and this was the antidote. The script was gone over with a fine-tooth comb by thirty different people, and I attended at least two meetings a day for over a week, taking down notes as to what had to be changed. My victim could no longer be anyone as specific as an old Jew. He was to be called an unnamed foreigner, and even this was a concession to me, since the agency felt that there should not really be a suggestion of a minority at all; this was too close to the Till case. Further, it was suggested that the killer in the case was not a psychopathic malcontent—just a good, decent, American boy momentarily gone wrong. It was a Pier 6 brawl to stop this alteration of character. The script was then dissected and combed so that every word of dialogue that might remotely be "Southern" in context could be deleted or altered. At no point in the script could the word "lynch" be used. No social event, institution, way of life or simple diet could be indicated that might be "Southern" in origin. Later, on the set, bottles of Coca-Cola were taken away because this, according to the agency, had "Southern" connotations. Previously, I had always assumed that Coke was pretty much a national drink and could never, in the farthest stretch of the imagination, be equated with hominy grits and black-eyed peas, but I was shown the error of my thinking. And to carry the above step even further, a geographical change was made in the script so that instead of being a little town of undesignated location, it was shoved as far north as possible, making it a New England town. It is conceivable that the agency would have placed the action at the North Pole if it hadn't been for the necessary inclusion of Eskimos, which would prove still another minority problem. For it to open in New England, with the customary spires of a white church in the background of the set—so typically Yankee and Puritan—was somewhat ludicrous to behold. But this was to be a total surrender, and there would be no concessions made even to logic.

Noon on Doomsday was, in the final analysis, an overwritten play. It was often tract-like, much too direct, and had a habit of overstatement. What destroyed it as a piece of writing was the fact that when it was ultimately produced, its thesis had been diluted, and my characters had mounted a soap box to shout something that had become too vague to warrant any shouting. The incident of violence that the play talked about should have been representative and symbolic of a social evil. It should have been treated as if a specific incident was symptomatic of a more general problem. But by the time *Noon on Doomsday* went in front of a camera, the only problem recognizable was that of a TV writer having to succumb to the ritual of track covering so characteristic of the medium he wrote for. It was the impossible task of allegorically striking out at a social evil with a feather duster because the available symbols for allegory were too few, too far between, and too totally dissimilar to what was actually needed. In a way it was like trying to tell a Jewish joke with a cast of characters consisting of two leprechauns. This track covering takes many forms in television. It is rarely if ever successful, and carries with it an innate transparency that shows it up for what it is.

When Reginald Rose, in an exceptionally fine play, *Thunder on Sycamore Street*, took an uncompromising swipe at a brand of lunacy in our country that recognizes equality as applying only to those whose roots are in the third-deck planking of the *Mayflower*, he had to couch his theme in a language acceptable on Madison Avenue. It was the story of a family in a residential street being bullied and pushed around by their neighbors because the guy happened to be an ex-convict. The story was originally written about a Negro family. The central conflict in every line of dialogue pointed to the Negro-White problem and the altogether basic premise that sooner or later human beings are going to have to live together side by side. Mr. Rose's enforced track covering was simply exchanging an ex-convict for a Negro. And this is a process a TV writer has to learn and to perfect. He must hunt and peck until he finds a more acceptable minority than the Negro—often the American Indian. This is, of course, somewhat limiting—since it is a difficult minority problem to play in New England—but television sponsors and agencies are prone to accept slight inconsistencies when it comes to skirting a sticky issue. I am afraid that eventually we TV writers may run out of substitutes. I suppose, then, because we are pretty inventive and imaginative guys, the standard minority scapegoat will turn out to be a robot, and this will step on no toes whatsoever. But in the meantime, a medium best suited to illumine and dramatize the issues of the times has its product pressed into a mold, painted lily-white, and has its dramatic teeth yanked one by one.

Sometimes television is faced with a problem where it is physically impossible to substitute an idea. Last year I was faced with such a problem when I wrote a script called *The Arena*, which was done on *Studio One*. In this case, I was dealing with a political story where much of the physical action took place on the floor of the United States Senate. One of the edicts that comes down from the Mount Sinai of Advertisers Row is that at no time in a political drama must a speech or character be equated with an existing political party or current political problems. Some of these problems, however, are now so hoary with age and so meaningless in modern context that they are stamped as acceptable. Slavery, for example, can now be talked about without blushing. Suffrage is another issue that need make no one wince. The treatment of the lunatic in chains and dungeons can no longer be considered controversial. But *The Arena* took place in 1956, and no juggling of Documentary of the year. It was a program on CBS called *Out of Darkness*, and it had been repeated three times. It was a moving, powerful and telling story of the effects and treatment of mental illness, and it also was the work of one individual—Al Wasserman, who conceived it, wrote it, and produced it. When the award was announced, the recipient was not Mr. Wasserman but one Sig Mickleson. Later on, in almost a bone-throwing gesture, Mr. Wasserman did receive a Certificate of Merit, but the major award went to one of the vice-presidents of the network, not to the man who was singularly responsible for the program itself. I have no doubt that Mr. Mickleson gave great moral and perhaps physical aid to the creation and ultimate production of *Out of Darkness*. But, as always, it is a fact that "first came the word" and that any kudos to be offered should have gone to the writer from whose mind and at whose typewriter the idea was given life and nurtured—not to a network executive whose major claim to recognition in this case was simply that he was permissive to the idea of the program.

I cite these Emmy and Sylvania Award dinners as somehow characteristic of the almost begrudging attitude the industry saves for its writers. For the rank and file among them never, or at least rarely, appear as an important adjunct to a press release. When a show is publicized, it is always the star, sometimes the story, and almost never the writer. And when the awards are made, despite the fact that every program owes its basic existence to the efforts of a writer, he himself stands nearest the end of the line to get his.

I cannot complain because of a lack of identity. I am one of a handful of fortunates who have been able to grub and battle our way into relative limelight. I get my publicity—perhaps too much publicity—with little effort. Chayefsky is the same way. And so are Reginald Rose, Gore Vidal, Bob Arthur and a few others. But to the average men or women who supply the raw materials of entertainment via the typewriter, recognition is sadly lacking, and if there are any fingers to be pointed, they must point to the networks and the agencies who cry for material, but at the same time find the name value of its creators immaterial.

The Anatomy of Success

ON JANUARY 13, 1955, the *Kraft Television Theatre* presented *Patterns*. One minute after the show went off the air my phone started to ring. It has been ringing ever since. There are two ways for a writer to achieve success. One is the long haul, the establishing of a record of consistent quality in his work. The other way is the so-called overnight success, charged and generated by a single piece of writing that captures the imagination and the fancy of the public and the critics. *Patterns* was that kind of piece. It came on the air unheralded, but pushed me into the limelight with a fabled kind of entry. In two weeks after its initial production (it was telecast again one month later), the following happened to me:

> I received 23 firm offers for television writing assignments.
> I received three motion-picture offers for screenplay assignments.
> I had fourteen requests for interviews from leading magazines and newspapers.
> I had two offers of lunch from Broadway producers.
> I had two offers to discuss novels with publishers.

In addition to the above, I sold six television pieces in a row—plays that had been knocking around for anywhere from six months to three years—and they all went quickly, with no price-haggling. All of a sudden, with no preparation and no expectations, I had a velvet mantle draped over my shoulders. I treaded my way through a brand-new world of dollar-sign mobiles hanging from the sky, shaking hands with my right hand, depositing checks with my left, watching my bank account grow, reading my name in the papers and magazines, listening to myself being complimented unreservedly and extravagantly. It had all the glittering, dreamlike quality of the sudden and spectacular rise to the top and it was great to live with for a while—very great. There were moments of disquiet in the beginning, the sudden cooling off of friends who were afraid to phone because they were afraid of misconstrued motives. They wanted to remain friends, not to be glad-handing hangers-on. Into the breach that they left came the other phone calls from the long line of phonies, the people who a month before didn't care if I lived or fell off a bridge. And now they were the loudest in their praise.

They were the perspicacious ones who had "recognized my talent many years before." Some of them weren't phonies really. This is a caste business. Sometimes you have to wait for people to get into your league before you invite them to play ball. And this was the case with me. Some producers' waiting rooms that had provided many hours of heel-cooling for me in years passed suddenly became my old alma mater, and I was the prodigal son when I walked through the door. These are some of the little accouterments to success that you never can prepare for but learn to get accustomed to damn quick once you've achieved it.

And then, almost according to plan, there are new aspects to your living and your writing that follow this success. For one thing, I had a spotlight on me and a spotlight on my work. It was constant, bright and revealing. Like a good horse, or a swivel-hip halfback, I was the guy to watch. I had the ball, I was up top, and I was fair game. I was studied, assessed, and dissected. In the month that followed, everything I had on television was plugged, bugled and advertised. It was also carefully watched and reviewed. The big thing, the important thing, was that whatever I had on was invariably compared to the one successful thing I had already done, and also, almost as invariably, the new piece didn't take to the comparison. Overnight successes are almost always something special. They hit some kind of basic nerve of reaction; they achieve some fantastic universality; they accomplish by accident so much more than can usually be accomplished by design. In my case, the first reviews of the shows after *Patterns* were charitable; benefits of doubt were freely exchanged. It was as if the critics were wary of throwing a brickbat at a successful author for fear that their own analysis might be incorrect. (After all, this is the guy who wrote *Patterns*.) But after a time, when the comparisons became even more obviously negative, the needle was unsheathed. It got longer, it probed deeper, and I began to bleed. For on the periphery of every success, in the shadows just outside the limelight, is a hulking, brooding monster known as a "flash in the pan"! Patterns wasn't my only success, but it evolved as the single standard by which I was judged. It was a point of comparison. It was the stock reference for quality. And where once its title conjured up the sweet smell of success, the odor now became just a little acrid and unpleasant and I began to get sick of it. I'd written other things, I assured people. I made it a point in interviews to slough off the title and I became preoccupied with the old plays that preceded it and the new ones to follow. And it wasn't too long before I realized that sometimes the writing that brought you success on a platter was also the writing that evolved as your principal competition. I now had to fight myself or at least something I'd done. I had something to prove, first to others and then to myself. I had to prove that *Patterns* wasn't all I had. There had been other things before and there would be other things to follow.

As it turned out, it took a long time to prove. Almost two years. I thought that *The Rack* was better written than *Patterns*. I thought that *Noon on Doomsday* had more innate power. I thought *The Strike*, done on *Studio One* in June 1954, had more universality and more appeal. But I was a minority of one. On a network radio interview a few months ago, I was introduced as "Rod Serling, the man who wrote *Patterns* and" (a long pause) "... and ... well ... here he is—Rod Serling." One of the plays in this volume turned out to be the one that, for the moment anyway, pushed back this specter of the "flash in the pan." This was *Requiem for a Heavyweight*. It appeared in October 1956 on *Playhouse 90* on CBS. In many ways it seemed to catch the public imagination just as *Patterns* had. Its reviews were fabulously good. And now in the columns I'm "Rod Serling, who wrote *Patterns* and *Requiem for a Heavyweight*."

To any writer, or to any human being for that matter, who has not slept with success, breathed its rich oxygen, and gamboled through the crazy, pink, whipped-cream world that it opens up, all this may sound carping and unimportant. I'll concede the point that a good bank account, a paid-for car, and a guarantee of your kids' education go a long way to compensate for some momentary hurt feelings and some bad reviews. But I guess it's part of the strangely complex human mechanism to want to savor success. Television makes this impossible. It changes its diet not only weekly and daily, but hourly. A writer's claim to recognition doesn't take the passage of time very well. This claim gets lost in the shuffle and is forgotten. *Marty* becomes obscure when *Twelve Angry Men* takes its place. And then *Patterns* takes over. It moves to the rear when *A Man Is Ten Feet Tall* comes to the fore. That, in turn, gets replaced by *A Night to Remember*, which is not long remembered when suddenly appears *Requiem for a Heavyweight*.

The challenge, the competition, the frenetic, staccato pace of television is forever pushing people off the pedestal, shoving someone else up there and continuing the process. To the viewing audience this is a guarantee—almost—of continuing quality or at least an attempt toward it. To the writer it dictates the purchase of a scrapbook, which is probably the only way he'll find permanence in recognition—in the written record of what he has already done. Because for better or for worse, television takes all its achievements and makes them history within a few hours of their presentation.

Whatever the psychological disturbances that stem from the overindulgences of the overnight success, there are obviously a lot of kicks to becoming known, financially independent and in demand. Here is a smattering of day-to-day accouterments to being a reasonably well-known writer.

1) I receive on the average of five to ten letters a week with offers of collaboration ("a guy who writes as much as you must certainly need some fresh ideas from the outside"). I invariably try to answer every letter, probably from a sense of compulsion and a good memory. I wrote a lot of correspondence myself with collaborative ideas before I was eating gravy.

2) I drive a 1957 white Lincoln convertible, so long, so garish, so obvious, that my wife blushes when she looks at it in the

driveway. It's the first big luxury car I've ever owned, and it's one of the few overt gestures of ostentatiousness on my part.

3) I fell almost immediately into the speech pattern of the theater with its propensity for terms of endearment ("sweetie," "baby," "darling," "dear"). I hate to hear other people use these terms, but I'm aware of using them constantly. Why?

4) I'm considered to be a co-operative writer—even now. I don't get my back up at requests for rewrites. I rarely, if ever, give producers or directors trouble. But now, as I never did in the early days, I'll at least speak my mind about what I consider to be a wrong approach or an incorrect interpretation. In the pre-*Patterns* days, I would unquestioningly do any rewrite, change or delete any conception without a single question asked.

5) I have never ceased liking publicity. This isn't ego for its own sake, because I don't drop names and I don't purposely seek it. But I still get a kick when I see my name in the paper, and I probably always will.

6) Bad reviews jar me down to the instep. I will never become philosophically resigned to a negative reaction to something I've written. The difference now is that I'm more prone to want to share the blame for a bad show. I try to analyze where the writing was at fault, as opposed to where the production let it down. In the old days, I invariably made the assumption that it was always uniquely my fault.

7) I have a hell of a schedule and I'm never without a writing project of some sort. If it isn't a screenplay it's a television play.

8) I discovered along the way that movies and television are separate entities, and each makes different demands on writing. You write "big" for the movies. You let your camera tell considerably more story than you do in television. You write with a much more pronounced sense of physical action than you're permitted in the electronic medium. Television also demands a visual sense, but very often the progression of a story must be indicated by dialogue. In the movies, it can often be externalized just by what is seen and not necessarily by what is heard.

9) I like Hollywood and motion pictures, though I felt intimidated when I went out there to do my first picture. I was at Metro at the time and was given an office 40 feet long and a secretary, both new to me. Sitting at my desk the first day, I was approached by a secretary from down the hall who had seen my coffee pot on the desk (I drink coffee from morning till night) and who asked me if she might borrow some sugar for a *Kaffeeklatsch* being held by some writers down the hall. I gave her the sugar with a little penciled note saying, "This sugar comes to you courtesy New York television." The next day the sugar came back, each cube marked with a skull and crossbones, with the legend, "TV writer—go home." This went a long way toward breaking the ice. The next morning I was invited to the *klatsch* and I began to make some good and lasting friends from that moment on. I'm beginning to feel that the Hollywood I felt so intimidated about is a Hollywood that in many ways doesn't exist any more—if it ever did. There once may have existed the Odets version of a phony, falsely glittering world full of sick people satiated with money, sex, and applause, a flimsy, unreal world that would disappear if someone were to yell "cut!" But the Hollywood of today, at least the one I found, had no more than its share of phonies or neuroses. It was no better and no worse than the New York television world or, for that matter, any area in the theater. I met a lot of adults in Hollywood—producers, directors, writers, and some agents whom I was proud to know. They were sober, intelligent, as-normal-as-I human beings. As in any social sphere or profession, you pick your own friends and your own social milieu. You don't walk on the wild side unless you choose to.

10) In looking back over the relatively short span of my career, I sometimes make mental notes of the people I'm indebted to. They are legion. But a few of them bear special mention. There was my first agent, Blanche Gaines, who took me on when no one else would have me, who browbeat me, mothered me, argued with me, and did some considerable swinging for me, and to whom I owe a great deal.

There was Dick McDonagh, already mentioned, who gave what is so much at a premium in this business—time and trouble. There were directors like Ralph Nelson, Johnny Frankenheimer, Dick Goode and Dan Petrie, who respected me long before a writer got much respect from most quarters. There were producers like Felix Jackson, Martin Manulis, Mort Abrahams, who judge a man several feet away from the bandwagon. And there were the editors like Florence Britton of *Studio One* and Ed Rice of *Kraft*, who professionally and personally gave me many a boost up the ladder. In the final analysis, it is relatively simple to buy properties from a well-known writer. I think it takes a helluva lot more insight and a much more knowledgeable feeling for the profession to buy scripts from unknown authors—which all of these people did, and continue to do.

11) I don't know where I'm going and I'm not sure where I am. My erstwhile success stems from a comparatively small number of plays—far too few, really, to lay any legitimate claim to permanence in the literary scene. I think it's really a moot question as to how I've got this far with the present track record that I lay claim to. I think that I'm a good writer but an undeveloped one. And I rather think that this applies to most young television writers. They have benefited enormously from the public attention that has come to them in far greater degree than that received by most writers in pre-television days. All of us have an obligation to our craft and to the audience to justify this attention. We must aim higher, write better, dig deeper. There are some basic values that apply to all writing, be it television, movies, the novel or anything else. A writer has to write as best he knows how. And ultimately, if this effort shows talent, he will be recognized.

Afterthoughts

TELEVISION is a potpourri of good things and bad, a medium of promise and intelligence and, at the same time, an electronic oat-burner in the always-always land of cliché.

On the negative side, here are some practices in television I feel strongly enough about to mention. For example, I find it shoddy and inexcusable for dramatic shows to pick up their actors and actresses after the curtain in the so-called "Star Dressing Room" and have them plug products. Whether or not their performances during the program were good, this is an absolute guarantee that they won't be remembered. All that remains is the memory of a gratuitous, phony pitch thrust in at the end.

I am embarrassed when movie actresses hired as "Show Hostesses" flounce into tacky living rooms on certain dramatic film anthologies against a background of oversweet violins. The embarrassment becomes even more acute when they launch into a patently ridiculous reason for the plot of the show that night. For example: "We got a beautiful letter from a farm woman in Idaho telling us of the romance of corn husking. It's called *She Found Romance While Corn Husking*, and we'll bring you Act I after this important word to you ladies about protecting your hands." I get a violent reaction to certain dramatic-show emcees who preface each act with a résumé of what happened in the previous act. I assume this is based on a belief that a one-minute commercial destroys memory and a recapitulation is necessary. But this carry-over of the old soap-opera technique has no place in the theater, and there is no excuse for it on television.

I hate most beer commercials, with the notable and refreshing exception of the Piel Brothers and the incomparable Bert and Harry. The majority of the cousin brews are littered with catchwords, slogans, and raucous singing jingles that dent the ears. Cigarette ads seem to be no less offensive on television. And the worst commercial of any, bar none, is the dramatized doctor-pitchman in a white medical coat who juggles test tubes and ponderously exhorts you to do what his "patients" do. Perhaps this is the natural evolution of the old traveling snake-oil shows, but then, at least, the hucksters did sleight of hand and a few buck-and-wings before launching into the pitch.

Probably because I am a writer, I am acutely aware of the next television fault, which makes me wince whenever it is in evidence. This is simply what I think of as the "oblique slant" of language or theme that is meant to be earthy, gutsy or tough. Since profanity is frowned on, the medium has devised its own compensatory language. "Devil" replaces "hell." "Blast you" is the alternative to "damn." And for anything with more passion, the actor just bites his lips in soundless fury. I remember an emotional second-act curtain in a television play called *The Strike*, which I wrote for Studio One in June 1954. An Army officer is called upon to ask for an air strike on an area where he knows twenty of his own men are. The scene calls for him to throw a bottle against a map board and say that he's just about to give the order to blow his own men to hell! It took exactly nine days to impress upon the legal department of CBS that in this given situation an officer wouldn't say "darn," "shucks," or "gosh." To retain the one word took all the efforts of the program's editor, Florence Britton, the producer, Felix Jackson, and the director, Frank Schaffner, but finally we won our little semantic victory. And I remember Floss Britton coming back into the studio the day of the show, bussing me lightly on my flushed and excited cheek and saying "We're in business, Roddy. We traded them two damns for the hell!"

This is a more specialized dislike, but very often the writer is called upon to pad a part to make it more palatable to a sought-after actor or actress. But this goes on all the time when a script is submitted by the writer and in turn sent over to the agency for the actors to read. These people owe their careers to exposure and the right kind of exposure, but many a good script has died a-borning because it has been constitutionally unable to withstand the onslaught of padding a role, or twisting a story line to change a characterization. In the miserably tight time framework of a television play, there is room for only so many lines and so much story. For every added line, one must be deleted, and it is this cycle of add and withdraw that does irreparable damage to a story.

But there are a lot of things in the medium I write for that I like and admire. They are more than things really; they are people as well. I like most of the editors I've worked with. The editor is in the totally untenable position of acting as a catalyst in a weekly situation that involves the writer on one end and the advertising agency on the other. His is the constant hassle of passing on the agency's fears to the writer with enough diplomatic finesse to keep the writer from cutting his throat. At the same time, the editor has to keep the script as intact as possible without the agency's yanking it off because of their fears. This latter action is not an everyday occurrence, but it does happen. One script of mine called *The Bomb Fell on Thursday* was cast and had one rehearsal, and the sets were ordered, when the agency yanked it because of a question of "taste." Writers and editors together have to face up to one basic truth: the agency is all-powerful. It is extremely difficult to cross the Young and Rubicam!

I also like the television directors. They are mostly a young lot. And if the reader has ever watched a television drama produced in a studio, he realizes the consummate talent required of them. They must know acting and actors, sets and designs, lighting and sounds, blocking and business, story and writer. And at that point where the legitimate play director quietly steals off into the darkness in the rear of the theater to entrust his work to the opening-night cast—this is when the TV director works the hardest in the most trying, frenetic, inhuman tension imaginable. At this point he's an obstetrician assisting at a birth, but he's also nurse, anesthetist and general manager of the hospital. When it's close to air time, and I happen to be on the set, I invariably break into a cold sweat, wondering how in God's name this show will ever get on the road. Nerves, like the common cold, are easily transmitted. I can remember one time on the *Danger* show when I was bodily removed from the set by John Frankenheimer (6' 5") because I was turning his actors' sense of well-being into a shambles by gratuitously reminding them of their cues and stage directions. A couple of years later, on another show directed by John, he saw to it that I received a little gift just prior to air time. It was a beribboned box that on being opened revealed a neatly wrapped package of adhesive tape.

I can't say that I "like" television critics because I really don't know many personally. But I respect them and I'm glad they're around. Their presence is a tacit assertion that the television program is an art form that warrants and merits critical analysis. The function of the television critic is somewhat different from that of his counterparts who review movies and plays. The latter are, in a basic sense, previewers. Their writing is read to determine whether a movie or play is worth the price of admission and the inconvenience of getting there. The television critic analyzes a play or program that is already a fact. He can bring no one in, and discourage no one to keep away. His is a critique and not a preview. It's a needle or a back-slap that can in no way affect whatever is in the record. My own feeling is that the television critic has one primary purpose. He's there to needle and prod the industry into quality. He's there as a reminder that nothing can be slipped by. His very presence sets up certain absolute standards to be aimed at. His approval is solicited, his disapproval keenly felt and pondered. When Jack Gould or J.P. Shanley in *The New York Times* dislikes something, this precludes the possibility of a "smash," and, conversely, their benign approval is cause for celebration on the part of the writer and all concerned. In the case of my own *Patterns*, the demand for a repeat was generated by the critics and columnists. Jack Gould's calling it ". . . one of those inspired moments that make the theatre the wonder that it is . . ." did more to make it a TV legend than the thousands of letters sent in by viewers. Critics, in short, pack weight. As to the legitimacy of the various analyses, this is not nearly so absolute as the standards the critic sets up for the industry he writes about. Ten different TV critics will come up with ten different reactions to a given television play. Check the following box score, for example, as it applies to the critical reaction toward one of my shows on *Studio One*.

HARRY HARRIS, Philadelphia *Inquirer:* "In *The Arena* on *Studio One* last night, Serling did much to regain his *Patterns* prestige."

ERNEST SCHIER, Philadelphia *News:* "I doubt if anything quite as childish transpires as that depicted in Rod Serling's contribution to *Studio One* last night . . ."

BURTON RASCOE, syndicated columnist: ". . . an instructive, semi-documentary on the initiation of a new senator in Washington, with a salutary and agreeable sermon, implied rather than stated . . ."

JAIK ROSENSTEIN, *The Hollywood Reporter:* "Rod Serling must have had to blast his way through the cobwebs with a blowtorch to get to the old trunk from which he resurrected *The Arena*. . . . An hour is a real long time for an issue such as this, with characters so conventional and with long maudlin speeches of mawkish idealism and pat dialogue."

DAVE KAUFMAN, *Daily Variety:* "Chalk up another powerful teleplay for Rod Serling. This time he incisively explores the practice and moral climate of politics . . ."

GEORGE CONDON, The Cleveland *Plain Dealer:* "Rod Selling's *Studio One* story, *The Arena*, turned out to be one of the finest dramatic productions of the year . . . it was thrilling to encounter a show that went past the superficial plot into the real dramatic conflict that rages inside men who are torn between good and evil . . ."

PATTERNS

CAST

FRED STAPLES: *A young, dynamic though extremely sensitive executive.*

FRAN: *Fred's wife. An attractive, hungering kind of woman whose appetite is that of the competitive American wife. A very aware person.*

RAMSEY: *A tough, icy, predatory but honest corporation head. In his early sixties.*

ANDY SLOANE: *A battered, dying and yet strangely resilient kind of man in his late sixties.*

MARGE FLEMING: *The typical professional secretary tied to one man by a bond of innate loyalty, habit and deep-rooted affection that is as sexless as the woman herself.*

MISS LANIER: *Ramsey's executive secretary.*

FIRST SECRETARY:
MISS STEVENS:
MISS HILL:
MISS EVANS: } Secretaries of Ramsey and Company.

GORDON:
JAMESON:
SMITH:
VANDEVENTER:
LATHAM:
GRANNINGAN:
PORTIER: } Executives of Ramsey and Company.

ROD SERLING

PAUL: *Andy's son.*
BILLY: *Fred's assistant.*
ELEVATOR STARTER
ELEVATOR OPERATOR
TELEPHONE OPERATOR

ACT ONE

Dissolve through film shot of Park Avenue traffic at Forty-fifth Street Pan up to Grand Central Building to feature clock. Cut to medium shot of clock reading a few minutes after 8:30 A.M.
Traffic noises.
Dissolve to bank of elevators, lobby, closed with only one in operation and no one about. Traffic noises out. Very quiet. One person is waiting inside elevator. Miss Stevens enters shot to go into elevator.

STARTER: Good morning, Miss Stevens. You'll have to take the local.

MISS STEVENS: Doesn't matter, Bill.

Bill gives snap of fingers, door closes, elevator up. Pan to huge board listing firms in building. Pan board to listing of Ramsey and Company. Other firms have office numbers. Ramsey and Company list fifteen floors with appropriate departments, then executive floors, thirty-fifth through fortieth. In tight on these listings.
Dissolve to electric clock on wall of telephone switchboard room, Ramsey and Company. Clock reading 8:40. Pan to see empty room, board clear of operators, a few lights indicating calls flashing on and off. Night lines plugged in. Dissolve tight shot grandfather's clock, elegant antique in very plush but ultraconservative reception room, main executive floor, Ramsey and Company. The clock reads 8:50. Back and pan to see Miss Stevens near her immaculately neat, totally uncluttered kidney desk. She is taking off her light topcoat and hat. Miss Lanier, Mr. Ramsey's

executive secretary, enters shot to go through door to offices. She is an older woman.

MISS STEVENS: Good morning, Miss Lanier.

MISS LANIER: Good morning, Martha.

Phone rings.

MISS STEVENS: Fortieth floor executive, Ramsey and Company, Miss Stevens. . . . I'm sorry, sir, our switchboard doesn't open until nine. . . . You should be able to reach Mr. Donaldson shortly after that. (*Jots down name*) I'll leave your name with his assistant, Mr. Phillips.

She hangs up. Pan to elevators, which open into room. Paneled and very discreet. They give a first impression of arches that have been boarded up in mahogany. Young girl gets out of elevator to go to door behind reception desk Miss Lanier went through.

MISS STEVENS: Ann . . .

GIRL (ANN): Yes, Miss Stevens?

MISS STEVENS: Leave this on Billy's desk for Mr. Donaldson.

GIRL: Sure thing. (*Going out, looking at slip of paper*) Mr. Fortisque?

MISS STEVENS: Inland Steel and Copper, I think.

GIRL: Oh, yes—they washed out. Too high a bid. . . . Billy can take care of it. (*Goes to door*) No sign of the new genius, I suppose?

MISS STEVENS (*Finding something to do at the desk*): It's 8:55, Ann.

GIRL: I know, but if you're that bright, you must be very eager. (*Going out*) Today's the day, and boy oh boy, it should be some day! (*Exits*)

Dissolve to Ramsey's office. Tight shot handsome desk clock reading 8:55. Pan to tight shot of silver cup on desk filled with pencils with dull points. Miss Lanier's hand enters, lifts cup to empty pencils in box, places new and sharpened pencils into cup. On the desk lie a bunch of fresh-cut jonquils, most probably from her garden. Looks up, sees Ann (GIRL) pass by door and calls to her.

MISS LANIER: Ann . . .

ANN (*Entering*): Yes, Miss Lanier?

MISS LANIER (*Taking up the flowers and handing her a small vase on the desk*): Would you fill this with water for Mr. Ramsey?

ANN: Certainly, Miss Lanier.

MISS LANIER: Thank you, Ann. It's such a long trip to the ladies' room, and I expect him any minute.

ANN: The new executive starts today, doesn't he?

MISS LANIER: Mr. Staples?

ANN: Yes.

MISS LANIER (*Sorting Ramsey's mail*): This morning most likely.

ANN: I hardly recognized Mr. Phillips' old office the way it's been fixed up for Mr. Staples. Real antiques. They look like they were handed down from . . .

Miss Lanier's attitude before should have left no doubt that this was a conversation topic that should be dropped. Here her tone makes the attitude definite.

MISS LANIER: Yes . . . Well, I understand Mr. Staples prefers Early American over contemporary pieces. Now I think . . .

ANN (*Her passion for some definite information too strong*): All the girls are excited, Miss Lanier. It's the first time since any of us has been here that a new vice-president has been brought in from outside the company, and—

MISS LANIER (*Cold and very clear*): Are you starting a rumor, Miss Evans, or merely repeating one?

ANN: We just thought that since he was being given an office so close to Mr. Ramsey's, and that every other executive on this floor is—

MISS LANIER: Mr. Staples' position in the company will be made known when Mr. Ramsey chooses to define it. A new vice-president isn't made until another is fired. Our guesses and faulty logic on even a secretarial level could cause others a good deal of embarrassment and possibly some harm.

ANN: I'm sorry.

MISS LANIER: I would appreciate it if you would make this very clear to the rest of the girls.

ANN: Yes, ma'am.

She exits, closes door and holds outside by other girl.

GIRL: What did you find out?

ANN: You never know when you'll strike a nerve.

Cut to film, medium shot clock on Grand Central Building. Nine o'clock. The bell strikes the hour.

Dissolve to bank of elevators in lobby; the jam is on. One elevator is packed and starter holds crowd back to get the door closed.

STARTER: Next car, please. (*To elevator operator*) O.K., Stevie.

Door closes. Elevator up.

STARTER (*Into phone on elevator call board*): Charlie, Phil, Steve . . . Express down. No stops. We're jammed.

Dissolve to switchboard room. Clock on wall reads 9:10. Pan to switchboard. Lights going, all the operators at work combatting the wave of incoming morning calls. Sound over telephone montage.

OPERATOR: I'm sorry, sir, every outside wire is taken, and they're waiting . . .

Dissolve to reception room. The morning has begun. Man is standing at desk.

MISS STEVENS (*Hanging up phone*): Mr. Davis will be out as soon as he is free. It shouldn't be long.

Man goes to sit down. Secretary enters obviously late. Miss Stevens makes a note of her arrival time on chart on her desk.

MISS STEVENS: Good morning, Miss Hill.

MISS HILL: Morning, Miss Stevens. (*Goes to desk. Quietly*) Is my boss in yet?

MISS STEVENS: You're lucky.

MISS HILL (*Going in*): The subway was tied up at Fourteenth Street for—

MISS STEVENS: Yes, dear. (*She exits. Ramsey enters*) Good morning, Mr. Ramsey.

RAMSEY: Miss Stevens. (*Exits*)

MISS STEVENS (*Dialing*): Miss Lanier, Miss Stevens . . . he's here. *Dissolve to Ramsey's office. He enters. Miss Lanier takes his hat and Coat to hang them in closet.*

RAMSEY: Good morning, Miss Lanier.

MISS LANIER: Good morning, sir.

RAMSEY: Any messages?

MISS LANIER (*Handing him pad with names*): No one important.

RAMSEY (*Looking over list*): Hicks, Martin Tool and Die . . . Van Buren, Bankers Trust Company . . . Romaine . . . (*Crumples paper, throws into basket*) You're right, as always. I finished my analysis last night for our factory in Portland.

MISS LANIER (*Incredulous*): All of it?

RAMSEY: Yes, my dear. It's in my brief case. I want it teletyped this morning to our Seattle office. Have someone there drive to Portland to get it to Johnson before lunch, their time. That's by far the quickest way. Then run off twenty copies, confidential mimeographing, to be ready by our board meeting. That's our topic for today, and it's a big one. (*Looks at appointments calendar*) No sign of Mr. Staples?

MISS LANIER: No, sir.

RAMSEY (*Checking his desk clock against his watch*): Delay the meeting for eleven this morning to give you time to get the report mimeographed and distributed. I want it read and carefully. Get word underground to their secretaries that they shouldn't count on making any early luncheon dates. Also that Staples is to sit one down from Granningan, on my right.

MISS LANIER: Yes, sir.

RAMSEY (*Noting time again*): Let me know immediately his arrival. *Dissolve to lobby. Tight shot of Fred Staples and Fran standing before board listing firms in building. She is fussing with his tie.*

FRAN: Freddy, let's pick you up for lunch after I finish shopping. I can't wait until tonight.

FRED: Will you relax? Will you do that?

FRAN: Maybe they were just joking. Maybe they don't even expect you.

FRED: Fran—

FRAN: You look wonderful—charcoal-gray suit, striped tie—no trace of Cincinnati.

FRED: Is that good?

FRAN: For the present. You've arrived, Mr. Staples.

FRED: I must have to get you to drive me in town to work.

FRAN: Only this once. Just to see my wonderful man step into that elevator and go right up to the sky.

FRED: Easy, girl. We're country people.

FRAN: That may be . . . Ramsey, Staples and Company.

FRED: Goodbye, dear.

FRAN (*Kissing him*): Goodbye, darling. Take such very good care of yourself.

He exits to the elevators. Goes up to starter.

FRED: Ramsey and Company. The board says—

STARTER: Yes, sir, executive or administrative?

FRED: Er . . . executive . . . Mr. Ramsey—

STARTER: Fortieth floor.

Fred starts into open elevator.

STARTER: You want the Tower, sir. (*Points out of frame*) First elevator on your right will take you up. It'll be down in a moment.

FRED: Thanks. I should see you every morning now. I'll be working here. You have a lovely building.

STARTER: Thank you, sir. Ramsey and Company is a wonderful outfit.

FRED: Glad to hear it. (*Holding out hand*) My name's Staples.

STARTER (*Shaking hands*): Mine's Tommy, sir. You're from Cincinnati?

FRED: Why, yes.

STARTER: There's your elevator, sir. (*Fred starts off*) We've been expecting you.

Dissolve to corridor before Sloane's and Fred's offices, which adjoin. Marge enters from Sloane's office with armful of office supplies which she takes into Fred's office. She is trailed in by Ann and another secretary.

FIRST SECRETARY: Mr. Ramsey really had this place fixed up for him.

MARGE: It's very nice.

FIRST SECRETARY: He's due in this morning. Very touchy subject. Miss Lanier snapped Ann's head off when she tried to get a little information.

MARGE: Good for her.

ANN: Thanks. Latest rumor is he's to be your boss's assistant.

MARGE: That may be.

ANN: Some office for Mr. Sloane's assistant. Just three down from the president.

MARGE (*With a shade of anger*): Ever hear of efficiency?

ANN: Yes, Marge.

MARGE: Mr. Staples goes into Mr. Sloane's adjoining office because they happen to be working together—or *will* work together. You girls see hidden meaning in wall colors!

FIRST SECRETARY: All I know is that the offices have always been in order of rank. And all of a sudden bright and early one Monday morning a desk from Ohio comes in and leap-frogs to number-three spot. (*Looking around*) You know, Margie, it's pretty much common knowledge that your Mr. Sloane isn't exactly the fair-haired boy around here.

MARGE (*Very defensive*): That's not common knowledge—it's common gossip! But you two harpies wouldn't know the difference!

She exits to hall for coffee from coffee wagon.

GORDON (*Approaching*): Good morning.

MARGE: Good morning, Mr. Gordon.

GORDON: When Mr. Sloane comes in would you ask him to have the Anderson plant inventory reports sent over to me?

MARGE: Yes, sir, I'll do that.

GORDON (*Going on in*): Thank you very much.

Marge enters Sloane's office with her coffee. Then Sloane enters.

SLOANE: Good morning, Marge.

MARGE: Good morning, Mr. Sloane. I put your messages on your desk, and here's your coffee.

SLOANE: Thank you, Marge. Mr. Staples hasn't arrived, has he, Marge?

MARGE: No, sir. Just the furniture.

SLOANE (*Vaguely looking at wall separating the two offices*): I see. There was talk of tearing down the partition—making this one large office for me. (*Turning to her; a forced smile*) Suppose space was a factor in that.

MARGE: I'm sure of it, Mr. Sloane. They're doubling up in personnel. Some of the girls have three and four people they're working for. (*A pause*) Mr. Sloane . . . nothing's been mentioned, sir, about—about Mr. Staples' secretary.

SLOANE: I . . . I assume you'll sort of handle things for both of us for a while. I'll check with Mr. Ramsey later on.

MARGE: There's some letters you have to signature, too, sir. I'll bring them in.

SLOANE: Thank you, Marge.

Dissolve to reception room. Miss Lanier enters from door to greet Fred, who is seated near the desk.

MISS LANIER: Mr. Staples, I'm Margaret Lanier, Mr. Ramsey's secretary.

FRED: How do you do, Miss Lanier.

MISS LANIER: Mr. Ramsey of course would be here to welcome you himself if you hadn't caught him on long-distance call. Let me take you back to your office.

FRED: Thank you very much.

MISS LANIER: Have you met Miss Stevens?

MISS STEVENS: I introduced myself, Miss Lanier.

MISS LANIER: Fine. Now if you'll just come with me, Mr. Staples . . .

They cross to the door.

MISS LANIER: And may I bid you my own personal welcome. We're very glad to see you.

FRED: Thank you, Miss Lanier.

They exit into hall, lined with office doors. As they reach the end a door ahead of them opens and Mr. Jameson enters hall.

MR. JAMESON: Good morning, Miss Lanier. (*Notices Fred. Holds*) Mr. Staples?

FRED: Why, yes.

MR. JAMESON: Henry Jameson. I'm head of purchasing. Welcome aboard.

FRED: Thank you very much.

JAMESON: See you at the meeting.

FRED: Right.

He and Miss Lanier exit frame. Mr. Smith enters from room as they leave. Stand looking after them.

SMITH: That Staples?

Jameson nods.

SMITH: Any first impression?

JAMESON: Nice guy. And young.

SMITH: How young?

JAMESON: About twenty years under what I had expected.

Dissolve to corridor facing Sloane's and Fred's offices. Miss Lanier and Fred enter to go into his office.

MISS LANIER: Here you are, Mr. Staples.

FRED (*A little overcome*): Great golly . . .

MISS LANIER: Mr. Ramsey found from somebody in your old office that you were especially fond of Early American.

FRED: Very, but always from a distance. Never been able to afford them.

Marge enters office.

MISS LANIER: Mr. Staples, this is Miss Fleming. She'll be your secretary for the time being.

FRED: How do you do.

MARGE: How do you do, Mr. Staples.

MISS LANIER: Now if you'll excuse me, I have to go along. Goodbye, Mr. Staples.

FRED: Goodbye, and thank you again, Miss Lanier.

She leaves. Marge watches him most closely. Fred walks about the room.

FRED: Some office, Miss Fleming.

MARGE: Mr. Ramsey tries to furnish each office to fit the taste of the person in it.

FRED: He flatters me. (*Sloane enters*)

ANDY: We will be sharing for a while the best secretary in the office. You're a lucky man. Let me be the last to bid you welcome.

FRED (*Rising*): Come in. You're . . . ?

ANDY: Andy Sloane, known as your immediate superior. Only as time goes by I get less and less immediate.

FRED: I think Mr. Ramsey said on the phone you'd been ill.

ANDY (*Quickly*): Oh, did he? (*And then recovering*) Actually just a—a pesky stomach that's been acting up on me.

Marge exits. Andy sits down, lights a pipe.

ANDY: You busy?

FRED (*Grinning, then laughing*): Yeah—very. I was going to arrange my desk. Then get busy trying like mad to look busy!

ANDY (*In answering smile*): From now on you won't have any trouble. Mr. Ramsey has very definitive ideas about Executive's working capacity. You'll be busy. (*He looks down at his pipe, and he forces a matter-of-factness into his voice*) You were in Cincinnati? That it?

FRED: Yeah. Little plant out there I managed. Did some subcontracting stuff for Mr. Ramsey. He . . . well, he seemed to think I'd fit in here. So here I am. He's quite a guy.

ANDY: Ramsey? He's very close to being a production genius. He's also no slouch when it comes to judging men. You must have blown a bugle in his ear out in Ohio. He brought you here in a hurry.

FRED: As I recall, my end of the conversation was principally shaking and nodding my head. Mr. Ramsey's a pretty dynamic man. As you probably know.

ANDY (*With a strained look, another forced smile*): Yes . . . yes, I know.

FRED: You've been with the firm some time, haven't you— (*Grinning*) Is it "Andy" to me?

ANDY: It's "Andy" to most people. Yep—twenty-four years. Twenty-four glorious years.

FRED: That makes you kind of an institution.

ANDY (*Bantering but with an edge of seriousness*): One of the security boys—that's me. "Stay-in-one-place Sloane."

FRED: You must like it.

ANDY: Sure. After twenty-four years. (*He turns away*) Twenty-four . . . glorious years. I seem to recall Mr. Ramsey talking about you as a production man. You're an engineer, aren't you?

FRED: Yes, but I think from what he said I'd be a little of everything around here—mostly in industrial relations.

ANDY: Oh? That's . . . that's been one of . . . of my specialties. We . . . we ought to work pretty well together.

FRED: I'm sure we will.

Marge appears at the door.

MARGE: Excuse me, Mr. Ramsey's called a meeting in the conference room, Mr. Sloane.

ANDY: Oh. Well, Fred, been a real pleasure meeting you.

MARGE: Mr. Ramsey's expecting Mr. Staples, too.

FRED (*Rising*): I'll go in with you if you don't mind.

ANDY: Not at all. (*They walk out into the outer office*) I've just got to pick up a few papers from my office.

He goes in. Fred, standing by the door, notices a picture of two boys on the desk.

FRED: Yours? (*Points to the picture*)

ANDY (*This time the smile is prideful and genuine*): Yep. Older one's Jack—he's twenty-three. Goes to State. Younger one is fourteen—that's Paul. Older one's a linesman. The little one has the making of a nice scatback. They're good kids.

FRED: They look it.

ANDY (*With a new interest*): You married, Fred?

FRED: Five years. Girl from my home town.

ANDY: That her picture on your desk?

FRED: That's my ever-lovin'.

ANDY: Very lovely lady. My wife passed away a couple of years ago.

FRED: I'm sorry.

ANDY (*As they walk out*): The boys keep me busy. When you get a couple of sons you'll realize how very restful and relaxing an office can be.

FRED: I hope Mr. Ramsey remembers hiring me.

ANDY (*Unsmiling*): Mr. Ramsey rarely forgets anything. (*At the door*) After you.

We cut to the interior of the conference room. The various executives are taking seats. Mr. Ramsey sits at the head of the table. His eyes dart about the room. He's aware of everyone and everything. When he speaks there's a certain ease of language—he knows what he wants said, and it comes out that way. It's only after you listen to him awhile that you get the force of the personality—disturbing and yet arresting.

PATTERNS

On location near the Beekman Downtown Hospital in New York. It was a scene that ultimately never got on the screen, the whole thing being played inside the bar at the right.

A movie cameraman's view of the "Night Scene" between Fred Staples and Andy Sloane.

PATTERNS

This was the night scene when Staples finds Andy Sloane alone in the office and in a halting, oblique way tries to talk him into resigning so that he himself will not have to administer the *coup de grâce*.

In the top picture, Richard Kiley plays the televison version. Van Heflin, who played the role in the movies, is shown below. Ed Begley played Sloane in both productions. Both scenes were almost identical in the two versions and in both cases this proved to be one of the most powerful moments of the play. When Jed Harris was on this picture (before litigation moved him out) he used to act out scenes with me while I was doing the screenplay. This was the scene that used to excite him so that he would bodily lift me out of the chair and shake me while I played Begley's role. Whatever the pros and cons covering his departure, I was down to three shirts when he left. If I were doing *G-Men* with him, I might not even be alive to write this book.

This is the conference-room sequence just prior to Andy Sloane's death. Like many scenes in the television play, it was transplanted onto the screen with few changes. It contained some powerful writing and exceptional performances by Everett Sloane, Ed Begley, Dick Kiley, and then Van Hefhn in the movie. But it was somewhat diluted in its over-all effect by an earlier conference-room scene that in the movie at least was played much too emotionally. I argued with the director on this but couldn't win my point.

This is Fred Staples on his way to the showdown with the boss. This shot is representative of the basic difference between television and motion pictures—simply that of physical flexibility. The long walk down the semi-dark hall, footsteps echoing hollowly as if in a mausoleum, the shrouded typewriters on the desks flanking the walls—all this was much better done on the screen than it was on television.

RAMSEY (*Looking around*): We all here? (*His eyes stop at Fred*) Welcome back, Sloane. Feeling better?

SLOANE: Much, thank you. A little stom—

RAMSEY: I'm glad it's cleared up. This will be a very brief meeting this morning. At the board meeting last Friday the purchase of the Anderson plant was discussed. We tossed it around awhile—made no conclusive findings. I've finished my analysis of the entire matter. I'd like you all to look it over, then come back to me. (*He hands out mimeographed sheets to either side*) How are you doing, Mr. Staples? One of us yet?

FRED: I think so, Mr. Ramsey.

RAMSEY: Fine. Before we go any further, gentlemen, I'd like you all to meet our newest member of the firm—Fred Staples. He's from Cincinnati. He's a production engineer by training, an industrial-relations man by instinct. I expect good things from him. Reading from left to right, Mr. Staples—Mr. Smith, comptroller; Mr. Jameson, head of purchasing; Mr. Vandeventer, chief engineer; Mr. Gordon, head of sales; Mr. Latham, head of service; Mr. Granningan, record control; and Mr. Portier, head of operations. (*Each in turn nods and Fred murmurs how-do-you-do's*) You've met Mr. Sloane—he's our assistant general manager in charge of everything everybody else forgets to be in charge of.

There's laughter, but it's pleasant laughter. Andy laughs with them, and then Fred chuckles along.

RAMSEY: Now back to this Anderson thing. Look feasible to you? Look practical?

There's general agreement, rather dutiful enthusiasm.

RAMSEY (*Looking at Andy*): How about you, Sloane? You look injured by it all. (*He says this absolutely pleasantly, and smiling*)

ANDY (*Wetting his lips*): You mention here probable time of purchase as sometime next spring. The plant'll be in receivership until then?

RAMSEY: That's what it says. Bother you?

ANDY: That means six months with improper maintenance of equipment. Loss of good will. Deterioration of—

RAMSEY: If you'll forgive me for interrupting, it also means a savings of a quarter of a million dollars in the purchase price.

ANDY: The plant employs two hundred men. That's half the working force of the village.

RAMSEY: So?

ANDY (*Sorry he's gone so far, but unable to turn back*): So it means the disrupting of an entire village's economy!

RAMSEY: That is very true. Anything else?

ANDY (*Flushing*): Aside from the . . . the consideration I mentioned, I think the purchase plans are adequate.

RAMSEY: Adequate? (*To the others, and amused*) Mr. Sloane thinks it's adequate. Well, Mr. Sloane, if I can't induce any more enthusiasm than that from you, I'll be satisfied with what little crumb of agreement you may toss at me.

ANDY: I . . . I didn't mean to imply just . . . just adequacy, though I must admit to feeling a concern for two hundred wage earners suddenly deprived of a livelihood.

RAMSEY (*This time nothing humorous*): Mr. Sloane, if you'd do me the goodness to listen closely to what I think is a fairly elementary thing. By putting two hundred men out of work, we ultimately may employ twice that number—by paying less for the plant, by being able to cut production costs as a result, by then competing more favorably in the market, we'll be able to sell more goods. We're not going to ruin that town; we're going to make it. I should think, Mr. Sloane, after twenty-odd years you'd be able to think beyond the tongue-clucking stage and come up with an analytical point of view!

ANDY: I was under the impression I'd given you a point of view.

RAMSEY: I saw none. I perceived what amounts to a little emotional tidbit that is decidedly more charitable than it is corporative, and by no means thought through. I asked, I believe, for an objective view of a business venture. From you I got—and I seem to be constantly getting a very negative response if any at all. Adequate, I think you said. Well, Mr. Sloane, this little move will save us two hundred and fifty thousand dollars, which we'll be able to put back in the business. Sloane, you take a liberal view of adequacy!

ANDY: I didn't . . . didn't mean just . . . just adequacy. I meant—by and large—it sounded very good. Very good, indeed.

RAMSEY: Thank you, and bless you, Mr. Sloane. (*To the others, grinning again*) Mr. Sloane approves.

There's laughter now, but a little forced, because the kidding has become something infinitely deeper, more cutting. Andy tries a grin, but it's sickly and fades fast.

RAMSEY: Now, Mr. Staples. You have an opinion?

FRED: I'm . . . I'm afraid not.

RAMSEY: And why don't you?

FRED: Well . . . frankly . . . because I've looked at this for just five minutes. I know nothing about the plant—its corporative set-up, causes of bankruptcy, or its product, for that matter. I'm afraid I'd have to pass on this one at the moment.

RAMSEY: I would call that a solid, intelligent and conservative answer. Had you come up with an intensive program of your own after five minutes I'd have wondered about your sanity. There are times, gentlemen, when dynamics are plain idiocy. I respect thoughtful judgment. Congratulations, Staples. That's it for now. I want each of you to try to pick this analysis to pieces—we'll discuss it further. If there are any flaws in it, I want to find them now.

He rises, and this is the signal for general exodus.

RAMSEY (*Walking over to Andy and Fred*): How is that stomach, Andy? Still acting up?

ANDY: I think . . . I think much better.

RAMSEY (*Patting him on the arm*): Good boy. Leave early this week. Get some rest. (*Turns smiling to Fred. Extends his hand*) Good to have you with us, Staples. Find a house, did you?

FRED: We're renting—out in Westville, Connecticut.

RAMSEY: That's beautiful country there. I think you'll enjoy it. Please give my best to Mrs. Staples. I hope we may have dinner together soon. (*Sees Andy heading out. Calls*) See you later, Andy. (*Andy goes out. Ramsey turns again to Fred*) Incidentally, Sloane there has a project being worked on now—sort of an end-of-year review of plant operations and suggested changes. I'd like you to get your finger in that. I think he could use your help.

FRED: I'll do that.

RAMSEY: Fine. I think you'll do all right, Staples. I'm sure of it.

FRED: Thank you, sir.

Fred exits. Ramsey holds, looking after him. Jameson comes up to him, looking for a lead.

JAMESON: Nice fellow, Staples.

RAMSEY: Umm . . . Howard, would you take another look at the cost accounting?

Cut to Andy's office. Cut to Fred's office. He enters to find Fran.

FRAN (*As he enters*): I'm early. I couldn't wait. Freddy, how is it?

FRED: Oh, kinda . . . kinda early to tell. (*He kisses her*)

FRAN: Your secretary said you'd been in a big meeting. Did you see Mr. Ramsey?

FRED: Yep. Just finished talking to him.

FRAN (*Catches his mood, tries to cheer him up*): Freddy, I think your office is lovely. And oh, Freddy, I bought curtains. The most gorgeous things. Very expensive but strictly rich! Oh, you—you—we're gonna love it here!

FRED (*Taking her in his arms. Then, as if to a little girl*): Where do you keep this vast reservoir of enthusiasm?

FRAN: Why shouldn't I be enthusiastic? I love you very much. I'm so very proud of you. I have been for years, remember? I'm expecting you to be president inside two years. It's in my master plan! (*A little smile as she takes out a thin box*) And in line with that—a little memento of the morning's shopping. Something you can have to remind you in a small way of how wonderful you are.

Fran hands him the box, opened. Fred takes out a watch—an expensive, very dressy watch.

FRAN: I had to buy it. I had to give you something.

FRED: Fran—it's . . . it's lovely.

FRAN (*Very intently*): Every time I hear you doubting yourself, wondering if you've done the right thing—coming east. Take a look at the time. It goes with the salary, so don't worry.

FRED: It's gorgeous. (*Puts it on*) I don't suppose you'd tell me how much it cost?

FRAN: Two hundred and thirty-eight dollars plus tax and please don't say anything. It's from me. (*Hugs him close*) If only Cincinnati could see you now!

FRED: Thank you. (*He crosses to door of office and sees Andy Sloane come out of his office with his coat and hat*) There's Andy Sloane. I'd like you to—(*At which point he sees Andy turn, top coat under his arm, walk off alone*) Well . . . you'll meet him next time. Ready?

FRAN: Take me to lunch? Feel like celebrating?

FRED: Sure—where would you like to go?

FRAN: Somewhere very elegant and very unlike Cincinnati.

FRED: You've come to the right place.

They exit. Marge is sitting at her desk, staring after them. She turns slowly toward Andy's office, rises, goes into it. She sees a bottle open on the desk, looks around, then closes it, puts it away. She slowly shakes her head—pityingly, sorrowfully, knowingly. Fade out.

ACT TWO

Fade in on Marge typing at desk. The time is three months later. A buzzer rings. Marge goes into office. Fred is standing near his desk with a young man, his assistant, going over some last-minute instructions before the kid leaves on a job for him. The boy is checking each report as it is handed him and putting it into a brand-new attaché case.

FRED: Let's see that breakdown again. (*Leafs through it*) That's the one. It's the only one I've got that's cross-indexed for divisions, so don't let them keep it. Marge, I want Billy to take with him my letter to Henry Jacobsen. (*She exits*) Henry's a very nice man. Spent a week with him last month. He's as hard as they come. Started out stoking coke furnaces at fourteen, was mill foreman at twenty, bought the company for his own fortieth birthday present. So look out. Give him these reports, remember what he says, make stenographic notes when you can, when you can't put it on paper, as soon as you can get out of the room. (*Marge has returned with the letter. Fred walks to his door with the boy*) I want to know what they're thinking, what they feel about every paragraph of my recommendations. I hope they'll open up more to you than for me, and I'll go down next week for their decision. (*Phone rings. He starts back for it*) Goodbye, boy. Come back Sunday night if you can. (*Picks up phone*) Hello . . . (*Hand over phone*) Don't go away, Miss Fleming. . . . This is Fred. . . . I'm sorry, Jud, I meant to call you back. That meeting on Atlantic States Nitrate has been set up for March the eighth, but I want a delay on it. . . . Yes, could you? . . . Thanks. It would help a lot. See you in the dining room at lunch. (*Hangs up*) Did those wires get out?

MARGE: Yes, sir.

FRED: Good. Now then, after lunch I would like to set up a conference call between Ramsey, Jameson and myself with Mr. Deering in Denver, Colorado. (*There's a knock at the door*) Come in. (*Andy enters*) Hi!

ANDY: You dictating? I'll come back.

FRED: Sit down. I can always do this.

Andy lights his pipe and sits down.

ANDY: How'd you know it was my Paul's birthday Saturday?

FRED: Because his old man told me one time—few weeks ago.

ANDY: It was kind of you, Fred. He goes to bed with that football. Said you came around Saturday to bring it and showed him how to pass it properly. And he also said you were an All-American. He read it in a book—some sports magazine.

FRED: That was a long time ago. I'm glad he got a kick out of it, Andy.

ANDY: He did. Very much so. Thanks a whole lot, Fred. Thoughtful of you. (*He rises*) Incidentally, I've got the first draft of that report done. Perhaps we can spend an evening on it soon.

FRED: Wonderful. And how about our party? Saturday night. I hope you're coming.

ANDY: I'm not sure yet. I planned to phone Fran this evening. Well, go back to work. Sorry for the interruption.

Andy smiles, waves, goes out. Fred watches the door close and stands there gazing at it in deep thought.

MARGE: Your last sentence was "Further, the set-up of—"

FRED: I'd like to knock that off until after lunch, Miss Fleming—if you don't mind.

MARGE: All right, Mr. Staples.

She starts to collect her things, then reaches for her coffee container.

FRED: Drink it here—relax a minute, if Mr. Sloane doesn't need you.

MARGE: Thank you. I will. (*A pause*) Where did you play your football, Mr. Staples?

FRED: Ohio State. But if you ask me the years, I won't tell you.

MARGE: Old man, huh?

FRED: Yeah, And three times as old as I was when I got here.

MARGE: They've kept you busy.

FRED: Yes they have, thank heaven! It's their secret. Always give a man more responsibility than you're sure he can handle. He'll grow with it, take that and more, and do you well.

MARGE: Or go under.

FRED: No, the doing makes you stronger. You give and give, and when even more is needed you find strengths in yourself that you would never have discovered otherwise. It's the doing! It can make you feel that nothing is impossible. It is a great excitement! The greatest! And you grow!

He looks at her. She has been watching him very closely.

FRED: Sorry. I guess I'm off again. I like it here. I enjoy the challenge. I used to yearn for the old Cincinnati days. We had an executive staff of three people—the president, me and my assistant. That makes for a simple operation. It's been like going from sandlots to major league.

MARGE: You've handled it very well. You've fitted in quickly.

FRED: Thank you. You know, Miss Fleming, I've been here three months. As I recall that's the first out-and-out kind thing you've said to me. (*She doesn't answer*) You resent me a little, don't you?

MARGE: Yes. It's very natural, Mr. Staples. You work with a fine man for a long while. You are part of his future as well. Then comes the new man.

FRED: You're loyal. That's pretty admirable—loyalty.

MARGE: I'm not complaining, Mr. Staples. You have been very nice to me.

FRED: I'm not complaining either, Miss Fleming. I'm just making some off-the-cuff comments about life and times in the office. (*He walks over to the window*) I like Andy Sloane. (*Turns to her*) That may be our only common ground. I don't know. But I like him and I have from the first.

MARGE: I think you do. He's . . . he's a fine man, Mr. Staples. He was with the firm when it was just a few frame buildings and twenty workmen. That was when Mr. Ramsey's father was in charge. Mr. Sloane is the last of the original bunch. That's not . . . not easy—to be the last of an old group.

FRED (*Looks at her a long while, then nods*): I know.

MARGE: If I seem . . . protective, defensive, it's habit, that's all. Just habit. He's not well. He has a bad heart. And the stomach ailment is really an ulcer. I guess that's par for the executive course, isn't it? At least one recognizable ulcer?

FRED: I wouldn't know, really. I haven't been an executive very long.

MARGE: That's obvious.

FRED: Yes?

MARGE: You're different than most.

FRED: In what way?

MARGE: I'm talking too much.

FRED: In what way? Go ahead.

MARGE: Well, when you make mistakes—

FRED: And I have.

MARGE: Yes, I know. But you don't do the usual thing. Put blame on others. Pass the buck. Blow your horn loud enough to drown out your occasional failures. That's different. In a way . . . That's the way Mr. Sloane is. Only . . . only before, he never gave in. If he believed in something, he'd fight for it. He's ill now . . . and older. He was once a wonderful fighter, too. (*She rises*) I really must go. Thank you for a mutual letting down of the hair.

FRED: Marge, why?

MARGE: Why what?

FRED: Why does Mr. Ramsey pin a target on him? On *him* so specially?

MARGE: This is Marge Fleming talking, not a secretary. Will you take it that way?

FRED: Just that way.

MARGE: Mr. Ramsey doesn't like his judgment constantly questioned. An old-fashioned point of view, a deep concern with ethics. It's this way with Mr. Ramsey. You go along, or you get off.

FRED: Andy Sloane never got off.

MARGE: You're here now. Maybe he's about to be pushed.

Dissolve to reception room—night—one light burning. Fred enters and crosses through room into dark hall. Cut to tight shot of Andy, bone-tired, working in his office. He looks up as he hears footsteps off, puts bottle into desk drawer. Cut to corridor in front of their offices. Footsteps come on mike. Fred enters shot through corridor B. Dark but for light in Andy's office. This is the place of busy, frenetic noise and motion, suddenly stripped of sound. Fred holds a moment, crosses to Andy's door, which is open. Andy is tired—tired and sick. He doesn't want to see anyone—even Fred. The scene is one of separation—by no means easy for either one.

ANDY: Hello, Fred.

FRED: Hello, Andy. Working late?

ANDY: Trying to. Come in.

FRED: Thanks.

ANDY: That new watch out of commission? It's ten o'clock at night.

FRED: I know.

ANDY: What are you doing here?

FRED (*Sitting down, his coat still on*): Nothing, really. Took a solitary ride. Wound up here. Magnetic place, isn't it?

ANDY: It can be. . . . Been looking over the supplements you did for the report. I think Mr. Ramsey's right. You're an engineer by diploma, but a cracker-jack industrial planner by instinct or something! Your suggestions were great, Fred. Really very good. I've incorporated them verbatim.

FRED: I'm glad for that. I didn't sleep last night.

ANDY: I liked your approach. You think of people in terms of a human factor. Not just logistically. That's something I've been trying to sell Mr. Ramsey for—I like your ideas.

FRED: Will he like them?

ANDY (*Smiling wanly*): Who's to say? One thing—he's been complaining I turn in the same report every year. He won't be able to say that this year. It had reached a point where I'd have to . . . to . . . (*He turns away*) . . . brace myself with about a half a bottle before I'd hand it in each year.

FRED: Andy . . . (*He stands*)

ANDY (*Pulls out a bottle, fingers it*): I've begun to use this as a morning cap as well—good for illusions. Not to dispel them but to conjure them up.

FRED: How many have you had tonight? Enough, maybe, Andy?

ANDY: Never enough—not lately. Sit down, Fred. Sit down quietly and be a nice sympathetic friend and associate. I'm wondering if you're as good a human being as you are an industrial-relations man.

FRED: He doesn't like you, does he?

ANDY: NO.

FRED: Why doesn't he fire you?

ANDY: On our level you don't get fired. You resign. They don't know how to say get out after thirty years of service, most of them productive. So they create a situation you can't work in and finally can't live in—tension, abuse, mostly subtle and sometimes violent. Chip away at your pride, your security, until you begin to doubt, then fear. . . . Ramsey wants me to resign. He wants me to get my craw so full I'll forget what his father meant to me, what this great company has meant to me, that I'll chuck it all and pull out. He thinks he can make me miserable enough to do that.

FRED: You take it.

ANDY: Sure, I'm the kind who does. The kind who gets into a rut and feels desperate about the job. The kind who gets used to a big salary and decides it's more important than his pride. (*Holds up glass*) The chain that binds. Habit. Pattern. So I conjure up another illusion. That the other morning didn't happen. And all the other mornings. All the other little humiliations. How I get sick when he insults me. And when everybody in the room is waiting for me to either collapse or get out. Because it's a moot question—how much can you take before you crack!

FRED: Why?

ANDY: Why?

FRED: *Why* do you take it?

ANDY: Because I'm a weak man. Answer your question? Because I'm scared to death he'll ax me one fine day and I'm sixty-six years old, have a boy ready for college, and I don't think I could get another job. How's it strike you?

FRED: How do you think?

ANDY (*Sits down. Puts the bottle away*): I have a dream—every now and then I dream I'm sitting in that conference room and he starts working over something I've done he doesn't like. Then I get up. I walk over to him and I spit right in his eye. Then I shout at him. Then I smack him and I scream at him, "Ramsey—"

FRED: Easy, Andy.

ANDY: I scream at him "Ramsey! . . ." (*He breaks. He doesn't really know what he'd say to him*) I'll be all right. (*Beginning to come out of it and smile faintly*) Except for two big bleeding ulcers, a bum heart and a permanent cringe. Thanks for sympathy extended.

FRED: Is there anything I can do?

ANDY: Just don't mention this.

Off we hear a kid whistling, footsteps approaching. In for Andy's tortured reaction. Cut to hall off reception room. Paul enters, whistling, crosses down hall. Cut to Andy's office. Back from close-up. Andy to see both.

ANDY: It's Paul. He's to pick me up. (*Turns off light. The office is dark*) Tell him I left early to go home to rest.

FRED: Come on, Andy.

ANDY: Do like I tell you, Fred. Help me.

Fred leaves office to enter dark corridor. Footsteps have been coming closer through scene. Paul enters frame. He stops suddenly as he rounds corner, sees no light in his father's office. He notices a shadowy figure standing by door.

PAUL: Dad?

FRED: It's me, Paul.

PAUL (*Crossing to him slowly*): Man, what a place by night. Where do they keep the caskets? And you guys work in this place?

FRED: How are you, Paul?

PAUL: Been to a show. Dad said I should drop in here when I got out. Guess he's gone.

FRED: Hours ago. Went home to rest, or so he said.

PAUL: Good. He's under orders not to work late. But he can't keep away lately. Always work, always worrying. No wonder he's the number-two man.

FRED: I'll drive you home.

PAUL: Swell.

They start out. Leave frame. Under following speech of Paul's we just hear their footsteps and his voice gradually disappear.

PAUL: Ever since I can remember he's been married to this place. Mom used to say the same thing. Two wives. Half the time growing up he'd be here before I got down for breakfast. Once he missed two Christmas Eves in a row and Mom threatened divorce. They were great together, Fred. Mom and Dad. Used to yell and argue and carry on. He was a fighter. It was great growing up. I remember . . .

A door opens and closes way off. Voices and footsteps out.

A beat. The light in Andy's office finally comes on. A beat, and dissolve to Staples' living room. Music behind from hi-fi. A party that is breaking up. Dissolve to Fred helping guests on with coats at door. Ad libs—"Nice dinner"; "How nice you could come." Cut to Fred's study. Ramsey's seated at desk looking over a heavy report. Fran enters.

FRAN: Some fresh coffee will be ready soon.

RAMSEY: Thank you, Fran. Now my father's recipe was to mix salt and chocolate in the coffee grounds. Cook them together. Wouldn't drink anything else.

FRAN: Sounds wonderful!

RAMSEY: They serve it at a restaurant I eat at frequently. I must mention it to Fred—two of us'll eat there. You say he's a confirmed coffee drinker?

FRAN: Dedicated!

RAMSEY: Fine. He's quite a young man.

FRAN: How do you like his report?

RAMSEY: Thank you for letting me see it. Not according to Hoyle at a dinner party, but most acceptable even so! Makes me extremely proud of my judgment, Fran.

FRAN: I'm so happy. He's been worried.

FRED (*Off*): Fran . . .

FRAN: Excuse me.

Cut to the front door. Fred is bidding goodbyes to several members of board. Fran joins him to ad-lib goodbyes—"I never liked office parties, but this has been great," etc.

FRED (*After the group has gone*): You hitting it off well with Ramsey?

FRAN: Delightfully. He's a tremendous person, Fred. Really!

FRED: Where is he? Spending the night? (*Laughing*)

FRAN: No, he's in your study.

FRED: That's cozy.

Gordon comes up.

GORDON: Wonderful party, Fran. Makes me think I should get married.

FRAN: Wonderful having you, Bob. Come again soon.

Cut to study. Ramsey is looking through the bookcase.

RAMSEY: I like your reading material, Fred. Good stuff here.

FRED: That Maugham book is new. Read it?

RAMSEY: Saw a few reviews on it. (*He turns to Fred. Motions toward the papers on his desk*) Also some interesting reading on your desk here. I took the liberty of accepting Fran's invitation to look over your report.

FRED (*Nervous*): Oh? How . . . how did it strike you?

RAMSEY: Good, heady stuff. Good, solid thinking. I don't agree with all your conclusions, but I'll hear arguments from you. It will be good to hear arguments for a change.

FRED (*Tremendously relieved*): That's the best thing of the evening!

RAMSEY: I like initiative, Fred. I like a person to think a new thought—take a different kind of step on his own.

FRED: Andy and I felt that—

RAMSEY: Andy? Come now, Staples—I know Andy's work. I've been exposed to it since I was of voting age. This isn't Andy's thinking.

FRED (*Hesitant, unsure*): I . . . I don't know what Fran may have told you, but—

RAMSEY: Fred, learn to accept success. Don't take half of your own accomplishments and gratuitously hand it out to a man on your left who hasn't the stuff to do it on his own. That's charitable and it makes you feel good, but it's not business. The meeting's tomorrow. We can talk about the report then.

FRED: I don't want undue credit.

RAMSEY: I never extend undue credit! Ask your friend Sloane. (*A pause*) You think I'm tough on him, don't you? I am tough on him.

FRED: He's a good man, Mr. Ramsey!

RAMSEY: He was. And grandfather clocks were good clocks. And Stanley Steamers were good cars. But you don't run them by competition today—Mr. Sloane now has a certain sentimental value. He's a sweet old keepsake—a sentimental carry-over from the old days. He can serve that kind of purpose.

FRED: I like his ideas—some of them.

RAMSEY: So do I. Some of them.

FRED: Still, a man with his experience . . . he'd be—be hard to replace. (*And then vaguely, anxious to shut this off now*) That coffee ought to be done! Perhaps it'd be more comfortable in the living room. (*He stops, sees Ramsey staring at him*)

RAMSEY: Are you serious, Fred? Sloane would be hard to replace? You honestly think that? Then why the devil do you think I brought you here from Cincinnati on a week's notice? You think that was a whim? Fred, you're Sloane's replacement!

FRED (*After a pause*): That is the deal, then.

RAMSEY: I assumed you knew that. I'm sure Sloane must realize it. I'm expecting his resignation. I don't like to prolong these things. And I don't want him to have to be fired.

Fran enters, perceives immediately that something's wrong.

FRAN: Come on into the living room and—

RAMSEY (*Looking hurriedly at his watch*): Good lord, look at that time! I'm awfully sorry, Fran, but I really must run. It's been a wonderful evening.

FRAN: For us too. I'm so sorry you have to leave.

RAMSEY: I really must. My coat's in the bedroom, I think.

FRAN: I'll get it for you. (*She goes out*)

RAMSEY (*Turning to Fred*): May I make a suggestion?

FRED: I realize I'm not acting grateful—

RAMSEY: I'm not looking for gratitude. You don't run a business with thank-you notes. That's Sloane's trouble, too. And God forgive me, that was my father's trouble. The fantastic conception that a big industry could be run like a soup kitchen—a welfare comfort station. I know what the old-timers think of me. I've grown up getting stared at by tongue-clucking old fogies who call me ruthless. I suppose that's why I find Sloane so completely irksome to me. He seems to represent everything my father left me that I didn't believe and kept our business from growing to anything like it's present size. This preoccupation with morality above profits. This stupid, black-and-white idea that honesty and profit are incompatible. (*Fran enters with his coat and now his voice is modulated*) I just happen to feel that the atmosphere of a big corporation can't be constantly churchlike. Thank you, Fran. (*He starts to button his coat*). Again, my thanks for a wonderful evening.

FRAN: It was wonderful having you—and we'll do it again soon.

They walk him out into the living room and to the front door.

RAMSEY (*Slapping Fred on the shoulder*): See you in the office tomorrow. We'll talk some more.

FRED: Good! See you then.

RAMSEY: Good night—and thanks again.

He goes out. Fred closes the door.

FRAN: What was all that about?

FRED: I'm in line for Andy Sloane's job.

FRAN: *A vice-presidency?*

FRED: You must have spread it thick this evening.

FRAN (*Pulling him close*): Listen, Ears—it takes more than a good dinner and some wifely pride to get *this* kind of promotion.

FRED (*Breaking away from her*): Yeah, it takes something more. A little misrepresentation, for one thing. (*Picks up the papers on his desk*) A little switch of authorship for another. (*Turns to her*) You told him I'd written the report.

FRAN: I told him Andy helped you on it.

FRED: That was a lie, you know.

FRAN: No, I didn't know. I knew you'd said that, but I know how you are. I know you can't stand winning because you hate to see a loser. And I guess that comes from that deep-rooted neurosis of yours that you're grade-B inferior and sooner or later everybody'll know it.

FRED: Whatever I am, I don't like lying into a capital-gains bracket. I don't like using a knife to pry open doors.

FRAN (*Hotly*): I didn't hear you tell Mr. Ramsey he was mistaken. I didn't hear any clear-cut defense of your bosom friend, Mr. Sloane. Don't rip out our lily-white banners and flaunt them in my face. If you don't want to be successful, tell that to Mr. Ramsey. He'll hand you a broom and you can check in every night at seven. But don't tell me. I'm sick to death of hearing it.

FRED: Fran, I don't want to argue.

FRAN: Neither do I. I just want you to answer me. Did you tell Mr. Ramsey that your wife was mistaken? Did you tell him you were taking bows you shouldn't be?

FRED: No. No, I didn't.

FRAN: Why, Fred?

FRED: Because . . . because I want to be a vice-president.

FRAN: I thank you for a straight and honest answer. I think we can both go to sleep now.

FRED: Tomorrow morning, in that meeting, in that conference room, he's going to whip Andy to death.

FRAN (*Handing him an ash tray*): Help me clear up. We can talk about it in the morning. Besides, that's Mr. Ramsey's responsibility—it's not yours.

FRED: It's mine, too. Tonight . . . all along . . . and just by coming here—I handed him the whip. Here's . . . here's to vice-president Staples! He finally made it.

He flings the ash tray against the wall and stands there with his head down. Fran, white-faced, quietly walks over to him, touches his shoulder, then softly lays her head against him.

FRAN: Oh, Fred . . . Freddy.

Fade out.

ACT THREE

Fade in tight shot of the report lying on Fred's desk at home. Same shot as close of Act II, except that now it is morning and the room is splashed with sunlight, a pattern across desk. A car starts off. Motor in gear. Backs up a bit. Horn blows impatiently.

FRED (*Off*): All right, all right.

FRAN (*'Way off*): Fred, if you miss the 8:02, you'll never make the office in time for the meeting.

FRED: I know, I know.

Door opens, closes on mike. Fred's hand enters shot, takes up report, stuffs it into brief case. Horn off.

FRED: I'd better not forget you.

Exits. Horn again. Door opens, close off. Car door opens-close, car in gear, backs out driveway, changes gears and off. Cut to tight shot of Andy's brief case on desk. He takes report out of it, hands it to Marge, who is waiting. Sound: Immediate blend on cut from car to office background.

ANDY: All done. Get Miss Lanier to initial it for confidential mimeographing.

Marge exits out of office, down hall to Miss Lanier's desk before Ramsey's office.

MARGE: Good morning, Miss Lanier. This is Mr. Sloane's report. It's ready to be printed if you'll—

Phone rings.

MISS LANIER (*Picking it up*): Take it in to Mr. Ramsey, would you, Marge? He asked to see it first.

Marge enters office.

RAMSEY: That the report?

MARGE (*Handing it to him*): Yes, sir.

He takes it, opens it to title page. Cut to close-up of page while she talks. He draws a line through Andy's name, leaving Fred as sole author.

MARGE: It's all ready for mimeoing, Mr. Ramsey, if you'll just initial and—

She sees what he has done. He hands her back the report. She opens it to title page.

RAMSEY: Print it.

MARGE: Mr. Ramsey, I'm sure that—

RAMSEY: Miss Fleming, I've seen the report and have discussed the matter thoroughly with Mr. Staples. Print it.

Marge turns and exits into hallway. She goes to Andy's door, finally enters.

MARGE: Mr. Sloane, there's something you have to know about.

Cut to hall. Fred enters, goes into office, leafs through notes on desk. He pushes buzzer. Finally calls.

FRED: Miss Fleming . . . Miss Fleming, any time set for the meeting this morning?

MARGE: Ten-thirty.

FRED: And is Mr. Sloane in?

MARGE: Yes, sir, he's busy at the mo—

FRED: I didn't ask you if he was busy. I asked you if he was in.

MARGE (*Hotly*): I'm so terribly sorry. In the future I'll—

FRED (*Wilting*): Marge, I'm sorry. Please . . . sit down for a minute.

She sits, but she doesn't relax, doesn't relent, and carries the same chip as she has in the beginning.

FRED: Very little sleep last night. That's never very good for the next morning's temperament. (*He awaits a reply, gets none*) The good executive never shows outward temperament, does he? (*Still no answer*) I suppose Andy . . . Mr. Sloane never raised his voice in any given situ—

MARGE (*Rising*): Why don't you ask him yourself? He's in his office. I'm sure he'd love to give you any information you'd like.

FRED: Marge!

MARGE: Only when you ask him, don't play the part of the wide-eyed disciple. We all know that doesn't fit any more.

FRED: What part would you like, Miss Fleming?

MARGE: The clever young executive—on his way up, kicking open doors and pushing people out of the way—keep it true to life! Subtle, Mr. Staples—always subtle!

FRED (*Very, very softly*): Anything else?

MARGE (*She looks at him intently, and then after a pause*): Yes. Yes, one other thing. Take a good long look at Mr. Sloane. That'll be you in ten years. Because I think you know that way down deep you're very much alike. A lot of the things, a lot of the good things he believes in, I think you believe in, too. You're inheriting his title, Mr. Staples, but it's a package deal. You'll get his heartache, too.

She walks out of the office, Fred staring after her. Andy comes out of his office, sees Marge quickly dabbing at her eyes. He turns to Fred, who comes out of his office.

ANDY: Ready, Fred? It's about that time.

FRED: Yeah. Yeah, I'm all set.

ANDY: Good.

They start up the corridor toward the conference room. Andy, as usual, pauses by the water cooler.

FRED: Andy . . .

GORDON (*Passing them*): You gentlemen ready?

FRED: We'll be right in. (*After Gordon's passed, he turns again to Andy*) I never wanted to knife you, Andy. I never wanted to—

ANDY (*His face is haggard. It shows strain, a mounting fear, a desperate apprehension*): I'm braced now. Don't make it any harder.

The last ten years—all pointing to this next minute—and I'm braced for it now. So for God's sakes, Fred, let's not have any unburdening now.

He walks on ahead and into the conference room. Fred follows him in and we cut to the interior.

RAMSEY (*As usual, studying the men as they take their places*): Let's begin. I've received each of the departmental reports turned in. By and large they show effort and thought. One in particular is unique in its effort—and ingenious in its thought. To Mr. Fred Staples of our organization goes my heartfelt thanks and congratulations. Besides being the newest member of our group, he also appears to be one of its most astute! His year-end report is ingenious, comprehensive and fresh. Congratulations, Mr. Staples. Your success is a reaffirmation of my own judgment. My own *good* judgment, I may add.

FRED: Mr. Ramsey . . .

RAMSEY: Now if you drench me with modesty, Mr. Staples, I'll have to re-evaluate that judgment.

FRED: This isn't modesty—it's just a clearing up of what appears to be a misunderstanding. (*Turns to Andy*) Andy here actually-

RAMSEY (*Throwing the paper onto the table*): I'm getting to Andy. You'll forgive me, Mr. Sloane, if I come to the point and if I appear direct and highly unflattering. (*To the group*) Mr. Sloane saw fit to add his name to this document. (*Holds it up*) Right here. You see? "Respectfully submitted, Mr. Andrew Sloane, Mr. Frederick Staples." You know what I call that, Mr. Sloane? I call that presumptuous. I dislike few things, Mr. Sloane. High taxes, low production—and coattail riding! Your taking credit for someone else's work is an example of the latter. Coattail riding. A man slips, he clutches. He loses his stuff—he tries to borrow someone else's!

ANDY (*On his feet*): *That's not true!*

RAMSEY (*After a long silence in the room*): How's that, Mr. Sloane? I'm mistaken, you think. You recollect, no doubt, that I built this business from a scratch pile of used lumber and one machine into a giant, and I made few mistakes doing it. Few mistakes in business and few mistakes in judging men! Your work hasn't shown this stamp of originality and talent in ten years.

ANDY: In this matter . . . in this matter you're mistaken—

RAMSEY: I'm mistaken. (*To the others*) Mr. Sloane believes me to be mistaken. You're sure, Mr. Sloane?

Andy is fighting a desperate, back-to-the-wall fight within himself—struggling for a strength that is fast deserting him.

ANDY: Mr. Ramsey, really I must protest that—

FRED (*Rising*): Mr. Ramsey, you're mistaken, sir. Andy had every right to put his name on that—

RAMSEY: And you're mistaken if you think I'll permit this meeting to turn into a private little personality clash! You'll be good enough to sit down.

FRED: Andy, this is ridiculous. *Tell him!* For God's sake, tell him!

Something happens to Andy at this one moment. I have to describe it this way: His guts cave in. His pride, or what was left of it, oozes out in a flood tide. His manliness collapses. And when he speaks now it's the voice of a panhandler begging a dime for coffee; and it comes from a hollow-eyed, gaunt ghost just cut down from a whipping post.

ANDY: Mr. Ramsey . . . Mr. Ramsey . . . the . . . the misunderstanding arose from a . . . a secretarial error. My name was not supposed to be put on that . . . that thing. It . . . it was a secretarial error.

RAMSEY: Thank you, Mr. Sloane. I've had Mr. Staples' project mimeoed so you can each have a copy. Take it to pieces. We'll meet again tomorrow morning at eleven. Be ready. I

> want to break that report into bits. I think it's good enough to stand it. Meeting's adjourned.
>
> *Andy has gone out of door. Cut to hall. Teletype very faint off. Crosses down. Door opens, girl out with teletype message, exits. Teletype up on mike. In on Andy. He is sick. In real pain. Slumps against wall. Sound of teletype up. Andy slides to floor. Fred and Ramsey are in door behind. Fred sees him, runs to him.*

FRED: Andy! Your heart?

ANDY (*Nodding*): Get my pills . . . top drawer, left . . . in my office.

RAMSEY: I'll get them. Smith, get an ambulance and don't move him. (*Exits*)

ANDY: Still giving orders. Do me a favor, Fred . . . tell him to go to

FRED: Just rest, Andy. Just don't move.

> *Slow fade out. Teletype hold strong through fade, one beat on black, out, one beat on black silence. Cut to Marge's desk. She is sitting, waiting. Jameson, Gordon are standing near Andy's office. The phone rings.*

MARGE: Hello . . .

> *All she can do is nod. She finally hangs up. Jameson comes over.*

MARGE: Fifteen minutes ago.

> *Jameson moves back to Gordon. Together they go down hall to Miss Lanier's desk. Then she rises and goes into Ramsey's office. A moment, then he comes out. During this time, Marge has covered her typewriter, taken a few personal things out of a drawer and put them into her purse. Fran enters frame.*

FRAN: Hello, Miss Fleming. Fred called me from the hospital. He left before I could get there.

MARGE: Why don't you wait in his office, Mrs. Staples?

FRAN: Thank you, I will.

> *She enters. Marge picks up a small, silly little plant growing on her desk and starts to go for good, when Ramsey enters from his office and walks down the hall toward Andy's office. Marge sees him and freezes. Pure hatred. Ramsey walks slowly into office and closes the door without even being aware she's there. She exits. Inside, he stands a moment*

looking at the desk. Opens drawer, takes out bottle, pours drink, takes it. Sits, drawn into knot. Cut to reception room. Fred enters through elevators.

MISS STEVENS: Mr. Staples, we're all so very sorry . . .

He can only nod, cross down long corridor. Cut to his office—Fran sitting, waiting.

FRAN: Where have you been?

FRED: I've been on the phone talking to his boys. And then in a bar talking to myself. So I've run out of conversation.

FRAN: All right.

FRED: I came back to see Ramsey.

FRAN: He's in Andy's office.

Fred is up like a shot. He goes to her.

FRED: Where?

FRAN: Right next door.

FRED: We're getting out, Fran.

FRAN: O.K. by me, darling.

FRED: I won't be long. (*He crosses to the door*)

FRAN: Hear him through, Fred.

He exits into hall. Goes to Andy's office, throws open door. It is empty. Turns back to hall, goes down to Ramsey's office and to door. Ignores Miss Lanier.

MISS LANIER: He's expecting you.

Fred enters office. Ramsey is standing near window.

RAMSEY: Andy was to go to Detroit tomorrow for a meeting with Phillips. You'll have to take his place. I believe I've already mentioned that.

FRED: Fair enough, Mr. Ramsey. You've got a great man. Andy Sloane and I were always two of a kind.

RAMSEY (*Turning slowly*): What was that?

FRED: Andy Sloane and I. We shared the same insecurities, Mr. Ramsey. The same sense of searching, worrying, apprehensions. So understand that before you put me in his place.

It wasn't Andy's weakness that bothered you. It was his strength. It was his ethics that kept digging into you. Every minute he was around, Andy Sloane was your conscience. A constant, irksome reminder that some things are *wrong*. They can't be shaded somehow or changed—they're wrong!

RAMSEY: Keep going, friend.

FRED: So you used Andy as your whipping boy to try to make him quit. You played through his strength to get at his weakness. You made him backtrack and knuckle down and beat him to death—because he had to compromise to stay alive. And for him to compromise kept him from living. You wanted him out, and you wouldn't fire him.

RAMSEY: That is true.

FRED: Now you've got me. Now I climb into the stocks because I'm the same kind of poor, weak human that Andy was.

RAMSEY: That's not true.

FRED: It was true. I was that kind of human. But I'm not now. Now I'm not afraid of anything you or anybody else can do to me. I'm not afraid of winding up like Andy did—tortured and frantic and desperate. And I'm not afraid to stand here and tell you to your face that it's a tragic renunciation of pride to lick a man's boots. But it's a lot more pitiable to be the man who has to have his boots licked.

RAMSEY: I'm not a nice human being. What else?

FRED: You're a washout! You're a genius, a production, organizational marvel with no compassion for human weakness! You drive and fight and tear your people into peak efficiency if they can make it, or a grave, like Andy, if they can't. Because he lacked the strength.

RAMSEY: And the capacity. He was third in command. That's a lot of responsibility to hold.

FRED: It was his business, too!

RAMSEY: It is no one's business! It belongs only to the best! To those who can control it. Keep it growing, producing—keep it alive! It belongs to us right now! In the future, to whoever can give it more. And as for you . . .

FRED: Now don't fire me—since I still hold the floor I've got a few more seconds to officially resign.

RAMSEY (*Rising*): What do you want from me—apologies? I don't apologize. What else? A nice unsullied conscience? You walk out of here with a halo because you spoke your mind. Then what do you do? You go work for a nickel-and-dime outfit run by "nice people" who won't challenge you, beat your head in and make your talent reach a height you never dreamed of. A company where you won't have to fight for anything, because you're the best and there's no competition. Where everything is handed to you and there's nothing important to fight for.

FRED: Now it's my turn. What do you want?

RAMSEY: I want you to stay. I need help on my level and you're the only one good enough to function there. You don't like me. I'm not a "nice person" in your mind. But you will learn more, grow more, do more with me than anywhere else because I'll beat you ragged until you do. I don't ask to be liked—fight me, take over if you can. And watch the business grow from your efforts beyond even our dreams. Be a conscience for me if you want. Be anything you like. And what I don't like you'll surely know about. But if you stay, you're going to have to fight for every idea and principle that's holy to you. I think you're strong enough to take it. If not, I'm sure you're strong enough to get out.

FRED (*After a pause*): I think that's acceptable.

RAMSEY: No reservations?

FRED: None. (*Then a pause*) Make that one reservation. Andy Sloane had a forlorn little wish—a little dream—that someday he'd come in here and break your jaw. I reserve that right to have that wish for myself—for him.

RAMSEY: I'll have it drawn into the contract, with a little rider that gives me the same privilege.

FRED: I'll see you tomorrow.

RAMSEY: You bet you will. And, Staples—Andy Sloane's kids are being taken care of.

FRED: Will that let you sleep now?

RAMSEY (*A grim smile*): It starts, huh?

FRED: It starts. Fair enough?

RAMSEY: Fair enough.

Fred goes out of the room. Fran is waiting for him in his office.

FRED: Let's go home.

FRAN: Fred, are you out of a job?

FRED: No. Not yet.

FRAN: Whose terms?

FRED: Mine—and his.

FRAN: Satisfied?

FRED: Yeah. Very.

FRAN: I'm very glad.

FRED: Want me to take you home?

FRAN: I can manage. Finish your work. I'm sure you have some.

FRED: A lot. Good night, darling. (*He kisses her and enters office*) Marge . . . (*To Fran*) I'll be late.

FRAN: Aren't you always?

She blows him a kiss and walks away. Fred continues deep in work, dictation, etc. Follow her through offices and fade out.

AUTHOR'S COMMENTARY ON PATTERNS

Patterns was written in the fall of 1954, shortly after I had taken my wife and family from Ohio to the East. It took me into television's elite quickly and fabulously. But actually, as noted by *Time* Magazine in its review of the program, it was a soundly built play that derived even greater impetus by the most uniquely consistent acting and production ever accorded a television play. Fielder Cook's direction was creatively and artistically a total triumph; the acting of Richard Kiley, Everett Sloane, Ed Begley, Elizabeth Wilson, and everyone else was almost unbelievably excellent.

As to the play—it was good, perhaps better than good. Quite mistakenly, people have attributed its quality to the author's keen perception about big business and its ramifications. Actually *Patterns* was not at all conceived as a big-business opus. I had never occupied a position in the upper-executive echelons, nor had I even ever functioned in what could be legitimately called a big business. *Patterns* is a story of power. It is also parenthetically a conflict of youth versus age. It is set against a background of big business and it utilizes some of the inherent problems that arise in that kind of a situation, but it is not truly a big-business story. There is no single character within it who could be considered a prototype of an economic system, or at least any distinct level of that system. The same kind of conflict could arise if this had been a war story, a political story, or the story of a foreman on an assembly line. I couched it in terms of big business because there is an innate kind of romance in the big, the blustering, and the successful. But there is, in the final analysis, nothing Marxist in the message of this play. It is not an indictment of our capitalistic system nor an exposé of the evils of big money. It is the story of ambition and the price tag that hangs on success. If it professes actually to have a message, it is simply that every human being has a minimum set of ethics from which he operates. This minimum set of ethics often injects itself into a man's own journey upward against competition. When he refuses to compromise these ethics, his career must suffer; when he does compromise them, his conscience does the suffering. There are tragic overtones to this because our society is a competitive one. For every man who goes up, someone has to leave. And when the departure of the aged is neither philosophical nor graceful, there is a kind of aching poignance in this kind of changing of the guard.

The success of *Patterns* was uniquely due to a kind of team effort. I have already mentioned the fabulous direction and acting but the support came also on an editorial level. A totally new conception of the ending came from the editor, Arthur Singer, and it proved to be perhaps one of the most successful and lauded moments of the play. Most television productions are collaborative but *Patterns* evolved, I think, a little more collaboratively than most.

In analyzing the writing of *Patterns*, you will note that though the dialogue is literate—sometimes almost archaic—there is still an over-all pattern of simplicity about it. There is a spare, concise measurement in the writing that gives it flow and legitimacy. You will note that in the final scene between Ramsey and Sloane the two forces clash head on, one with a violence and anger generated by disgust and the other with a zealous fanaticism that is neither blind nor illogical. When these two giants tangle, it is still a scene of comparative brevity. In fact, with the exception of the conference-room scenes, no individual section of the play seems prolonged or padded. Each has its place, its function, and its own particular meaning within the scheme of the story. It follows the classic lines of the tragedy in a way that could be plotted on a graph. There is the step-by-step culmination of all the ingredients. The arrival of Staples; the establishment of his talent and strengths; the subtle overtones of Andy Sloane's worn-out usefulness; the duplication of the two men's positions; the stalking specter of progress that pushes Staples and seeks to pull down Sloane; the agonizing inevitability of Sloane's demise along with the jarring, wrenching ambivalence of Fred Staples' hunger for success that is nonetheless not so bright as to blind his own awareness of another man's agony—all this is the pattern of a handful of lives with the prime mover, Walter Ramsey, at the helm, pushing, prodding, squeezing, in the name of progress and profit.

Underlying all this is the subplot. There is the ambition of Fred Staples' wife; there is the poignant sort of half-groping understanding of Andy Sloane's young son; and there is the despairing dignity of Marge, now Staples' secretary, who has come over to him from Andy Sloane—perhaps the only one who clearly sees that whatever Staples' intentions, and no matter the depth of his sensitivities, he's there as a spoiler and Andy Sloane is his victim.

As you read *Patterns*, you will note that there is little fuzz in the dialogue and in the characterizations. This is a well-defined story with well-delineated people. But the power that is derived from its very simplicity also helps to hide the fact that while there is a vast complexity and depth in its theme, this probing does not extend to its people. With the exception of Walter Ramsey, you'll note a thinness to some of the others. For example, the part of Fran, Staples' wife, is badly drawn. At no single point in her development do we get a reasonably accurate picture of this woman and her motivations. We know that she is ambitious and that her ambition is what prods her husband. We never discover, however, whether or not she shares her husband's sensitivities. We don't know whether she blithely and deliberately chooses to recognize what her husband must do to another fellow human being, or if she realizes this will be one of the by-products of his success and she chooses to discount it in the name of her ambition. She is a charming, rather glib, but, in the final analysis, hard-to-understand young woman. The writing makes her hard to understand.

Staples, on the other hand, is much more a known quantity. He is written in such a way that we readily perceive the diverse pulls on his conscience. We know that he shares his wife's ambition and that with it is a sensitivity. We know that he genuinely likes the man he's been called upon to replace. But in the end of the play we are never given a really definitive explanation of what he feels the moment he walks away from his moment of truth. Or even if it is a moment of truth. He walks into Walter Ramsey's office after Sloane's heart attack to read a riot act in the name of simple, basic, decent justice. And when he walks out he has decided to stay and fight, supposedly on his own terms. There is clarity here in his actions, but not in his motives. Whether it stems from belief or rationalization I have not made clear. Actually, in my own mind I must excuse this lack of a clear-cut direction, because I feel that Fred Staples is himself unsure as to his reasons for staying. When he walks out of Walter Ramsey's office his battered conscience has not been assuaged; but the tense and taut emotions of the past few hours, along with his fatigue, have taken away some of his own awareness. He is not certain at this given moment whether he has won or Ramsey has conned him into *thinking* he's won!

In the motion-picture version of *Patterns*, this vague disquiet on the part of Fred Staples is more clearly shown. When he greets his wife waiting for him in the lobby he says something about it being easy enough to chuck something, suggesting that he is already rationalizing away a gnawing and persistent little doubt that his victory was nothing more than a sellout.

It is interesting, particularly in the case of *Patterns*, to review its transition into terms of motion picture from its original television form. There was no basic ingredient left out for want of time in its original television form. Consequently, when I translated it into terms of motion pictures, there was little in the way of expansion needed, except a more or less horizontal expansion. Many scenes could now be prefaced by a physical introduction—i.e., Wall Street before we enter the offices. Right now, my feelings (subject to change) are that this additional horizontal scope added nothing to the over-all quality and effect of *Patterns*. If anything, some of its incisiveness, its sharpness and clarity and some of its taut kind of understatement seem to have been somewhat diffused. Only in the board-room scenes did the story seem to gain in the movie. In television, because of its time limitations, there exists the necessity for showing a part to suggest the whole. In the case of a board meeting, which in the context of the story is of vital importance, we do not have time to show the entire board meeting. We can show only a few dibs and dabs of the proceedings, and then get right into the action that is important. Thus, though an audience knows that any board meeting must last at least an hour or so, in television it lasts but a few moments and, if successful, gives the illusion of lasting longer. This illusion was sustained somewhat in the television performance. There was a suggestion of things on the agenda that were properly vague and complex, but it wasn't long before the conflict at hand was introduced with the colloquy between Ramsey and Sloane. But though few people were aware of the approximately six-minute board meetings, there was an over-all effect of staccato and hurry-up that did not enhance the realism of the performance. In the movie this effect has been aided. Though the scenes are not in themselves much longer, the illusion of length and an agenda seems better drawn. It comes more from camera than from writing. The corridor, the room, and the visual play on the characters add a dimension that was lacking on television.

As of this writing *Patterns* has proven no boon to the motion-picture exhibitors. Rather, it has played to only sporadically good houses, with a record of financial return that has been sparse and disappointing. Its reviews as a motion picture matched their television counterparts. These have been with only one or two exceptions consistently fine. If we can utilize this as a measure we can make a further assumption that *Patterns'* comparative failure is more economic than artistic. Perhaps an audience, however taken with the television show, is not so prone to spend money to see it again in another form. This suggests further that the relationship between motion pictures and television is so close in terms of technique that there is little to choose between the two. Basic in any play is its story, and this is the one area which will require the least change in taking one vehicle over from one medium to another.

From a writing viewpoint, time is the only big difference in creation. The movies permit more by-play, perhaps a bit more subtlety, and, as I indicated before, more horizontal freedom. Scenes can play longer, and characters can say and do more. But the story unfolds in much the same way. Its physical trappings are extended, colored and costumed, but it is questionable how this will implement a dramatic effect in a story, if the story itself has an innate power that has previously come through without those trappings.

But with all its faults and foibles, *Patterns* must have hit on a truth, and this truth had its roots in the behavior of men and women. Almost half of the several hundred letters I received after *Patterns'* initial television performance pointedly asked if this wasn't really the story of so-and-so company with Mr. A and Mr. B. This was, then, no indictment of big business. The characters in *Patterns* have their counterparts in real life on many levels. If, on the other hand, any indictment is suggested, it is simply an indictment of the imposed values of a society that places such stock in success and has so little preoccupation with morality when success has been attained. And this is not the morality of good and evil, not the black-and-white of what is fundamentally right and wrong. This is the morality of the fringes, the plowing under of human dignity in the name of progress, and the mass-production attitude toward the individual because his goods and services happen to be efficiently produced by mass-production methods. This is morality's shady side of the street. The patterns of which this piece speaks are behavior patterns of little human beings in a big world—lost in it, intimidated by it, and whose biggest job is to survive in it.

THE RACK

CAST

CAPTAIN ED HALL, JR.: *A Regular Army officer in his late twenties; a good officer if a sensitive one. A very astute, intelligent man but one who has succumbed to fear and its consequences; one whose nerves are taut and thin.*

LIEUTENANT STEVE WASNIK: *Just a little older than Ed. His defense attorney. He's brusque, with a sense of humor and a "not give a damn" about conventions and protocol. A very human and a very likable guy.*

CAPTAIN SAM MOULTON: *A little like Wasnilk, he's the trial counsel. But he's older and he thinks things out a little more and he's a searching kind of man. He's in his middle to late thirties. Regular Army.*

COLONEL EDWARD HALL, SR.: *Ed's father A Regular Army colonel, retired.*

AGATHA (AGGIE): *Ed's sister-in-law. An attractive young woman full of sympathy and awareness.*

COLONEL SMITH
COLONEL FIELDER } Old cronies of Colonel Hall's.

LIEUTENANT ANDERSON: *A young platoon officer.*

COLONEL HANSEN: *A G-2 officer*

SERGEANT
CORPORAL } Witnesses for the prosecution.
PRIVATE

ROD SERLING

Gateman *at the railroad station*
President *of the Court*
Law Officer
Soldier *(Court Recorder)*
Chaplain

ACT ONE

We open on a long shot down a semidark, bare corridor of the Pentagon building. On the wall is a sign reading "CORRIDOR NINE-BAY FORTY-FOUR. J.A. SECTION. AUTHORIZED PERSONNEL ONLY."

We go down the hall to an office door marked "J. A. office . . . trial counsel section."

Dissolve through to the interior—a small outer office where Captain Sam Moulton sits on the corner of his desk. He canies a large brief case. He looks at his watch. Then toward the door leading to the adjoining central office. It opens. Colonel Hansen sticks his head in.

HANSEN: You want to come in please, Sam?

Sam nods, walks on into the colonel's office. He takes a seat near his desk and opens up the brief case. He takes out a thick bundle of papers, holds them up, puts them on the desk. The colonel goes over to a table nearby and pours some coffee into a paper cup. He turns to Sam.

HANSEN: Want some coffee?

SAM: No, thanks.

HANSEN (*Sitting down at his desk*): You got a brief?

SAM (*Motioning to the papers*): Pretty much. One-o-four, one-o-five and one-thirty-four. Nine specifications. We can take our pick of fifty witnesses and dig for more if they're needed. (*He rises, lights a cigarette*) It's not open and shut. But it's close to treason and we can ask the limit. Thirty years, maybe.

All this time he's in the act of lighting his cigarette, and his hands shake noticeably. Finally he lights it and tosses the match into an ash tray. But he remains standing.

HANSEN (*Briefly looking through the papers*): I told Colonel Gregor that we'd be checking with G-2 in the morning for interrogation transcripts. Let me know what's needed. (*He looks up. His expression changes when he looks closely at Sam*) Nervous?

SAM: Hmm?

HANSEN: You nervous?

SAM: Nervous? Tired is all. I've been at that sixty-odd hours.

HANSEN: If it makes you feel any better, G-2's been at it for two years. (*Leans back, sips his coffee*) Thirty-three hundred army POWs repatriated. Two hundred-odd cases investigated for trial. Forty of those approved for further action. They're throwing just *one of them* at you. One of the cut-and-dried ones at that.

SAM (*Looks at him a moment, then slowly takes the cigarette from his mouth*): An infantry captain with a silver star and a cluster, a commendation from the C.G. of his division for exemplary conduct under fire—that's not cut-and-dried.

HANSEN: An infantry captain who collaborated with the enemy while a prisoner of war—and thirty different men will swear to every single specification. I'd call that cut-and-dried.

Sam squints into the blight fluorescent light of the desk lamp. He motions to it.

SAM: Mind if I turn that down?

HANSEN: Please.

Sam turns off the light, leaving one small bulb burning in a table lamp across the room. He sits down in the chair near the desk and rubs his jaw.

SAM: I'll tell you frankly, sir. I'd have just as lief not had this one.

HANSEN (*Nodding*): Some are pleasanter than others—or at least not as *un*pleasant. You're a good trial counsel, Sam. A very good one and your S.J.A. knows it. That plus the fact that there are three of you attached to your office. You take the cases in order.

This is an ugly one—that's unfortunate—but you were in line for it. Are you telling me you want to hand it back?

SAM: No, sir. I'm telling you it . . . it hasn't got a pleasant taste.

HANSEN: Some cases don't.

SAM: Some cases aren't just cases. They've got first and last names. They're people. They've got identity. (*Looking off*) They've got silver stars with a cluster and no matter what else they've done, that man who has to prosecute has to look into his soul—he has to count up his doubts.

HANSEN (*Nodding slowly*): All cases have identity. First and last names as you say. Any prosecutor, Army or civil, has to count up his doubts. If an accused suddenly doesn't have a name; if he's just a case and not a human being; and if his prosecutor sticks him on a chair without a doubt or a single concern—(*Shakes his head*)—then it's not a trial. Then it's an inquisition. (*A long pause*) They wouldn't force this one on you in the form of an order. You can probably take it or leave it. (*Pause*) You've spent sixty-odd hours planning it. Now go home and spend a hundred and sixty more searching your conscience. If you take the case *I want you to have regrets—but not remorse*. It's as simple as that.

SAM (*Rising*): That's fair enough. (*He looks down at the papers. Musing*) Edward Hall, Jr., Captain, United States Army. It's nice and impersonal when it's on paper, isn't it?

HANSEN (*Deliberately lights a cigarette, very steadily looking at Sam, pacing the whole thing slowly*): This man is accused of collaborating with the enemy. The people who were hurt by this—they had names, too. And their names look impersonal on paper. Pick it up from there, Captain Moulton.

Sam nods. He's very thoughtful. He picks up his brief case and walks out.

SAM: Good night, sir.

HANSEN: Good night, Sam.

Hansen leans back, slowly draws on his cigarette and studies the door. Fade out.

Fade in with a shot through an iron gate in a train station late at night. Through the grill we see the approaching figure of Captain Ed Hall as he walks slowly, limping slightly up the ramp toward the gate. He carries a half-filled duffel bag and when he reaches the gate he pauses, stands there, looks resigned, as if the gate being shut were an accustomed thing, an expected obstacle and there's little he can do about it. A gateman at our side of the camera walks into the frame, looks at Hall, then grins and opens the gate.

GATEMAN: Not locked, Cap'n.

Hall nods—a forced, weak grin. He walks through the gate and into the waiting room. Behind him we see a soldier engulfed by relatives. Much jabbering as the group walks away. Hall heads toward a bench. The gateman watches him intently, sees the limp, sees the strain of carrying what is not a heavy duffel bag, shakes his head, closes the gate. Hall sinks down onto the bench with what is a massive and sudden fatigue. He leans back, closes his eyes, lets the sounds wash over him and his body go limp. It's a thin body. It was obviously at one time a wiry build. Now it approaches emaciation.

We cut to a shot of Aggie entering the station. Her eyes sweep about searchingly. She sees Ed on the bench. Sudden delighted excitement, then her eyes narrow and she reacts. There's surprise and then deep concern. She walks toward him, obviously steeling herself at the closer and closer look, until she stands just a few feet away. Then she stops.

AGGIE (Very quietly): Ed. (*There's no answer. She moves to within a hand's reach*) Ed—it's Aggie.

He opens his eyes, blinks, looks at her, first blank and then a slow smile. He sits up and holds out his hand. She takes it and presses it hard.

ED: Aggie.

AGGIE (*Blinking back tears*): Welcome home, stranger. Long time.

ED: Aggie. (*Smiles again*) Aggie—

AGGIE (*Close to tears, she sits down beside him still holding his hand*): We got your wire. Some wire after four years. "Arrive 12:07, Capitol City Limited. Don't bother meet me." A barely literate wire—you know that?

ED: Aggie—you're pretty.

AGGIE: And you're tired, aren't you? You're dead tired. I've got the car outside.

ED: My father—?

AGGIE: He wasn't home when your wire got phoned in. I ran right out. Left a note. He's probably so excited he'll be potted by the time we get there and up the driveway.

ED: How is he?

AGGIE (*With deep affection showing*): A little older. But still the Colonel. (*The smile fades. This is the difficult part*) Ed, you . . . you heard about Peter?

ED: A year ago. Just that he was killed. One of your letters . . . one of the ones that got to me a long time afterwards. Inchon? That where? (*She nods*) How did my father take it?

AGGIE: Very, very bravely. You'd have been quite proud.

ED (*A pause*): And Peter's wife? How did she take it, Aggie?

AGGIE (*A quick biting of the lip, then control*) Not as bravely—because I'm a woman, I guess. I loved your kid brother very much.

ED: I know that. (*He rises and wavers momentarily, gripping her arm for support*) I'm . . . I'm O.K. A few excess emotions. They seep in suddenly.

AGGIE: Ed—how bad was it? (*He looks down into her face and his expression is totally unfathomable*) Can you answer it in just a word or a sentence? Just so I'll have an idea?

ED: Let's just say . . . let's just say it was very bad. Very, very bad. Now—you said the car was outside?

AGGIE (*Rising and taking his bag*): Out this way.

ED (*Quickly taking the bag from her*): I'll carry it. (*He laboriously hoists it up*)

AGGIE: Why don't we get a redcap, Ed? Why don't—

ED (*Interrupting, not with anger but quick resolve*): No redcap. Carry it myself. Which way now? Over here?

AGGIE: That's right.

He motions her ahead and follows her out. We get a brief tight shot of his face—full of strain and weariness, the duffel bag much too heavy for him. Then a shot of Aggie watching him. Her face shows concern as she looks at him over her shoulder, then quickly faces front, not wanting him to see the concern.

Dissolve to the Hall living room and the Colonel. He's in mufti but is obviously field-grade Regular Army. This is obvious in his posture, his whole bearing, his close-cropped steel-gray hair. The air about him is that of a man accustomed to giving orders, and the orders involve masses of men and big decisions. He pours a small brandy, sips at it and then drains it at a gulp. He Crosses the room rather nervously and looks out the window. He is retracing his steps across the room when the sound of a car rolling into a gravel driveway makes him stop in dead center of the room. He turns toward the front hall. Offstage is the sound of a car pulling to a stop. Doors open and close, then footsteps up the porch steps. The door opens. Aggie enters, motions to the door.

AGGIE: Presenting . . . Captain Hall.

Ed enters, puts down the duffel bag, looks across the room at his father. The two men stand there motionless, silent, and the Colonel looks him up and down. His reaction is similar to Aggie's—a kind of slow shock. The difference lies in the relative degree of restraint. Aggie, as a woman, could fight back tears but not worry about losing that fight; the Colonel, on the other hand, must maintain an iron grip on his emotions. At this moment the father shows through the officer. After this interminable pause, Ed enters the room and stops just a few feet away from his father—perhaps a long arm's length.

ED: Hiya, Dad. You potted? Aggie said you'd be after you read the note about my wire.

This breaks the strained silence that sometimes happens in reunions between men who are very fond of each other. The Colonel holds out his hand. Ed grips it and they hold the handclasp for a long minute.

COLONEL: You're thin. You're too damned thin. You look like a scarecrow. My God, we'll fatten you up! Won't we though? Won't we fatten this scarecrow up, Aggie? (*He talks to prevent tears*) Why, we'll turn this regimental puppy into a mastiff! By God we will! (*Laughs*) Ed—you know how long it's been? You know it's been four years? (*Laughs again—short, high, only barely controlled*) Four years you lie in a sack in some comfortable Oriental converted teahouse while I worry myself sick about you. (*To Aggie, because he has to turn away*) Now I think I rate a full report, don't you, Aggie? Was it some Korean nurse? Was that the deal? (*Laughs*) Or some big cloak-and-dagger assignment that even I couldn't hear about! (*Turns back to Ed, puts his hands on his shoulders, shakes him*) By God it's good to see you! It really is, Ed! (*He snorts into a handkerchief. The flow of words is stopped and he recovers*) Aggie, my dear, I hope you showed more restraint in public than I was able to in my living room!

AGGIE (*Smiles, hugs Ed*): Ask him! I almost strangled him!

ED (*Walking over to the cocktail table or bar*): May I? (*Holds up a bottle*)

COLONEL (*Scoffing*): May he! May you indeed! Ed, you and I are going to sit in front of the fire and put a dent in those millions of words we've got to speak. So much . . . so much to ask you. And Aggie here'll put us to bed about six A.M.

AGGIE (*With a look at Ed*): Why not tomorrow bright and early? It's so late, and Ed's awfully tired. That was a long train trip, you know.

COLONEL: A long train trip . . . and four years in a camp. (*Nods slowly*) We'll make it up, Ed. (*Suddenly remembering*) Ed . . . (*Looks at Aggie*) Did anyone tell you . . . did anyone—

AGGIE: He knows, Dad.

ED: How was Pete killed?

COLONEL: Mortar shell. During an attack. At Inchon.

ED: Instantly.

COLONEL: He never knew what happened. His C.O. wrote me a letter—a long letter. It seems your younger brother was quite a soldier. As good a soldier as his older brother was. Pour me one too, will you, Ed?

Ed pours two glasses, pauses over a third. He looks up at Aggie, who shakes her head.

AGGIE: Excitement's just too much for me. I'm going to bed. (*Goes over to Ed and takes one of the glasses. She takes it over to the Colonel and gives it to him*) Follow soon? He needs rest.

COLONEL (*Kisses her*): Very soon. (*Holds up his glass*) To my son, Ed. To his return home.

Both men drink. The Colonel's eyes never leave Ed's face.

AGGIE (*Crosses over to Ed and kisses him*): Good night. You're in your old room. You remember your old room?

ED (*Nodding*): Second on the left.

AGGIE: That's the one. Good night, soldiers. Sleep tight, both of you.

COLONEL (*Reaches for her hand as she goes by him*): Good night, Aggie, dear. You, too.

Aggie exits.

ED (*Sits down, holds his glass tightly*): She and Pete, they were together for how long before he shipped out? A month?

COLONEL: Just about.

ED: And Pete must have been . . . twenty-two. All of twenty-two.

COLONEL: Not quite.

ED: You took it well, Aggie said.

COLONEL (Rises, crosses to the bar, pours a drink): I took it well . . . because I had another son still living. I couldn't spare the time to grieve when there was so much hoping to do. (*Holds up his glass*) This time—to a hope realized!

Ed rises, closes his eyes, blinks, crosses the room.

COLONEL: Ed?

ED: Yes, Dad.

COLONEL: When you want to—understand? When it's far enough away from you for you to talk about it, I'd like to hear.

ED: Sure. Sure. Fair enough. When it's far enough away, I'll oblige. (*Looking away, touches the light switch on the wall*) Only . . . only right now, right at this given moment, I've got it on my back and it's dead weight. (*He flicks the switch on and off and it lights the hall light*) You know, over there, in the camp, there was just one light in this big, long room. One light. In the center. It had a string on it. That's how you turned it on and off. I used to think—the first thing I'll do when I get out . . . if I get out . . . I'll use a light with a wall switch. (*Turns to his father*) That's nuts, huh? Not a blonde or a thick steak, or a big, shiny convertible or twenty hours of sleep. (*Turns, flicks on the switch, over and over again. And then, sobbing, he leans against the wall*) A light switch. A lousy light switch.

COLONEL (*His face white*): Ed . . . oh, my God, Ed—

Aggie comes down the stairs.

AGGIE: Say, I forgot. It seems the towel situation is—(*She stops dead, seeing Ed. Then she looks at the Colonel and hurries down the steps to Ed. She puts her face against his shoulder*) Ed, come to bed, darling. Let it all out, then come to bed.

Ed moves away from the hall. He wipes his eyes with the back of his hand and starts up the stairs, then stops.

ED: Dad . . .

COLONEL (*At the foot of the stairs*): Yes, Ed. Yes, son . . .

ED: Good night. I'm . . . I'm sorry.

COLONEL (*After a pause. Shakes his head*): Don't be. Please don't be.
Ed goes on up the stairs. The Colonel stands there stock-still long after he's disappeared.

AGGIE: How about a cup of coffee? I'm not as tired as I thought.

COLONEL: Good. Sounds good, a cup of coffee. And a . . . a chat.

AGGIE: It's already made. I'll heat it up. (*She starts to go, stops, comes back to him*) He'll be all right. We can only guess what he's been through. But if we bear with him, he'll do fine.

COLONEL: When he went away, he used to walk so straight. Now he's hunched over—like some old man. And he limps, too. Did you see him limp going up the stairs? Aggie? Did you see him limp?

AGGIE (*Softly*): I saw him.

COLONEL (*Half a roar, half a cry*): Well, goddamn it, Aggie, what did those . . . hounds do to my boy? What did they do to him?

AGGIE (*Takes his arm, puts her face against it, then smooths his hair*): We won't think about that now, Dad. He's home. He's back with us. He's alive. Sit down now. Sit down and I'll bring you some good hot coffee and we'll talk. We'll talk as long as you want . . . and make some plans.

The Colonel nods numbly, walks into the living room, half stumbles over the duffel bag. He looks at it and sees the "Captain Edward Hall, Jr." stenciled on the side. He grins slowly, pats it, goes on into the living room. Aggie's gone into the kitchen. The door chimes ring. The Colonel heads back into the hall.

COLONEL: I'll get it, Aggie.

He goes to the door, opens it. Two colonels are outside.

SMITTY: Saw your lights, Ed. May we come in?

COLONEL: Sure, come in. Come on in. Smitty . . . Fielder . . . good to see you. What brings you out in the snow? Lemme take your coats.

They enter the hall as Aggie comes out from the kitchen.

COLONEL: Aggie, you've met Colonel Smith and Colonel Fielder—
AGGIE: Of course. I was just making some coffee. May I offer—
SMITTY (*Interrupting*): No, thank you. We can only stay a moment.
COLONEL: I'll have mine hot, black and strong. (*Leads them into the living room, points to the bar*) My boy came home tonight. I've been celebrating. I *need* black coffee. Sit down, both of you.
The two men exchange looks, stiffly walk over to chairs and sit down.
COLONEL: Now! What can I do for you? If you've come to get me out of retirement and take over a regiment, the answer's no. I'm needed here—for a change. I'm a father again. Now listen to me. Here I stand and not even offer you two old war horses a drink. Now what'll—
FIELDER: Ed, this isn't social.
COLONEL (*Looking from one to the other*): Oh?
SMITTY: It's about your son, Ed.
COLONEL: I told you. He just came home. And you two temperate mossbacks won't even drink to it—and if either of you had a boy back from four years in a POW camp, I'd—
SMITTY: Ed, sit down. Listen to us.
COLONEL (*A pause. He sits*): All right, Smitty. I'm sitting . . . and I'm listening.
SMITTY: What we've come to tell you you'd hear through regular channels in a day or so—three days at the latest. Fielder and I heard about it tonight. Just a few hours ago. We're old friends . . . and you're a valued old friend. And we decided it'd be better if you heard about it from us.
COLONEL: Heard what?
At this moment Aggie appears in the hall carrying a tray. She stops, unnoticed.
FIELDER: There'll be charges preferred against your son. And a General Court-Martial.
COLONEL: On what grounds? What charges? (*Rises*) What kind of stupid, red-tape nonsense is this? He's just come back from

four years in hell. Now what's the problem—improper uniform?

SMITTY: Collaboration with the enemy.

We get a very tight close-up of the Colonel's face as this registers. His mouth tries to form words but none comes immediately.

FIELDER: Three charges and nine specifications. All having to do with collaboration.

COLONEL: Collaboration? *Collaboration?* Ed? My son—collaborate with an enemy (*Whirls around at them*) That's a dirty, shameless, bare-faced, rotten lie! It stinks up the room with the very word! Now you two gossipy, lousy midwives get your carcasses out of my living room and get back into the cold and cleansing winter air. You must be out of your minds to make a statement like that to me about my son! You must be drunk and I'm being charitable in that surmise!

FIELDER (*Very quietly*): Ed. Ed, ask him!

COLONEL: I won't insult him by giving a lie like that the credence it would gain from the question!

FIELDER: There are 50,000 witnesses, Ed. Men who were imprisoned with him. And there are more if they're needed. They tell the same story. He signed enemy surrender leaflets. Gave lectures for them. He even—(*Stops, wets his lips*) It isn't a lie, Ed. Though we wish to heaven it were.

The Colonel walks over to the fireplace, his back to them. He believes them. He knows they're to be believed. Finally he's able to speak.

COLONEL: In combat . . . he won a silver star. Two. He got a cluster. He . . . he honored me.

FIELDER (*His head down*): In the camp, Ed, it would appear . . . he didn't honor you. (*Pause*) If we were wrong in letting you hear it this way, we're sorry, Ed. We talked about it. We talked about it for two hours before we decided to come. And we decided . . . it might be better if you heard it this way, from us.

They rise, wait for him to speak, but he doesn't. They pick up their coats, go out into the hall, pass Aggie, who doesn't look at them, then go out the door. We cut to them on the front steps, the snow falling heavily in the darkness. Fielder takes out a pack of cigarettes, hands one to Smith. Lights it.

FIELDER: You know, once I heard a guy, a supposedly very astute citizen, talk about the Regular Army. He said that only weak and essentially uninspired men became Regular Army officers because it was reverting to the womb. It was a sacrifice of all initiative for three meals a day, a uniform, and some minor prerogatives. (*He looks at the glowing end of his cigarette*) The guy who handled the initial interrogation of Captain Ed Hall, after he was released, said that he looked fifty years old. He happens to be thirty-one. And he looks fifty. And a year from now—if he's still alive—he'll look seventy-five. This very bright guy . . . this astute citizen also said that the Regular Army was a gravy train. Somebody ought to show him Captain Ed Hall, Jr. Then they ought to take him out and shoot him. Let's go.

He flings his cigarette away, and the two men head out into the darkness and the falling snow.

Dissolve to the door of Ed's bedroom. The Colonel steps into the frame, opens the door softly, looks inside. Ed's cigarette can be seen in the semi-darkness. He's lying on the bed.

COLONEL: May I turn on the light, Ed?

ED: I like the dark, if it's all the same.

COLONEL (*Approaching the bed*): For what I'm going to ask you I want a simple, brief, to-the-point answer. Understand?

ED: Who was at the door? M.P.s? I hope you pulled rank. I'd like one night in my own bed before I got stuck away in the poke.

COLONEL: Don't get cute with me. Just answer my question.

ED: Which is?

COLONEL: Did you collaborate with the Communists?

ED (*After a long pause, with him staring straight ahead. Finally he looks at his father*): Yes. (*Pause*) Any more questions?

COLONEL: Yes, one more question. (*He turns his back*) One more question, God forgive me. Why didn't you die an honorable death in action? It would have been preferred. Much preferred! (*He walks out*)

ED: Dad! (*Ed gets up, goes to the door, sees the Colonel going down the steps*) Dad!

The Colonel stops midway down the stairs, stands there, looks back up toward Ed.

COLONEL: Go on.

ED: It would have been much preferred by me, too! Understand? Make sense to you? A nice, clean, acceptable death with dignity. *Much preferred!*

COLONEL (*Nodding slowly*): I certainly understand.

AGGIE (*At the foot of the steps, hand to mouth in a shocked gesture*): Dad! This is Ed you're talking to!

ED: Would it interest you to know that there are reasons?

COLONEL: For treason? I'm sure there are reasons. What were your reasons, Ed? They must have been of earth-shattering importance to make you crawl on your belly, renounce your country, break faith with me and everyone who loved you.

ED: You know what I got for that crawl on my belly? You know what I got? I'll tell you, Dad. I sold my soul for a dirty blanket that smelled of fish and urine and three hours of uninterrupted sleep. And you know what else, Colonel? At the time . . . at the time I thought it was one helluva bargain. (*He lowers his head, stands like a statue at the top of the stairs*)

Cut to a tight close-up of the Colonel's face. The certain softening is not sympathy; it's more puzzlement. It's more a simple lack of understanding, a groping for clarification, a great pronounced effort to fit what he's heard into a frame of reference he's familiar with, a set of rules and motives he knows. But he fails in the process. He can only stare at this man who was once a son and who is now a stranger.

COLONEL: What a fortunate woman you are, Aggie. Your husband could die with few regrets. You are not related as closely as I am to a man who must live with many.

ED (*His head goes up slowly*): First and foremost among them—that I was born into the Army; that my father was a uniform and three tiers of ribbons; and that this Army could perform only one human function. It could bleed—but it couldn't weep!

Dissolve to a bed in a darkened bedroom where Captain Sam Moulton lies propped up against the headboard. His coat's off, his shirt's open. His face shows the strain of a protracted introspection. He rises, flicks on a bed table light. He walks over to the dresser for a cigarette, pauses and looks in the dresser mirror, then down to the pile of papers he's been working on earlier. He picks one up, studies it, puts it back down. He rubs his face, opens and shuts his eyes.

SAM: Captain Hall, deep inside my gut I ache for you . . . but I think you're guilty. I know now—you're guilty. (*He goes over to a phone, lifts the receiver, dials a number*) I want the C.Q. at the Transient Barracks. Yes, that's right. (*A pause*) This is Captain Moulton. You received a list of names of men on temporary duty there—you have the list there? (*Pause*) All right, these men are to be government witnesses; they're to report to the Staff Judge Advocate's office at 0900 tomorrow. That's right. (*A pause as he wets his lips*) And Captain Edward Hall, Jr.—this officer will be under restriction to post from then on. That's right. Good night.

He hangs the phone up, goes back to the dresser, looks at himself in the mirror, then slowly puts his face into his hands and leans against the dresser top as we fade out.

ACT TWO

Open on a shot through the living-room window of the Hall house. Outside it's a midwinter, sullen gray. Pull back until we're behind Aggie. She leaves the window when the chimes ring, goes hurriedly to the front hall, opens the door. Wasnik stands outside.

AGGIE (*With obvious disappointment*): Yes? What is it?

WASNIK: Captain Hall—he home yet?

AGGIE: No, he's not. Would you care to leave a—

WASNIK (*Stepping inside*): I'll wait for him. (*He takes off his cap, unbuttons his coat*)

AGGIE: I'm not at all sure when he'll be home. He's at the Staff Judge Advocate's office.

WASNIK: I know. (*Looks at her*) Wasnik's my name. I'm the captain's counsel. He knows me.

AGGIE: *You're* his attorney?

WASNIK: You were expecting Clarence Darrow? Living room this way? (*He goes on in. Aggie follows him*) And who are you?

AGGIE: I'm Captain Hall's sister-in-law.

WASNIK: I'll tell you, Captain Hall's sister-in-law, your brother told the J.A. he'd take any counsel given him. I came in the box. For better or for worse. You think I'm worse—but just between you and me and Ridgway, I'm a hot lawyer. You got a name?

AGGIE (*Sore*): I'm Agatha Hall—if that's apropos of anything as far as you're concerned.

WASNIK: Everything connected with Ed Hall is apropos of something from here on in. (*A crooked grin*) As far as I'm concerned. I'm charged with trying to save his skin. Can I sit down now?

AGGIE: Go ahead.

WASNIK (*Grins, sits down*): Lousy weather, huh?

AGGIE: I haven't been out.

WASNIK: It's lousy weather—you can take my word for it. (*Looks at her intently*) You on his side?

AGGIE: That's a ridiculous question.

WASNIK: Maybe. But you see I talked to his father—or tried to talk to him. From the way I saw it, the Colonel's on the opposite side of the stadium. He's got it all prejudged.

AGGIE: Don't a lot of people?

WASNIK: Maybe. But there's pros and cons—that's why we got a judge and a jury. But a man's father . . . (*He stops when he sees her turn away*) You want it straight? No frills?

AGGIE (*Looking at him intently now*): Go ahead, Lieutenant.

WASNIK: Captain Hall has about the same chance as the Cleveland Indians in the ninth inning of the fourth game. You get the idea?

AGGIE: If you feel that way, why are you defending him? You could refuse, couldn't you?

WASNIK: Sure. I could plead prior prejudice, then take a long walk. My old man was a coal miner. He was real hot at anthracite, but he was better at philosophy. He used to say to all of us, "Never get scared at an unpopular cause—as long as it's popular with you." I have a prejudice, you see—in favor of Ed Hall. I want to help him.

AGGIE: Why?

WASNIK: Simple. A man is accused of a crime or a misdemeanor. You establish guilt so the man can be punished. I happen to think four years in a POW camp is punishment enough.

I don't think it's right to take this man after four years of that and sentence him all over again. I think that's double jeopardy. Now, that's no legal basis for a case, but speaking personally it's the way I feel.

AGGIE (*Nodding*): You've got a disciple for this unpopular cause. Those are my sentiments.

The door opens. Ed enters, walks into the living room, sheds his coat, nods briefly at Wasnik.

AGGIE: Ed, this is Lieutenant Wasnik.

ED (*Curtly*): You defending me?

WASNIK: I left you a note at the—

ED: I read it. (*Pours a drink*) What ax are you grinding, Wasnik? Or is it just some strange perverse penchant for lost causes? (*He gulps down his drink*)

Wasnik's eyes narrow, a thin smile. He rises, goes over to Ed, pours a drink, uninvited, and gulps it down.

ED: Well?

WASNIK: Let me put it this way. (*He lashes out with both hands and grabs Ed's lapels, pulling him toward him*) With anybody in the whole world—except me—you can toss off your liquor, look railroaded, disillusioned, self-pitying and racked up. But not with me! With me it's eye-level and straight. With me it's honest. So from you I want co-operation and belief and trust. When I walk into that court-martial I want a team, not a reluctant, lost generation and a passing stranger called in to go through the motions of his defense. You understand me, Captain?

ED (*Sitting down heavily*): I'm guilty. You know that.

WASNIK: There are degrees of guilt.

ED: Is that our case? (*Looks at Aggie*) That's some defense!

WASNIK: Check me, Captain. In your case, there isn't a defense. There's only an explanation. And *that's* our case! (*He rises*) Did they tell you when you went into restriction?

ED: Tonight.

AGGIE: Restriction? Why can't you—

WASNIK: You know where?

ED: Fort Hanford. Transient Barracks.

WASNIK: I'll be there first thing in the morning. In the meantime, make no public statements. Commit yourself in no way. Just rest and eat. (*Points to the bar*) Not liquid.

AGGIE: They won't let him stay here?

ED: I might kill you in your beds, or maybe sell you to a Communist caravan heading for Siberia. I'm a very dangerous rebel, Aggie.

Wasnik goes out into the hall, leaving Ed sitting there.
Aggie follows him out.

AGGIE: Lieutenant . . .

WASNIK: Yes, ma'am?

AGGIE: Thank you.

WASNIK: I'm sorry I can't say it's a pleasure. It isn't. (*Then softly*) Stick with him. I got a hunch he needs somebody like you.

AGGIE: Isn't there anyone for him?

WASNIK (*Turning to her*): Yeah. You, me, and God. I think we're for him. So long, Mrs. Hall. Let him know he's loved. (*He sticks on his cap and exits*)

Aggie walks back into the living room.

AGGIE: You . . . you didn't see your father? (*He shakes his head*) I thought maybe . . .

ED: You thought maybe what? Reconciliation outside on the parade ground? Blood is thicker than regulations? What did you think, Aggie? Did you ever think . . . (*He turns away*) Did you ever think that they can put a man's brain on a rack. And stretch it? Pull it. Yank it. Squeeze it out of shape! (*Turns to her*) Four years I was on that rack—my *brain* was on that rack. Now I'm home. And this rack is red, white and blue and it comes all wrapped up in a flag and sanctioned by Washington. A rack, Aggie! A *rack*!

AGGIE: Ed . . . listen . . . Ed . . .

ED: The Army. The pat, black-and-white, all-in-order Army. They could never understand that what's cowardice in one man . . . is Just simple collapse in another. (*Shakes his head*) How could they understand? A machine with three million parts. A machine can't understand. How could it?

We fade out on Aggie's face, frightened, tormented, desperate to help and being totally unable to.

We fade in with a shot of Sam's room. There's a knock on the door. Sam turns from his writing table.

SAM: Yeah, come in.

Anderson, a young lieutenant, enters. He walks with a cane.

ANDERSON: Captain Moulton?

SAM (*Rising*): Yeah. Come in. You're Anderson?

ANDERSON: Yessir. Sorry I couldn't be at your office this morning. Medics said I oughta be at the hospital for the X rays.

SAM: How is the leg? Better?

ANDERSON: Much better.

SAM: Sit down. We won't stand on ceremony. I assume you've been briefed by Captain Gavin about your role as a witness for the prosecution.

ANDERSON (*His face freezes*): Yessir.

SAM: Then I won't have to add much, except . . . tell the truth as you know the truth—as you remember it. I'll make it as quick as possible. I did want to go over with you the possible cross-examination you'll be subjected to—(*He stops, looks at Anderson*) This go down hard? (*Anderson nods*) Anything special?

ANDERSON (*Looks up, and then without thinking he blurts this out*): He's a human being. Does it have to be more special than that?

SAM (*Nods slowly, sits on the bed*): Hall's a friend of yours.

ANDERSON: He saved my life once. He was a brave man.

SAM: He was a brave man. (*Picks up the papers*) He gave aid and comfort to the enemy. He fell apart at the seams. He was directly responsible for the mistreatment of two fellow prisoners. All right, Anderson. He was a brave man once. But he can't ride to glory on that.

ANDERSON: I saw him today. In the corridor. I talked to him. He ... he looked like a ghost. He thinks this is a railroading—and I can't help it, sir, I think I agree with him. Despite everything he's done, I agree with him.

SAM: All right. You agree with him. You think this is a travesty. You think the Army has some set, prearranged words dragged out for certain occasions. Army words. All very orderly, all very categorical, everything in its proper place. A man does this, he's therefore that . . . he's sentenced thus. I want to tell you something, Anderson. When it comes to its own, the Army walks tiptoe and in agony looking for justice. That's right. Agony. Two years they've been checking you guys' stories. Two long years of days and nights. They didn't point any fingers until they decided a wrong was done. Then they went to work.

ANDERSON: Big project, huh? Knock him down, set somebody else up in the other alley—

SAM: The boys in here this morning . . . the boys from your compound didn't think like that. One in particular would have been all for going after your Captain Hall with a pistol butt and three hours of free time.

ANDERSON: There's people and people. Me—I don't like informing. You see, Captain, you guys behind desks—you don't know what it was like. You put in your nine-to-five behind your inkwells and when somebody says "compound" to you it's just a word. You don't know what it was like!

SAM (*On his feet*): You silly little punks! You think you were in the first war ever fought by the U. S. Army? That what you think? Listen, Lieutenant—on a hot afternoon in '42, I took a long walk from Bataan through Manila on one glass of muddy water. I visited a lot of resorts called Cabanatuan and Santo Tomas and Formosa. I got strung up by my thumbs for six hours one time because I spilled water on a Jap corporal's pants. When you say "compound" to me, little buddy, I don't have to imagine a thing. I got it burned deep inside me and I know of what you speak! Three years, five months, sixteen days—I know of what you speak.

Anderson seems to shrink into his chair. Finally he looks up.

ANDERSON: I'm sorry. I didn't know.

Sam relaxes, walks over to Anderson, puts a hand on his shoulder.

SAM (*His voice is quiet now*): I'm not asking you to inform. I'm asking you for the truth. I want Hall to have the benefit of truth where it helps him . . . and I want him hurt by it when it damns him. (*A pause*) But I won't call you as a witness unless it's essential. This much I'll guarantee.

ANDERSON: Captain Moulton, sir . . . (*Looks up at him*) You like your job?

SAM (*After a pause*): If what gets proven in that courtroom will help one kid . . . just one . . . years from now maybe—if it'll help one kid who's captured keep faith with his country and his Army—(*Nods*) I'll like my job.

We dissolve to the Hall living room. The Colonel has obviously just entered. He has his coat over his arm. He looks at Aggie, who comes down the stairs, and then to Hall's duffel bag set up in the entrance foyer.

COLONEL: Is he leaving tonight?

AGGIE: They're picking him up at eight. (*Turns away*)

The Colonel nods, looks toward the stairs at Ed, who comes down now.

COLONEL (*As Ed walks past him*): Got everything you need?

ED (*Tersely*): Yes.

COLONEL: Tell me, Ed—don't you think you're getting fair treatment?

ED (*Stops short, turns to him*): Are you serious?

COLONEL: In another country, another Army—say, Red China's—do you think you'd get the consideration you're getting now? A chance for defense? An opportunity to be heard? A jury of open minds—

ED (*Interrupting*): Open minds? I'll ask you again—are you serious? Open minds like whose? Like yours? You heard one word—"collaboration." And that was the case as far as you were concerned. Prosecution . . . defense . . . summing up . . . the works. Just the one word!

COLONEL: Not altogether. There was one other thing.

ED: And that was?

COLONEL: When I asked you if you collaborated—and you said yes.

ED: You didn't want any explanations—you wanted yes or no.

COLONEL: Simply because treason is to a country what murder is to an individual . . . and I can't accept any extenuating circumstances for that kind of crime. If you were a stranger, Ed, a total stranger, it would be a vast disappointment to me that an American officer would willfully collaborate with an enemy.

ED: But unhappily I'm your son.

COLONEL: You're my son, so added to my disappointment . . . is heartbreak!

Ed shows reaction—almost as if he were searching to find a softness that should go with his father's words. But somehow there is no softness.

ED: May I make this a matter of record? I know how this hits you. I wish it weren't this way.

COLONEL (*Picks up a glass*): Add this to the record. I agree. I wish it weren't this way. But since it is . . . (*He turns and faces his son*) I hope they find you guilty as charged—and sentenced accordingly! (*He drinks, then flings the glass into the fireplace*) *We lap-dissolve from the broken glass in the flames to a glass of water in front of the president of the court at the head of the table. Pull back for a cover of the room, taking in the trial counsel at one side, the Defense on the other. The president of the court is a colonel; beside him is the law officer, a lieutenant colonel. There's an undercurrent of voices as in the background. We hear a swearing-in ceremony. When over, the hum of voices subsides into silence, and the trial begins.*

LAW OFFICER: The Court is now convened. (*Nods toward Sam*)

SAM: The general nature of the charges in this case is collaboration with the enemy; the charges were preferred by Major General Anthony Roedel, forwarded with recommendation as to disposition by Colonel Richard Hansen and investigated by Colonel John Paulding. Neither the law officer nor any member of the Court will be a witness for the Prosecution. The records of this case disclose no grounds for challenge. (*A pause*) If any member of the Court is aware of any facts which he believes may be a ground for challenge by either side against him he should now state such facts.

PRESIDENT: Apparently there are none.

LAW OFFICER: I know of no such grounds.

SAM: The Prosecution has no challenges for cause. Does the accused desire to challenge any member of the Court for cause?

WASNIK: No.

SAM: Does the accused object to being tried by any member of the Court now present?

WASNIK: He does not.

PRESIDENT: The Court will seat itself.

SAM: With the consent of the accused I shall omit the reading of the charges, a copy of which is before each member of the Court, the law officer and the accused. The charges signed by Major General Anthony Roedel, a person subject to the

Code, as accuser, are properly sworn to before an officer of the armed forces authorized to administer oath, and are properly referred to this Court for trial by Commanding General, Fort Hanford, the convening authority. The charges and specifications, the name and description of the accused, his affidavit, and the reference for trial will be copied verbatim into the record.

WASNIK: The accused consents.

SAM: The charges were served on the accused by me on February 26, 1955. Captain Hall, how do you plead? Before receiving your pleas, I advise any motions to dismiss any charge or grant other relief should be made at this time.

WASNIK: The accused, Captain Edward Hall, Jr., pleads: To all specifications and charges: Not guilty.

SAM: The Prosecution desires to make an opening statement. The Prosecution will endeavor to prove that the accused, while a prisoner of war in Chang-ni (Chang-nee), North Korea, and Pyoktong, North Korea, during the period between January of 1951 and July of 1953 did willfully and willingly give aid and comfort to the enemy. He did this under no legally acceptable form of duress.

Fade out.

Dissolve out on a shot of the court reporter opening to a new page. Fade on with a close-up of many pages having been written on. Pull back for a shot of the witness during the course of his examination.

SERGEANT: He come out here and he says to us, "You guys better sign the leaflet." So I look at the leaflet and I see what it says.

SAM: Is this the leaflet here?

SERGEANT (*Looks at it*): Yeah, that's the one, sir. And so I says to him, "Captain Hall, sir," I says, "I can't sign this thing. It says for our side to give up. That's a crook," I says to him. "Ex-excuse me." He looks at me real mad and he says I better sign it or he'll see to it I get tossed in the hole. He was real scared, sir-different from what I'd seen him before.

Dissolve to a private on the stand.

PRIVATE: They got this interpreter on the stage and he introduces somebody he calls our . . . our "comrade in arms" and out walks Captain Hall. He gives us a lecture on how the gooks are really our friends tryin' to help us and for us to do like they say. A bunch of guys think maybe he's got somethin'. Oh, not a bunch of guys—two or three maybe—well, they figure it's a captain, he oughta know his business and it made 'em think pretty hard about what they *should* do.

Dissolve to a corporal on the stand.

CORPORAL: I seen him go up to Lieutenant Anderson and order him to sign this leaflet. And if Lieutenant Anderson *didn't* sign it, I heard Captain Hall say that neither of them would get medical attention. They both had leg wounds.

Dissolve to a shot of Wasnik sitting down following examination of Ed himself.

WASNIK: Your witness.

SAM (*Approaching the stand*): Captain Hall, we've heard testimony to the effect that on at least five occasions you gave lectures to men in your compound advising them to co-operate with the Communists. Further than this on at least two occasions you were overheard threatening fellow prisoners that unless they signed surrender leaflets that would be used for Chinese Communist propaganda purposes, you would in one case see that one man would be placed in solitary in a cellar known as "the hole," and on another occasion you would see that the officer involved would receive no medical attention.

ED: I didn't say that. I told him unless he signed neither of us would have our wounds looked after. The Chinese had told me that. I was repeating *their* warnings.

SAM: In the case of a soldier known as "Tony"—

ED: Sergeant Scalpone.

SAM: You knew Sergeant Scalpone?

ED: Yes, sir, I did.

SAM: State your relationship with Sergeant Scalpone.

ED: He was a platoon sergeant in my company. We were captured together.

SAM: On the night of August 11, 1952, you went to Sergeant Scalpone and insisted he sign a surrender leaflet—a leaflet which urged our men to lay down their arms and refuse to fight. You told Sergeant Scalpone—and I believe these were your words . . . (*He reads from a paper*) "Tony, you better get wise and sign this thing. If you don't it's going to be the hole for you." Those were your exact words?

ED: I don't know. Something like that.

SAM: Is it not a fact that that very night Sergeant Scalpone was thrown into the hole and remained in solitary with no food or water for three days?

ED: I guess so.

SAM: You guess so? Is it or is it not a fact?

ED: It is.

SAM: And is it not a fact that you never saw Sergeant Scalpone again alive?

ED: Not alive.

SAM: The next time was when you served on his burial detail. He had died of exposure and malnutrition. Now is *that* a fact?

ED: Yes, sir. They said it was pneumonia—

SAM: They said. Meaning the Communists?

ED: Yes, sir. (*He looks up*) If he'd signed the thing he wouldn't have been sent to the hole.

SAM (*Quickly*): But he wouldn't sign it, would he?

ED: No, sir.

SAM: And you didn't make a single move to *prevent* his being sent to the hole. Did you, Captain Hall, try to prevent Sergeant Scalpone from being thrown into the hole?

ED: No, sir, I didn't. It would have been futile.

SAM: So you merely signed the required document and watched your sergeant get what would nominally be called a death sentence.

WASNIK: Objection. May I respectfully request the trial counsel to confine his remarks to questions instead of trying to fabricate the entire story based on—

SAM: I'm not fabricating, Lieutenant Wasnik.

PRESIDENT: Objection sustained!

SAM: I'll rephrase the questions. What did you do about the leaflet, Captain Hall—and about Sergeant Scalpone's punishment?

ED (*After a pause*): Nothing.

SAM: Speak up, please!

ED (*Too loudly*): I signed the leaflet. I didn't do anything about Tony—Sergeant Scalpone.

SAM: Sergeant Scalpone weighed roughly 120 pounds at this point, suffered from dysentery and was running a high fever. Is this true?

ED: Yes, sir.

SAM: But he could not be induced into giving aid in any minute measure to the enemy, now could he?

Wasnik starts as if to object, then shrugs. The point has been made.

ED: No, sir. He signed nothing.

SAM: Now, Captain Hall, may I ask you this: In the period prior to August 7, 1952—the date you first affixed *your* name to a surrender leaflet—what had occurred to change your political views?

WASNIK: Objection. The defendant has never stated that his views changed.

LAW OFFICER: Sustained. Strike the question.

SAM (*A smile*): I'll ask it this way, Captain Hall. Did you not change your political views prior to August 7, 1952?

ED: I did not.

SAM: You did not. And yet that date you affixed your name to surrender leaflets, acted as a lecturer for the Communists, and had your voice on a recording broadcast over the Chinese Peking radio. Tell me, Captain Hall, why were you designated to perform these various acts?

ED: I don't know. I was ranking officer in my group. They tried to get others. Some didn't. I did.

SAM: And what made you accede to their wishes?

ED: I . . . I refused. Consistently. Many times. But they kept after me—

SAM: They "kept after you." I ask clarification of that term. What do you mean They "kept after you"? In what way?

ED: Long periods of questioning. Long periods without adequate food or medical attention. Threats, lack of sleep—I . . . I finally agreed to do as they asked.

SAM: Were you physically mistreated during this period, Captain Hall? Were you struck or subjected to torture?

ED: I wasn't struck. Not that sort of thing.

SAM: But you were questioned at length under adverse physical conditions.

This was Captain Hall's first night home just prior to admitting to his father that he had collaborated. This was done far more effectively in the movie version written by Stewart Stern. In the television play it seemed rather pedestrian and more than one critic called it "routine."

PATTERNS

Captain Hall is found guilty by the court-martial. Both the television and motion-picture versions stopped at this point, leaving the actual nature of the sentence up in the air. This was more acceptable in the motion picture version because there was a stronger resolve in the personal lives of the people, and this permitted a less explicit denouement.

Wasnik, the defense attorney, forces out of Captain Hall a graphic and brutal description of a death march in North Korea. For both men—Keenan Wynn as Wasnik, and Marshall Thompson as Captain Hall—it was one of their best moments of performance.

I loved this scene, but nobody else seemed to. Wasnik, the defense attorney, meets his client for the first time. His dialogue was flip and sometimes funny, but the critics felt that it muddied up the character.

ED: Yes, sir.
SAM: Speak up, please.
ED: Yes, I was.

SAM: Now, Captain Hall, I will ask you—how many men were in your compound?

ED: There were forty of us. Twelve officers, twenty-eight enlisted men.

SAM: Would you say, Captain Hall, that the thirty-nine other officers and men received approximately the same treatment that you did?

ED: Yes, probably about the same.

SAM: Then you would not care to testify that you were singled out for any harsher treatment than the rest?

ED: I think not.

SAM: Captain Hall—(*He turns and faces the Court*)—how many others in your compound gave lectures for the enemy?

ED: None.

SAM: Louder, please.

ED: None that I know of.

SAM: None that you know of. They were subjected to roughly the same treatment that you yourself received, but not another man committed treason—

WASNIK: Objection!

SAM (*Quickly*): But none saw fit to serve the Communist cause as you did. No further questions.

The law officer and president exchange a whispered conversation. The president then bangs the gavel.

PRESIDENT: The Court will be closed for today. Reconvene tomorrow morning at 0900.

Men rise in various parts of the room. Ed remains seated. He looks across at his father in the small handful of audience. The Colonel deliberately avoids his look.

The room empties. Ed remains seated. Finally when they're all alone Wasnik walks over to him.

WASNIK: Rough afternoon. Feel boxed in, Captain?

Ed doesn't answer. He rises, crosses the room, looks out the window. Wasnik follows him over.

WASNIK: I got a wire from your former regimental CO. He's flying in to take the stand. On your behalf. Then I got three more wires in affidavit form from three battalion officers testifying to your personal courage and efficiency. (*A pause. Still no response*) I also got a cablegram from Marilyn Monroe. Wants to know if you're busy tonight. (*Pause. Grins*) I didn't think you were listening. (*He pours water out of a cooler, holds up the cup*) How about it, Captain Hall—to better days?

ED: Wasnik, would you do me a favor? Would you stop acting like a high-school coach during the half of a bad game?

WASNIK: Sure. Anything at all.

ED: Will it all be this bad?

WASNIK: Not necessarily. It might be worse.

ED: Worse, huh. Sure—it probably will get worse. They love it, don't they?

WASNIK: Who loves it?

ED: The Court. The brass. The shiny field-graders with the fruit salad and the bravery that just plumb oozes out of their eyes. Don't they love it, Wasnik? (*He goes back to his seat*)

WASNIK: I think they're wrong, Captain Hall. But there aren't any kangaroos in this room. Every man in here is doing a dirty, unpleasant and unasked-for job of judging a fellow officer. No, Captain, they don't love it.

ED: I'll tell you . . . I'll tell you what I got figured out. I think I'm getting the dirty end of the stick. I think the Army is so goddamn orderly that it has to stick a tag on everything and label it. So when a man takes as much as he can—when he cracks into pieces—they look real wise and they head into their Army ledgers and they run their fingers down the page and they come to the word "treason." "Treason's" a fat, meaty, understood word. We'll tag this guy with treason. We'll fit him into a nice recognizable mold. Henceforth, skip the complexities of motives and personality and psychology. Just label him! Label him and act accordingly. My God, Wasnik, do you know what you're doing? You're trying to add a supplement to the ledger! You're trying to complicate the tag-sticking routine. You're—I swear to God—you're trying to wreck the whole bloody Army by suggesting there's a human factor. Wasnik, you poor slob, you're going to wind up a lieutenant if you stay in for fifty years. You know that? (*He slumps forward, head in hands*) You know that, Wasnik?

Wasnik doesn't answer. He can't answer. The man next to him is beyond logic, beyond expectation. He is full of hurt and self-sympathy and nothing can transcend these. Wasnik pats him gently on the shoulders, rises, puts on his cap, walks out.

We pan over to Ed, who sits there. He rises, starts out, passes the court table, looks slowly around the empty chairs, then walks out. Dissolve to the interior of a small bar. At a table at the far end Sam Moulton drinks a beer and in front of him lies a stack of papers. Wasnik enters and sits at the bar. He sees Moulton's reflection in the mirror, turns, walks over to his table.

WASNIK: Captain, buy you a drink?

MOULTON: Sorry. That'd be out of order and you know it. A trial counsel and defense attorney meeting socially while a case was on. You better do some reading.

WASNIK: I haven't got time. (*With a nod toward the papers*) My client's got a name for it. For this. A rack. His mind's on a rack. Four long, dirty years of fear—and he's come back to another rack.

MOULTON: Lieutenant, everybody I meet, even my own witnesses, the papers, mothers, fathers—everybody and their brother—they've got this case pegged as David and Goliath. The wicked Army and the poor lone man. Tell your client this: Look at the faces of the men on his Court. Have him look at my face. Let him try to understand that those men who sit in judgment on him have sons of their own. Let him try to look beyond his own misery just long enough to know that he hasn't got a corner on the market. And tell him for me I took his case after I sat in a chair for a day and a night and dug into myself to see if what I pulled out was a big doubt—or an honest principle.

WASNIK: Captain, there's a difference, you know—a difference in misery. Yours can end after the sentencing. His has to go on—because of what you're doing to him. Or let's say what the Army's making you do to him.

MOULTON (*Shaking his head*): The Army's not *making* me do anything. I've got justice on my mind now. I could strip off this uniform and walk into that court-martial in a bathing suit—and I'd use the same principles, the same arguments and come up with the same plea! Justice, Lieutenant Wasnik, doesn't dress in a uniform. Nobody's getting crucified in there. This I know.

WASNIK: This you'll have to prove to me.

MOULTON (*Going back up the steps*) All right, Wasnik. We let him off. Understand. Verdict innocent—specifications and charges. You know what then? wasnik: What then?

MOULTON: From that second on, no member of an armed force would have any compunctions about dealing with an enemy. We set-a precedent that says if a man must break, he must break—that's all there is to it. And why? Because in that court-martial we excused a man for collaboration and maybe worse. We're not crucifying a man. We're trying to put a little muscle into every other man who may have to face the same things he did.

WASNIK (*This is a quiet kind of rage that now has worked its way out*):
So when we smack him down, when we ruin this man for good and all, we have to tell ourselves it's not a punishment inherent in the crime. It's simply a case in point. An *example*. We sentence a man as an example. We put a man on a rack for want of an alternative! Captain, that may be law, but it's a helluva long ways from justice!

SAM (*Very quietly*): You might add this to what you tell your client, Lieutenant. That this rack he's on—it's a big one. It isn't just for the accused—it's for the people who accuse as well. And if all this sticks in your craw, Lieutenant, maybe you can give me an alternative.

There's a long pause, with Wasnik just staring at him. Then Sam nods, picks up his beer without looking at Wasnik.

SAM: Good night, Lieutenant.

Wasnik turns and walks out. We get a shot of Sam looking up and watching him. And there's sympathy in the look as we fade out.

ACT THREE

We fade in with a shot of the courtroom in the middle of a session. This is about the fourth week of the proceedings and it's nearing the end. Wasnik rises.

WASNIK: I call Captain Hall for redirect examination.

Ed rises, goes to the witness chair. Sam stands nearby.

SAM: Captain Hall, you are reminded that you have been properly sworn and are still under oath. (*Nods to Wasnik, then sits down*)

WASNIK: Captain Hall, can you tell the Court precisely the regimen involved in questioning and persuasion?

ED: They'd . . . they'd call me out of the barracks—any hour. Lead me to an interrogation shack. The night . . . the night I . . . I cracked, it was cold. It'd been raining for two weeks. They had me remove all my clothes. I walked through the mud to get to the shack. I was freezing, shaking all over, and I was scared. (*Wasnik nods*) When I got to the shack, I had to stand in a puddle of water. Then they started.

WASNIK: For how long?

ED: Usually for a couple of hours. That night they kept on—oh . . . maybe five hours. It seemed like . . . like a month or more. I fainted once. I don't know if it was from cold . . . from fear—I don't know. When I woke up, they had these . . . these pamphlets. The interpreter said I was the only man in the compound who was being so stupid. That if I signed, everybody'd sign. I knew . . . I knew that wasn't so, but then . . . that minute . . . I could feel my mind going soft. Crazy, disjointed thoughts. Nothing was clear at all. I didn't answer him. Then I asked him if I could think it over. He motioned to a guard. The guard pointed his gun, said to go outside. I followed him. He handed me a shovel. Said to dig a grave. And after it was done . . . they were going to shoot me. It was to be *my* grave.

We cut to a shot of the president of the court as he reacts to this—ever so slight a change of expression but nonetheless a change. Then a brief shot of the Colonel as, very slowly, he lowers his eyes.

WASNIK: They'd done this before?

SAM: Objection. He's leading the witness.

LAW OFFICER: Sustained. Strike the question.

WASNIK: Had they ever done this before?

ED (*His voice harsh now with the strain of telling and remembering*): Once. Not in the camp. On the way there. The week we were captured. They were marching us to Pyoktong—Camp Number Five. They'd told us that in each group of POWs, one of us would be in charge. And if any man in any group dropped out, the officer in charge would be shot.

We pan around the various people in the room. It's deathly still.

ED: A lot of the boys had been wounded—some not even tended to. Bad wounds. Running wounds. One boy—he'd lost a lot of blood. I didn't know who he was. He kept falling down. A lieutenant in charge of his group was half carrying him, and then this kid fainted dead away. And he couldn't be carried. They stopped the column. (*His voice falters*) They stopped the column. A guard went up to this lieutenant. Motioned for him to step out. He gave him a shovel. Told him to dig. Like . . . like they told *me* to dig. (*He looks up, around the room, then straight at his father*) Then, after he'd finished, they put a gun to his head. The lieutenant . . . the lieutenant looked the Korean right in the face and . . . and he said, "Mister . . . Mister, where I come from, they call this lynching."

There's an audible gasp from the court.

WASNIK: Go on.

ED: They shot him in the head. My group had to fill up his grave. That night, the night I cracked, all I could remember was the face of this lieutenant as he dug that grave—dug it knowing that in three minutes . . . he'd be lying in it. (*A deep breath. His voice rises an octave, still in control, but slowly losing it*) I remembered his face. That's all I remembered. I looked into the hole I'd dug and I thought—this one *I'd* be lying in. (*Looks around*) That's all. And later on, in the interrogation shack, I was standing in that puddle of cold water, and my leg—I'd been hit by mortar in the leg—it started to hurt like it never hurt before. And then I heard this interpreter say something about a warm blanket and my going to sleep. (*A long pause as he looks around again, and his voice rises almost to a shout*) I said yes! I said O.K. I said tell me what I have to do, or what I have to say, and I'll say it! I'll do it. Anything! Germ warfare, dope peddling, informing, surrender leaflets—anything! Only I've got to sleep and I can't be afraid any more. I've just got to sleep now and get warm! (*Then his voice gets quiet*) Lieutenant Wasnik, members of the Court—if this incriminates me, I'm sorry. But . . . but if it happened again tomorrow, I'd very likely do the same thing.

WASNIK: Do you wish the witness for recross-examination?

There's a murmur as Sam heads for him, passes Wasnik, and they look at each other. Then Sam stops in front of Ed.

SAM: Captain Hall, in any camp you were in, did you ever see anyone shot?

ED: They threatened to shoot a lot of—

SAM: I didn't ask you that. I asked you if you saw anyone actually shot.

ED: No, I didn't.

SAM: Only on the march to the camp—and by North Koreans. Is that your testimony?

ED: That's right.

SAM: Was any man ever actually willfully hurt for refusal to collaborate, to your knowledge?

ED: In my sight—no.

SAM: Who was in charge of your compound—Koreans?

ED: No, sir. Chinese.

SAM: No further questions.

WASNIK: No further questions.

SAM (*Very pointedly*): Call Lieutenant Anderson.

SOLDIER: Lieutenant Anderson.

A door is opened at the far end of the room. Anderson comes in, takes his place in front of the witness stand.

SOLDIER: You swear that the evidence that you shall give in the case now in hearing shall be the truth, the whole truth, and nothing but the truth, so help you God?

ANDERSON: I do.

SAM(*Without waiting for him to be seated, starts the questions as he sits*): Lieutenant Anderson, you testified prior to this that you knew Captain Hall, the accused, well before and during your captivity. Is that correct?

ANDERSON: Yes, sir.

SAM: Then you were familiar with what occurred on the night of August the seventh. The grave he dug. Their threatening to shoot him. The rest of it.

Anderson: Yes, sir.

SAM: You know the story to be the truth.

ANDERSON: Yes, sir.

SAM: *Why* do you know it to be the truth?

ANDERSON: I'm not sure I understand the question.

SAM: His story is gospel, Lieutenant Anderson, and you know why. Because the same thing happened to you the next night! Isn't that so?

WASNIK (*On his feet*): Objection! The questions are leading. The entire line of questioning!

SAM: Did you receive similar treatment—not similar—exact treatment?

ANDERSON: Yes, sir.

SAM: Shovel, grave, threats—the whole thing?

ANDERSON: Yes, sir.

SAM (*Facing the Court*): Lieutenant Anderson, I would ask you, how many surrender leaflets did you sign?

ANDERSON (*His head goes down*): None, sir.

SAM: Speak up, please. How many?

ANDERSON: None, sir.

SAM: How many lectures did you give to fellow prisoners with the speeches prepared by the Communists?

ANDERSON: None, sir.

SAM: How many broadcasts did you make—recordings telling American troops in the field to lay down their arms?

ANDERSON (*Looking at Ed*): None, sir.

SAM: Why, Lieutenant Anderson? (*He turns to face him again*) Why? Was it because you were a much braver man and much finer officer than the accused?

WASNIK (*Shouting*): Objection!

SAM: Go ahead and admit this fact.

PRESIDENT (*Pounding the gavel*): You're out of order, Captain Moulton. You must strike the questions.

Sam walks away from the witness and goes close to Wasnik.

SAM (*Without blinking an eye*): All right, sir. I withdraw the question. I have nothing further to ask this witness.

Wasnik rises thoughtfully.

WASNIK: The Defense has no questions at this time.

PRESIDENT: This Court will recess until 0900 tomorrow.

We cut to a tight close-up of Anderson as he rises. His features work and suddenly it comes out.

ANDERSON: Ed! As God is my witness, a thousand times I thought I'd break! A thousand times I didn't think I could stick it out! Ed—

The president pounds the gavel.

PRESIDENT: The witness is out of order. His remarks will be disregarded!

WASNIK (*Looking straight at Sam and in a voice only he can hear*): Disregarded on the record. But in the minds—try disregarding it in the minds!

We take a slow dissolve to the interior of an Army post chapel—almost empty save for a few soldiers widely dispersed. In the background is the sound of soft acappella of male voices—quiet, lovely, serene. We get a shot of Ed in a seat by himself. Wasnik enters, removes his cap, looks searchingly around the room. He spies Ed, then quietly goes out to the small lobby adjoining. In a moment a chaplain walks out.

CHAPLAIN: Hello, Steve.

WASNIK: Hello, Chappie. I'm just . . . waiting for a friend.

CHAPLAIN: Captain Hall is inside.

WASNIK: I know. I suggested this place to him, Chappie. He'd find peace here.

CHAPLAIN: For a moment, I think he has.

WASNIK: Tomorrow's the last day.

CHAPLAIN: I've been following the trial.

WASNIK: I think I know what it is now. We pass laws. We pass laws as just as possible. Because no country can condone treason and exist. But we base these laws on certain truths that we think are permanent. One of the truths is that there's a certain level of morality that all men must recognize. Then we find a group of men who'll threaten and browbeat and mentally torture to get what they want and who don't recognize that morality. And now we find ourselves having to judge a man who committed a crime only because under unusual circumstances he had no benefit of that morality. (*A pause*) They're going to find him guilty, Chappie. It's all they can do. And when he asks why, what do we answer?

CHAPLAIN: May I tell you what *I'd* answer? (*Ed comes out now, unnoticed*) I'd answer, Captain Hall, morality is not a weakness—morality is a strength. For a man to break because his captors do not share his humanity—this is a reason . . . but not an excuse. (*He sees Ed standing there, and he looks straight at him*) But I'd add this: You have a guilt, Captain Hall, but it's in some ways partly a guilt of all of us. You'll bear the cross because of this guilt—the verdict, the sentence, the stigma, perhaps. But the conscience you can share—*with* all of us. This you needn't bear alone. For this weakness is not yours alone, though you succumbed to it. Not your weakness alone, nor your Army's, nor your country's, nor the weakness of the men who sit in judgment on you. I think this is a weakness of the race of men—who may believe in a God but who don't act as if they believed.

When Ed looks at the chaplain he has tears in his eyes.

ED: Chaplain, if I have children, how can I admit this . . . or explain it, even?

CHAPLAIN: When you have children, you *must* admit it. But we pray that we'll live in a time when there'll be no need to *explain*. They'll understand.

Ed puts on his coat, starts out, and Wasnik follows him. Dissolve to the courtroom, the trial in progress.

SAM: The Prosecution has no further evidence to offer. Does the Defense have further evidence?

WASNIK: It does not.

SAM: Does the Court wish to have any witness called or recalled?

LAW OFFICER: It does not.

SAM: The Prosecution desires to make a closing argument. (*He walks closer to the table*) Gentlemen, the press, the public, and the Defense have a single, basic argument. They say that for any group to draw a line of resistance and to declare criminal any weakness beyond that point is a prerogative that must come from God and not man. Who are we, they say, to arbitrarily say how much a man must legally take before his will is not his own. But, gentlemen, on this stand we have talked to other men. Men who went well beyond the accused's threshold of pain and resistance—went beyond it and came out unbent and unsullied. Gentlemen, if we excuse Captain Hall we tell these men that their pain and their sacrifice was a waste. This, we tell them, is the point you can break. This, we say to them, is the prescribed fear you must feel before breaking. And what happens, gentlemen, is that allowing one man to go free is to arbitrarily limit the necessary courage of every other man who might ultimately face the enemy. This is the precedent you establish. You point to Captain Hall and you say, Take only what he took; suffer only to the extent he suffered—then you may give up. You may collaborate. You may sell your soul, your loyalty and your birthright, and we'll understand. (*A pause*) Gentlemen, when you do this you impair the morale of every man in the United States Army—the principle of leadership for every officer, and the respect for the military code. If you find Captain Hall innocent of collaboration, you find three thousand *brave* men who did *not* break guilty of stupidity. You must find Captain Edward Hall, Jr. guilty as charged.

He turns, walks back to his seat and sits down.

WASNIK (*Rising, faces the Court*): Gentlemen, the Defense wishes to make a closing argument. Before we judge this man, we must weigh the evidence not as it sounds inside this room but as it might sound in a POW compound in North Korea. We must alter values; we must re-evaluate certain human assumptions; we must draw on a new frame of reference. We must judge Captain Hall in terms of a situation where a cigarette—one cigarette—is of monumental importance. Where a hot meal is a basic thing like breathing. Where fear is not a momentary pang but a blanket that attends a man every passing second. Where uncertainty is a haunting, wailing ghost that pervades sleep and wakefulness. In these terms, gentlemen, we must judge Captain Edward Hall, Jr., and, in doing so it is most apparent that words like "courage," "bravery," "self-sacrifice" may apply to courtrooms and battlefields but take on new and unfamiliar dimensions in terms of a Communist prisoner-of-war camp. To condemn a man for cowardice is altogether right and just. But under the conditions of captivity that I have mentioned, cowardice does not occur when bravery ends. It is not either-or. For if it were, all men would be heroes or cowards. And I submit most humbly that there *must* be an in between.

We pan up to a clock on the wall. Lap-dissolve to the same clock reading several hours later.

SAM (*Rising*): All parties to the trial when the Court recessed are now present.

PRESIDENT: The Court has reached findings in this case and requests the law officer to examine them and see if they are in proper form;

LAW OFFICER (*Looks at two typewritten pages handed to him, returns them to the president*): They are in proper form, sir.

PRESIDENT: Captain Hall, will you appear before the Court?

Ed rises, walks to the table.

PRESIDENT: Captain Hall, it is my duty as president of this Court to inform you that the Court in closed session, and upon

secret written ballot, two thirds of the members present at the time the vote was taken concurring in each finding, finds you—of all charges and specifications—guilty.
There's a barely perceptible murmur that dies out into silence.
PRESIDENT: The Court will adjourn to meet at my call for sentence. *Very quietly men rise and start out. Ed remains seated, and he looks around him—at the president, who studies the papers in his hands and who, when he looks up, bears the features of sudden age and sudden deadening fatigue; at Sam Moulton, who rises, sticks some things into a brief case and, as if forced by some unseen hand, walks a few feet toward Wasnik. He stands there looking at him, then at Ed, and then slowly turns and walks out. Ed looks at the Colonel, who rises and stands alone in the area in which he'd been sitting and looks across the room, meeting Ed's gaze, then turns and walks out. Inside Ed's mind are voices, and we hear these voices:*
PRESIDENT (*Filtered*): Of the charges–guilty.
CHAPLAIN (*Filtered*): You have a guilt, Captain Hall, but it's in some ways partly a guilt of all of us.
PRESIDENT (*Filtered*): Of the specifications–guilty.
CHAPLAIN (*Filtered*): For this weakness is not yours alone, nor your Army's, nor your country's, nor the weakness of the men who sit in judgment on you. This is the weakness of the race of men–

Ed finally rises, turns to Wasnik, and the two men look at each other. Ed sticks his hand out and Wasnik grips it. And this is an eloquent affirmation of an understanding and an acceptance. Ed walks from the room. Outside the Colonel waits for him. Aggie stands at the far end of the Corridor. Ed walks out into the corridor. Wasnik is behind him. The Colonel walks up to him.
COLONEL: Ed, I think . . . I think the verdict just.
ED (*After a long pause. He nods*): I think so too . . . now.

COLONEL: You've been punished enough now. I'll not add to it. (*And then, as if to himself as a reminder*) You're my son, Ed. You're my son.

Ed looks up at him, smiles, and the Colonel grips both his arms. They turn and walk down the corridor toward Aggie, who waits for them. We cut to Wasnik watching them. He stands there until they've disappeared. Then he turns and looks into the courtroom—at the empty table, the empty chairs, the empty benches—and then he slowly closes the door as we fade out.

AUTHOR'S COMMENTARY ON THE RACK

AMONG the hundred or so television plays that I have written and had produced, *The Rack* holds a number of distinctions. It was nineteen months in creation, which is the most time I have ever given to any single play; it took the most number of rewrites– seven–and when it was finally produced it was the closest to what I had imagined it would be of any other play I had ever written. Add to these technical distinctions an almost universally favorable audience and critical reaction. There are a number of reasons, I think, why this is so. First, I will not hide behind any curtain of modesty and pretend that it's not a well-written piece. It is. It's tough, terse and human. It took an agonizing national problem, the root of which dug deep into the morality and conscience of a country, and treated it honestly, fairly, and effectively.

But its success lay also in the fact that the problem was so inherently dramatic that the writing at times merely augmented the stark and moving drama that was so apparent in the theme. Alex Segal gave it fine direction, and the cast, with few exceptions, was top-drawer. There were moments during the rehearsal of *The Rack* when I and others doubted that we could sandwich in the play within the allotted fifty minutes. It was a monumental problem to treat in that arbitrary time frame. As it turned out, *The Rack* came in just under the wire. Its final curtain speech occurred just about thirty seconds before the program went off the air. The credits were deleted and the final commercial speeded up almost to unintelligibility—but the play, thank God, was done in its entirety with no overtones of undue haste in the production.

Authors vary as to the source material for their writing. I will often borrow from the newspapers if the problem seems particularly timely and dramatic. I first got the idea for *The Rack* from reading newspaper accounts of the first return of POWs from Korea. In the reporting of these accounts, it was obvious that, even making the normal allowances for the inherent emotionalism of the situation and modern journalism's propensity for overdramatization, here was a problem both vital and tough, and a problem we were unprepared to meet. The treatment of prisoners has always been one of the attendant problems of warfare, but in the prison camps of North Korea and Communist China our captors embellished this problem in a manner we had not anticipated. At best, Korea seemed to be an inconclusive, muddled, indecisive and bloody affair that we were unable to win and couldn't afford to lose. And from this particularly ugly and uninspired engagement came the disconcerting spectacle of Americans informing on Americans. To compound this, the informing seemed not a result of the expertly conceived notion of torture that the Oriental ostensibly is the master of, but a much more frightening and a much less familiar technique of mental duress that broke men's spirits without laying a hand on them. We were a nation priding ourselves on the moral fiber of our fighting men, and suddenly we were given a torturous exhibition of the disintegration of that fiber—not only on specific individual levels but operating within whole groups of American men.

With our own natural bent for the handy phrase, we came up with a label known as "brainwashing." The term was sufficient for identification, but it belied the complexities of the problem. At the outset, returning POWs talked of torture, physical privation and cruel excesses. Gradually a pattern of treatment and behavior became evident and we were face to face with a problem that was as much moral and ethical as it was military. Americans were "confessing" monstrous and unbelievable falsehoods that were used as major propaganda instruments by the Communists. This resulted in the obvious reduction of the influence and prestige of the United States and the United Nations to an extent almost unimaginable. The involuntary character of these statements, as well as their complete falseness, could not be questioned. But it was an incontestable fact that American officers and men were supplying aid and comfort to the enemy, and the precedent established was nightmarish in all its ramifications.

At the time of the writing of *The Rack*, 3,500 POWs had been repatriated. Of these, 255 cases of defection had been investigated, with forty of them held up for further action. Since that time I understand even more have come up. The nightmare that I mention comes from the fact that this was the result of a police action in which only a fraction of our services were utilized. If we were to project these percentages in terms of a major war, we would suddenly find ourselves having to try men in Army courts by the thousands. Paradoxically, the average American has an abiding concern for fair play. But along with this is a sentimentality and a concern for human feelings. In assessing the problem of the Army informant in the POW camp these two frames of reference clashed and fair play was subordinated to what could only be called simple basic humanity. Americans could not find it in their hearts to judge and prosecute American soldiers physically and mentally weakened for betraying fellow prisoners. The Army, as has so often been the case, was "the heavy." They were the persecutors. With few exceptions, in every case tried in an Army court the defendant was uniformly given the benefit of the doubt in opposition to the Judge Advocate's office.

This, then, was the background of *The Rack*. The basic and underlying problem could be stated simply: Was it morally right to punish men for breaking under a form of duress which was not physical when they were exposed to an enemy whose frame of moral reference was totally unlike our own? Public opinion seemed to think not.

As an ex-soldier and aware of the frightening connotation of the word "capture," I think quite naturally the initial question asked of myself was "What would I do?" It's the same question probably asked by a lot of Americans before they sat in mental judgment on some of the men who stood trial. I must admit to sharing the majority opinion. The initial answer that I came up with was that we simply could not prosecute these men, not under our form of government and not within the rules of human behavior that a democracy sets down. The first draft of *The Rack* was written with this in mind. The fictional character accused and tried was found guilty, and the implication was that it was an expedient verdict and, though not ill-conceived, was probably basically unjust and incorrect. It was this draft that first went to the Theatre Guild of the *United States Steel Hour*, and it was on the basis of this draft that I was given an option payment and asked to go down to Washington and talk to some of the men in the Pentagon.

Now as a vet and a civilian, I shared the so-called popular idea of the Army as a big, massive, formless, impersonal glob of left-footed protocol, particularly on the Pentagon level. But after spending three weeks working with these men it became obvious that I was dealing with human beings who had more than a fair amount of sensitivity and awareness. They shouldered an added burden to the already pressing problem at hand: national survival. They were in the position of having to try and convict men under a set of rules forced on them by precedent. It was an Army problem because it involved Army men; it was an Army problem because the morale and well-being of the United States Army were victimized by the informants. But these were sober, thoughtful men who talked to me across their desks and discussed the cases one by one. These were Americans aware of the fact that they were sitting in judgment on other Americans in situations that, but for the grace of God, might have been theirs. I talked to a number of the officers from the Judge Advocate's office who had served as prosecutors at some of the trials, and from these meetings came one of the best definitive lines of drama that I had ever used. You'll find it in a speech by Captain Sam Moulton in Act Two when he is talking to one of his witnesses. He says, "I want to tell you something, Anderson. When it comes to its own, the Army walks tiptoe and in agony looking for justice."

In three weeks this is what I observed, the Army walking tiptoe and in agony looking for justice. At no time did they try to dictate to me a point of view or a conclusion. They were concerned that I get all the facts in each of the cases, and they were further concerned that in any of the fictional cases I used in the play there was no obvious connection between it and one of the actual cases tried. In a sense they told me it was not their business to tell me how to write *The Rack*. All that concerned them was that I realize that I had an obligation to study all the facts before coming up with my own conclusion. After three weeks at the Pentagon talking, reading, interviewing and becoming probably one of the best-informed civilians on the matter of prisoner-of-war treatment, I knew essentially what I was going to write in terms of the problem at hand. I was at a loss to know then how I would answer that problem. I read classified information having to do with some thirty cases of men who had already been convicted; I saw motion pictures captured from the enemy where American soldiers were filmed broadcasting to the enemy; I became personally and intensively acquainted with every single case and, in a sense, with every single man involved. And throughout all this my emotions rode on a pendulum. My resolve fluctuated from day to day. For unlike the usual situation in which an author writes a problem play, I had no ax to grind. I had an abiding interest in and concern for the problem at hand, but I had no answer for it. I wanted to pose the problem dramatically, but there was no preset idea to precipitate the writing. Rather, the complexity of it denied any clear-cut resolve, and *The Rack* evolved as more the presentation of a problem than the answer to it.

By and large I think *The Rack* is one of the most honest things I have ever written. It throws its characters into impossibly tough situations, but these characters are legitimately drawn and point up the problem even more effectively than if they were special cases. It proved one of the Army's main points: there was no racial, social or color group more prone to weakness than any other. Actually, I used as my "case" a composite of the thirty actual cases shown me at the Pentagon. The character of Captain Ed Hall was drawn from several Ed Halls. The only unique aspect of the individual that was unlike most of the cases shown me was the military background of his father and his family. There was an actual case somewhat like this in the files. But as to his age, background, and the nature of his activities while a prisoner of war, this was a composite of the others. And the fact that this was a normal, unspectacular kind of man seemed to illustrate the universality of the problem at hand. It proved that any man can break and that every man has a breaking point. There was variance as to where this breaking point occurred, but weakness was not an inheritable trait that could be equated with any particular group.

When I say that I felt *The Rack* was an honest story with "few exceptions" I do have one reservation. It was an honest deck but there was one case of card-stacking. I made the character of Sam Moulton, the Army prosecutor, a former POW himself. This provided a kind of sympathetic saving grace to the one man in the play for whom sympathy would be hard to come by. In the same scene, in Act Two between Moulton and Anderson, the witness, I gave the former a kind of artificial justification for his role as prosecutor. He was not simply a desk officer with the case thrown at him. He was a man who had suffered as his own victim suffered, but, unlike him, had not broken. Dramatically this proved effective, but it was the one area of the play where I stacked the cards.

Two days after the play's production on the *United States Steel Hour*, Metro-Goldwyn-Mayer purchased the motion-picture rights. I was unable to do the screenplay because of a previous commitment, but it was interesting to see the treatment that M-G-M used when they made the motion picture some months later. For the most part they hewed to the major line which I had used, but they failed to touch upon the one physical area that I felt obligatory. For were I to have done the screenplay, I should have started *The Rack* in Camp Number Six in Manchuria. I wanted to show this technique of so-called "brainwashing" as set down for me by several Army psychiatrists who had studied the cases intensively and interrogated the men involved. The action in the motion picture begins in almost the identical spot where it began in the television version.

The Rack was not a pleasant story. It was not a satisfying story either. One wonders, in thinking of the nature of it, whether it could even be classified remotely as entertainment. But it did create thought; it was provocative; it laid a painful, agonizing problem on the table to be stared at, analyzed and dissected. In this respect it was eminently successful. It was a play as much of ideas as emotions and it proved one fundamental thing to me. It established beyond any doubt that the medium for which I write need never shortchange itself by assuming an audience of escapist idiots who would rather gasp at contestants in sound booths than expose themselves to a life-and-death problem, however ugly and however unpleasant. There will doubtless be other plays of ideas in the mass media. The only deterrent is not the audience, it's the medium itself.

OLD MACDONALD HAD A CURVE

CAST

MAXWELL MACDONALD: *An ex-major-league pitcher. He's funny, pathetic, irascible and wholly lovable.*

MOUTH MCGARRY: *Exactly as his name implies. He's the manager of the Brooklyn Nationals.*

RESNICK: *A fast-talking, acid-tongued publicity man.*

BERTRAM BEASLEY: *The general manager of the team.*

CAROL ADAMS: *A young nurse at the Home for the Aged; pretty, understanding.*

DOCTOR: *The doctor at "The Home"–much like Carol.*

MR. PORTER: *A sort of male Mrs. Guerney; he's the superintendent of "The Home."*

GART: *One of the comedians at the home.*

PETERS: *Still another, but the "brain" of the group.*

SLOANE: *And still another.*

TWO OLD MEN CHESS PLAYERS

MONK: *The Brooklyn catcher.*

CHAVEZ: *One of the Brooklyn infielders.*

ANDERSON: *One of the Brooklyn infielders.*

MR. PINCHES: *A bespectacled little man from the ad agency.*

HIS PHOTOGRAPHER

REPORTER

RADIO ANNOUNCER

ROD SERLING

VARIOUS REPORTERS
VARIOUS OLD MEN
TRAINER
LOUD-SPEAKER VOICE

ACT ONE

We fade on with a shot of a glass door with a sign: "The Brooklyn Nationals." Dissolve through to the interior to the paneled walls of an office. We pan around the room, taking in various team photographs. First a handle-bar-mustached crew with the caption "Brooklyn Nationals . . . World's Champions . . . 1908"; pan further to a similar picture with the caption "World's Champions, 1912"; pan to a few others, none later than 1921, then to an entire wall with no pictures, panning down to a 1953 calendar. Dolly back for a cover shot of three men sitting dejectedly. Beasley, the general manager, methodically rips a paper into shreds; Mouth McGarry, the team manager, tortures a pencil, breaking it into pieces; Resnick, the publicity man, drums a staccato on the desk.

BEASLEY (*With a heavy sigh*): Well?

MOUTH: Well, what?

BEASLEY: Mr. McGarry, I'm only the general manager of this ball club. That's why I called the meeting of team principals. Why don't you take it from there?

MOUTH: Where do you want me to take it?

RESNICK: How about a critique of where we stand? Let's see–it's now July. We're twenty games out of first division. We're riding the crest of an eleven-game losing streak–

MOUTH: Ten-game!

RESNICK (*Unruffled*): We're playing tonight. And we've got a manager who handles a ball club like a bull handles a shrimp cocktail!

MOUTH (*Angrily*): And a publicity man with an I.Q. of a first-class idiot. Resnick, you handle your typewriter, I'll handle my ball club!

RESNICK: Why, you fatheaded, garbage-brained jerk, I'd like to see you turn out ten thousand words a day on a baseball team that when it wins one game I gotta call it a streak!

MOUTH: Beasley, I'm not gonna put up with it!

RESNICK: Beasley, where'd you find this? (*Points to Mouth*) Twenty games out of fourth place and the only big average we got is a manager with the widest mouth in either league. I know ten baboons who could do a better job than he can.

MOUTH: Leave your family out of this!

BEASLEY: He's right, Mouth. We've had slow teams before. But *this* year . . . (*Slaps his forehead*) This year, I've never seen anything like it!

MOUTH: Look, Beasley—I manage the club. You get the material. Have you looked at the roster? Our heaviest hitter is the bat boy —and he's ineligible. We got a pitching staff consisting of seven scarecrows. The only thing they got that other pitchers got is two arms. You know where we got one of 'em? He was mowing the infield and we were still lookin' for somebody within ten miles of our dugout who could reach home plate from the mound with less than two bounces. You want a winning club—get me some pitchers.

BEASLEY: Where you gonna find 'em? The only thing we got left to trade is a section of the left-field fence! Go get pitchers . . . go get pitchers—*where?* Order 'em from the factory? Dear sir, send me three left-handers C.O.D. Face it, Mouth, what we have is all we're going to have!

RESNICK: Ever thought of a new manager?

MOUTH: Yeah, this one may soon be in jail on a murder charge. He hit a publicity man with a bat.

RESNICK: Which is the only thing you *could* hit! Beasley, where'd you get this?

MOUTH: Beasley, I'm not gonna put up with this!

BEASLEY (*Rises, rubs his jaw contemplatively*): A pitcher. One good pitcher who'd be good for about fifteen wins. That's all. Just fifteen complete ball games. One pitcher!

MOUTH: Just my luck to get tied up with a baseball organization whose farm system consists of one silo and a McCormack reaper. The only thing we get sent up to us in the spring is a wheat crop.

BEASLEY: Just one pitcher. One good pitcher. He doesn't have to win fifteen games. Maybe twelve games–or ten. One lousy pitcher! A hundred and seventy million people in this country– there must be one guy out there who can pitch a baseball game! Now where do we find him?

RESNICK (*Pointing to Mouth*): Isn't this a beagle you've got here? Why not send him out on a scent?

MOUTH: Beasley, I'm not gonna put up with this!

RESNICK (*Walks over to the 1912 picture, taps it*): I wonder if we could get one of these guys out of retirement? I'll bet there's at least one sittin' in a rocker some place who's still got some stuff. (*Chuckles*) Lefty MacDonald. Wonder what ever became of him? (*A deep sigh*) Beasley, you're getting a leak in your attic. You honestly are. (*Chuckles*) Lefty MacDonald. Why, he must be sixty years old!

We pan up to the picture and dolly in for a tight close-up of old MacDonald in the front row–a goose-grease hair comb, parted in the middle, with the exaggerated stance of the old-time athlete. We take a lap-dissolve to a sign reading: "Carterville Home for the Aged." We pan down for a cover of a front porch. Two men sit motionlessly by a chessboard. MacDonald rocks in a rocking chair, listening to a baseball game on a small portable radio.

ANNOUNCER'S VOICE: That brings up Ted Kluzewski. He singled his first time up. Spahn gets the signal . . . the pitch . . . (*There's a loud crack*)

MAC (Shouting): That's sockin' her!

The two men at the chessboard start violently, glare at MacDonald, then go back to staring motionlessly at the board.

ANNOUNCER'S VOICE: Foul by inches. That ball was well hit. But for a strong northeast wind, the Reds would have had themselves a ball game at this point. Spahn gets his signal again. And here's the pitch! (*Another loud crack*) A line drive going way out into left field. Bruton goes back for it . . . back . . . back . . . and it's over the left-field wall for a home run!

MAC: E-e-e-e-yow!

The two men at the chessboard start violently again, upsetting the chessmen. They turn, glaring at MacDonald, who looks innocently over at them.

MAC: Troubles, boys?

OLD MAN: Young whippersnappers! Got no respect!

The other nods and they start setting up the game again. Mac looks at them. His smile fades. He shuts off the radio and is about to rise when a contingent of three men come up the steps facing him. One carries an almanac.

MAC (*Grinning*): What's up, boys? Little horseshoes, mebbe?

PETERS: MacDonald, you're hurtin'!

GART: Yep, yuh are!

SLOANE: We got the goods on yuh!

PETERS (*Nodding vigorously*): Go ahead, Mr. Gart.

GART (*Steps to the front*): MacDonald, at dinner last Thursday you made a coupla public statements concernin' your pitchin' record when you was alleged-like in the major leagues!

MAC: Now hold on. I wasn't alleged-like. I was–*actual*! Brooklyn Nationals–1903 to 1912. They useta call me Firebrand Lefty MacDonald.

GART: Mebbe. But you made the followin' statements. You said you was voted the most valuable player in the National League in 1912.

MAC: And I was!

GART: And that that year you struck out 477 men for an all-time record. Never been repeated.

MAC: And it ain't, neither!

GART: An' further–you was elected to the Baseball Hall of Fame!

MAC: That's gospel. That's honest-Injun!

Gart turns to Peters, tongue in cheek.

GART: Go ahead, Mr. Peters. You may puncture when ready. The old gas bag is waitin'!

PETERS (*Solemnly opening the almanac*): Number one. Wasn't no most-valuable-player awards made until 1924. In the National League that year it was won by Dazzy Vance!

MAC (*His jaw drops*): Well, now, I . . . that is . . . they give it to me kinda unofficial like.

PETERS: The strike-out record–all-time–is held by Bobby Feller. Struck out 348 men in one season an' that was in 1946.

MAC: Pshaw!

PETERS: An' as far as the Baseball Hall of Fame goes–I got it right here. Under M–M as in MacDonald– (*Peers over the book, then reads*) Mack, Matthewson, McCarthy, McGinnity, McGraw. (*Points to the page*) Look here, Mr. Sloane. You see the name of MacDonald?

SLOANE (*Looks, shakes his head*): Hide nor hair.

PETERS: Mr. Gart?

GART (*Looks, shakes his head*): Never happened!

PETERS: So, Mr. MacDonald, don't start makin' claims till yuh got the facts to prove it!

MAC: You gonna take the word of that fool book . . . in place of mine? You think I'm a liar?

PETERS: Wasn't you the man who said the most famous double play combination was Tinkers to Evers to MacDonald? Whatever happened to Chance?

MAC: Never leave nothin' to Chance. (*Grins weakly*) That–thatsa joke!

GART: If you was a pitcher, how come you was part of a double play?

MAC (*Without batting an eye*): 'Cause I was so fast I could pitch a ball, then cover half the infield. You can find it in the records! (*Points quickly*) But not in that there book. That's outa date!

The three men exchange caustic looks.

PETERS (*Loudly*): Let's go, boys. Next thing yuh know he'll be tellin' us he struck out Babe Ruth!

MAC: You think I didn't? Struck him out four times in one game. World Series against the Yanks. Three straight pitches each time. Blinding fast balls. I didn't fool around with none of these silly modern curves an' hooks . . . an' . . . an' . . . (*He lets it drift off. The others have gone down the steps. Weakly*) Hey . . . fellas. (*Rises, goes to the rail*) Fellas–no hard feelings. I mean . . . how's fer some horseshoes? Fellas?

There's no answer. He turns and sits back down. We cut to a shot of Carol Adams, one of the nurses, who stands near the porch steps. She's seen the episode. She looks from where the three men walked, then back to Mac–a slow, compassionate smile. She walks up the steps and sits on the top one.

CAROL: Hi, Mr. MacDonald. How are we today?

MAC (*Glaring straight ahead, mumbling*): Cussed doubtin' Thomases. I got more time in a bull pen than they got in life. I . . . (*Looks at her*) Fine! I was pitchin' baseballs when they was buggy-ridin', pitchin' woo. I don't have to take no gaff from–

CAROL (*Smiles*): Mr. MacDonald?

MAC: Wha-?Huh?

CAROL (*Quietly, thoughtfully*): Would you mind very much if I were to give you some advice?

MAC (*Looks at her*): Advice?

CAROL: In a lot of ways, you keep asking for what just happened. You see, Mr. MacDonald, some of the other men—most of them, for that matter—haven't done as much as you have. They haven't been famous or well known. So when you constantly . . . well—

MAC: Brag?

CAROL: In a way, yes. And when you do, it makes them feel unimportant and . . . and old. You don't want it to, I know. But it does.

MAC: I'm just statin' what's true. What's on the record.

CAROL (*With a smile*): All the time?

MAC: Wal, mosta the time. I . . . I exaggerate a little sometimes.

CAROL: You don't need to. You were a major-leaguer—and that speaks for itself.

MAC: Does it? Know somethin'? (*A pause*) I ain't braggin' just for them—the others here. I'm . . . I'm braggin' a mite for myself. I gotta keep remindin' myself that I was somebody once. I did have my name in the newspapers. I was famous. (*Looks at her*) Don't you see? I look in my scrapbook, and I see Lefty MacDonald. Pitcher. Then I look in the mirror. (*His voice lowers. He turns away*) I look in the mirror and I see an old man. Just one of the people at the Carterville Home for the Aged. (*He looks at her again, his face grim and set*) I don't wanna be just one of the old men, livin' in the past. I wanna be *somebody* today! I want people to know who I am . . . and who I was. (*Rises*) I wanna be alive and fer people to know I'm alive. I don't wanna be old. I don't wanna sit in a rockin' chair dyin' a little every day.

He breaks now. His shoulders move spasmodically as he grips the railing, head down.

MAC: Just once more. Just one more time, I'd like to . . . like to get cheered.

Carol shakes her head. There's tremendous understanding and sympathy in her expression as she pats his arm gently, then leaves him there by the railing and walks off the porch. After a moment he lifts his head, sniffs, takes out a handkerchief and blows loudly. He hears the offstage sound of horseshoes, wipes his eyes and walks off the porch. We cut to a group of old men watching another throw horseshoes. Mac joins them.

PETERS: Wal, look what just fell off a pedestal at the Hall of Fame!

GART: Ole marblehead himself!

SLOANE (*Who's throwing, says this between throws*): Figures he's gonna win the quoit trophy from ya this year, Pete. Bet he does at that.

PETERS: I see ya comin' in my room alla time, MacDonald, lookin' at it.

MAC: Pshaw. You think that tin cup means anythin' to me?

GART: Why yuh come into his room alla time to look at it, then?

PETERS: Won't do you no good, anyhow. I'm gonna win 'er again this year.

SLOANE (*Wipes his forehead, walks over to them*): Not if I got somethin' to say about it. (*Points behind him*) See them two ringers I got? Looks like Mrs. Sloane's little boy is gonna win it! (*Looks around*) That's me.

Mac walks past them to the stake. He picks up three shoes, throws one, then massages his arm.

MAC: Not that I care about that tin cup. But I got a empty place on my bureau where it'll fit in. (*Throws another, stops, listens to their laughter*) An' the day I can't beat a bunch of old men, I'll just go get me buried someplace. (*Throws with tremendous effort*)

We cut to a shot of the infirmary, Carol looking out of the window. The doctor sits on a stool reading a chart. The sounds of the horseshoe game are audible through the window.

DOCTOR: I think we better put Mr. Huber back on a salt-free diet. I don't like the looks of his pressure. (*Looks up at her*) Carol . . .

CAROL (*Turns quickly*): Mr. Huber?

DOCTOR: What's so interesting out that window? You've been standing there for ten minutes.

CAROL: They pick on old Mr. MacDonald so much.

DOCTOR (*Grins*): Old Mr. MacDonald invites it. He sends out engraved invitations for collective ribbings six nights a week. Ever hear the old guy tell about his baseball experiences? That's six pages out of Ripley.

This was a funny moment. The league president insisted on a daily physical examination of "Firebrand" to make sure not only that he was fit but that he was alive!

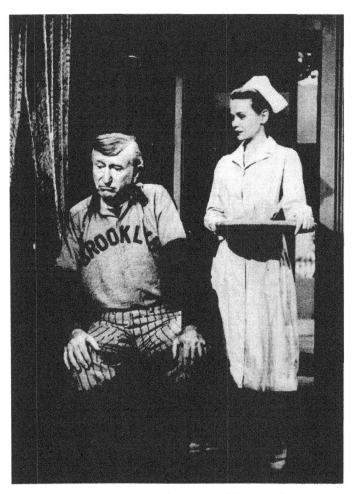

A little human moment in *Old MacDonald* when the nurse at the Home commiserated with the aged southpaw. His problem was the symptomatic problem of age: not to get shunted off to the sidelines of obscurity because the muscles become antiquated. The mind and heart, inconveniently enough, don't age along proportionately.

CAROL: But he was a pitcher.
DOCTOR: Sure he was–fifty years ago.

He walks across the room to get a cigarette out of a pack on a table. Carol goes to the stool and sits down.

DOCTOR: Darn good, too. And that's not just my opinion. (*Laughingly*) That's his, too. (*His laughter fades. He's serious as he lights his cigarette*) That's the pity of age. You can't do a thing about it. You can't turn in your life on a new one . . . or get a retread on your years. You just have to grow old and pull your memories out twice a day like a pocket watch.

CAROL: That's not a very happy time, is it?

DOCTOR: Old age? I'd say it was in the way you lived it. You can understand it, accept it, live it graciously or–

At the moment a horseshoe sails through the window and lands amidst several bottles of medicine. We can hear shouts outside the window as Carol and the doctor rush to it.

DOCTOR (*Angrily*): Which one of you threw that thing?

GART'S VOICE: I cannot tell a lie, Doc. It wasn't me!

DOCTOR: Then who did? Does he want to kill someone?

MAC (*Entering the room, holding his shoulder*): It was me, Doc. An' I wasn't tryin' to kill nobody. It was an accident!

DOCTOR: D'you hurt your shoulder? Let's take a look at it, Mr. MacDonald. (*He goes over to Mac, sits him in a chair, bends over, feeling of his shoulder*) Hurt, does it?

MAC (*Puzzled*): Nope. It don't hurt. It . . . it just feels kinda funny. Kinda . . . well, I guess you'd say . . . detached from my body.

DOCTOR (*Kneading it*): Probably strained it. (*Looks up suddenly*) But what's that got to do with your throwing a horseshoe through my window? You almost hit Miss Adams.

MAC: That's just it. I threw the blame thing and it curved. Musta curved twenty feet. I was throwin' the shoes like always–I threw one . . . oh . . . mebbe a mite harder–then doggone if my shoulder didn't start feelin' funny. An' after that, everything I threw–*curved*!

DOCTOR (*Rubs his jaw*): A curved horseshoe. Now I've heard almost everything.

MAC: Not just a horseshoe–anything! I can curve anything.

Mac looks around, spies a tennis racquet and a container of tennis balls. He takes out one of the balls.

MAC: Watch now.

DOCTOR: Tell you what, Mr. MacDonald–try it outside, huh? (*Points around the room*) I've still got a few breakable objects in here–even after your horseshoe!

MAC: This is the blamedest phenomenon, Doc. I got perfect control–except everything curves. Now watch. I can make this here ball almost go in a perfect circle. All I gotta do is give my shoulder a little twitch. Now watch . . . I'll fling 'er and you catch it. Stand right where yuh are.

He throws the ball and we cut to the doctor's face following it in a circle, then to him as he catches it. He looks down at it completely nonplused, then looks up at MacDonald.

DOCTOR: What's the gag? Where'd you learn that?

MAC: I'm tellin' yuh! I didn't learn it no place. It just all of a sudden latched on to *me*!

DOCTOR: That's the most amazing thing I've ever seen! Throwing a tennis ball in a circle! Curving it 360 degrees!

MAC: Not just a tennis ball. Anything! I threw a stick. I threw a stone. I threw that there horseshoe. They all curved. I can curve anything. An' I can curve 'em as much as I want. (*Points to the horseshoe*) Ahh . . . that there was 'fore I realized how much I could curve.

DOCTOR (*Pointing to his shoulder*): I think I better get a picture of that shoulder, though, Mr. MacDonald.

MAC: Don't that beat all! Why, pshaw, I never curved nothin' in my life before now. I was a fast-ball man. I didn't need nothin' else. Just fast balls. Firebrand Lefty MacDonald.

DOCTOR: Just take your shirt off, Firebrand, and Miss Adams'll–

MAC: Wait a minute, Doc. (*Scratches his cheek*) Hold up on the medicine. Bein' as it don't hurt, I'll just let her stay just as she is. (*Practices twitching his shoulder*) Kinda interests me. (*He struts around the room, twitching and winding up*)

DOCTOR (*Amused*): All right, but if it gives you any pain, I want you back here. Understand? Meanwhile you can try out for your old ball club. I take it the Brooklyn Nationals aren't doing so well this year. (*Hands him his horseshoe*)

Mac looks at the doctor and then looks through him, a rapt expression, then dreamily takes the horseshoe and starts slowly out. He stops at the door and turns back to them.

MAC: Short on pitchin', aren't they?

DOCTOR (*Who has busied himself sorting the broken bottles*): Quite short, I understand.

MAC (*Twitches once more, looks down at his arm*): That mightn't be a bad idea! (*Nods*) Not a bad idea at all.

DOCTOR (*Only half listening*): No, it wouldn't.

Mac goes out the door. The doctor looks at Carol suddenly at the sound of the door being closed.

DOCTOR: Wha-what'd he say?

CAROL: He said it wouldn't be a bad idea. Then you said the same thing.

DOCTOR: But I was kidding. I . . . oh, my back.

CAROL: What's wrong? All you suggested was that he– (*And now she realizes it and her voice is strained*) try out for the Brooklyn Nationals! Oh, Doc!

DOCTOR: He wouldn't do that. He has too much sense.

CAROL: And he's sixty-seven years old.

DOCTOR: This–this is his home here.

They look at each other, then start running out of the room.

BOTH: Mr. MacDonald! Mr. MacDonald!

We pan down to the tennis ball on the floor and take a slow dissolve to blank.

ACT TWO

We fade on with a shot of the porch, the two old men poised over the chessboard. Pan right for a shot of the steps, Carol standing there. The doctor comes out of the house.

CAROL: Well?

DOCTOR: He says he owes it to the team. Sixty-seven years old—and he owes it to the team. (*Looks at his watch*) Said he was going into town with the laundry truck and take the 1:40 train into the city.

CAROL: You told him you wouldn't be responsible?

DOCTOR: Among other things. But no—he's going to New York to pitch the Brooklyn Nationals out of the cellar. I'm quoting him now. Maybe he'll listen to you. Go ahead in there.

She nods, goes up the steps and through the door. We cut to a shot of the interior of Mac's room. He's packing a little overnight bag on the bed. A scrapbook is also on it.

CAROL: Mr. MacDonald?

MAC: Come in, come in, Miss Adams.

CAROL (*Steps inside. Her words come blurting out*): The doctor was saying that he felt that—well, it occurred to me that—

MAC (*Faces her, scratches his cheek*): Big girl like you oughta be able to finish a sentence. Now what's the trouble? I'm not supposed to leave? That the idea?

CAROL: Mr. MacDonald, you're not a young man. You can't play baseball. Not any more.

MAC: Crazy, huh? Lemme tell you somethin'. Johnny Mize is still pinch-hittin' fer New York. He's at least forty. Look at Satch Paige pitchin' fer Cleveland. An' how old was Bobby Fitzsimmons when he won the championship? An' Louis–thirty-seven– and still fightin'. Look at Sammy Baugh. He only retired from playin' football last year, an' . . . an' . . . (*He looks at his reflection in the mirror, then sits down on the bed, nods slowly*) It is crazy. Man my age. I know it. (*Looks up*) But I gotta give it a try. I gotta! (*Points to the scrapbook*) You can't live out of a scrapbook. It don't work. As long as there's somethin' still bubblin' underneath, man's gotta use it. (*Zips up the bag, rises*)

CAROL (*Unhappily*): We'll have to tell the superintendent.

MAC: You can send a wire to the chief of staff of the U.S. Army. They'll have to lick me to stop me.

CAROL: Mr. MacDonald, you may lose your place here.

MAC: Pshaw. Then I'll set up a tent at Ebbets Field.

The doctor and the superintendent, a fidgety little man, appear at the door.

PORTER (*The super, very condescending*): Well, now, Mr. MacDonald, who's being a very bad boy today!

MAC (*Gives him a withering look*): I'd hate to hold my breath since I was a boy. Or since you was a boy, fer that matter!

PORTER: Now you put down your satchel and lets you and I have a little heart-to-heart. A little tête-à-tête.

MAC: I'll give it to you mouth-to-mouth. I'm pullin' outa here on the laundry truck and goin' to the train station. Then I'm gonna get on a train and go out to Ebbets Field and show those kids how to pitch a baseball game. Way I feel right now I could go a hunnert an' four innings without havin' to wipe my brow. Now, Mr. Superintendent, stand clear of that door, or you'll get trampled in the rush. Old Curveballer MacDonald's comin' through!

PORTER: Mr. MacDonald, you are not leaving this room!

We cut to a shot of the door leading to the porch as Mac storms through it, followed by the doctor, nurse, and Mr. Porter.

PORTER: Mr. MacDonald! You'll lose your place here. We have rules, you know.

MacDonald stops, turns, and in one loud, jarring, all-encompassing reaction:

MAC: Pshaw!

The two men at the chessboard start violently. They all watch him from the porch steps. We hear the offstage sound of a truck starting up. Peters, Gart and Sloane enter from the left. They look interestedly toward the truck.

PETERS: Where's MacDonald off to, Mr. Porter?

PORTER (*Resignedly*): He's going to Ebbets Field to pitch for the Brooklyn Nationals!

All three nod, look in unison back toward the truck. Then all three take a simultaneous double-take, looking back at Porter, and then as one toward the sound of the fast-disappearing truck. We dolly past them to the chessboard. One of the old men looks off into the distance, listens.

OLD MAN: Quiet. (*The other nods*) MacDonald left. (*The other man nods in understanding*) Your move.

We pan down for a close-up of the chessboard. Lap-dissolve to a slip of paper in Mouth McGarry's hand as he laboriously writes on it. We dolly back for a cover of a baseball dugout. There are sounds of batting and catching. Resnick comes on from the left.

RESNICK: Got tomorrow's line-up?

MOUTH: Working on it.

RESNICK: Who starts?

MOUTH: I just feel 'em one by one. Whoever's warm pitches.

RESNICK (*Nods toward the field*): Practicing late today.

MOUTH: Batting drill. And I'm tryin' to loosen up Fletcher's arm. He throws like a shot-putter.

A phone rings. Mouth reaches down to a shelf, picks up the receiver.

MOUTH: Dugout. (*Pause*) What? Who? A pitcher? How many arms? . . . Awright. Send him down. (*Replaces the receiver*) Guy wants a tryout.

RESNICK: Who is it?

MOUTH: I didn't ask. If they got more than one arm and less than four, I look 'em over. Who knows—maybe we got another Lefty Grove.

RESNICK: We better get somebody who'll draw a crowd. For the past two weeks we've had more guys on our bench than we've had paid admissions. Current plans call for giving away a set of dishes with each ticket. Next week we'll give away you!

MOUTH: Go die someplace. (*Cups his mouth, calling out to the field*) Hey, Monk.

MONK'S VOICE (*Offstage*): Yeah, boss.

MOUTH: Fletcher can quit now. I got a new boy comin' down. Catch him for a while.

MONK (*Off*): Check. O.K., Fletch. Go get a shower.

MOUTH (*Yelling again*): Chavez, bat awhile.

CHAVEZ (*Offstage*): O.K., boss.

MOUTH: Anderson, pitch a few in for Chavez.

ANDERSON (*Offstage*): Check.

We hear the sound of batting offstage. Mouth and Resnick watch the playing field, unaware of MacDonald entering the dugout wearing a vintage early 1900s baseball uniform. The old man waits a moment, starts to tap Mouth on the shoulder, but pulls his hand back when Mouth yells.

MOUTH (*Cupping his hands*): Chavez, pull all the way around. Choke that bat. I've told you that before!

Once again Mac starts to tap Mouth, and again pulls back when Mouth yells.

MOUTH: Monk, make a target behind there.

MAC: Ah, Mr. McGarry.

MOUTH (*Shouting*): Yeah! (*Quieter, without turning around*) Yeah.

MAC: I'm the curve-ball artist.

Resnick turns around, gapes.

MOUTH: Curve, swerve, hook or crook—can you reach home plate?

MAC: I could try.

Mouth turns, assumes Resnick's incredulous look.

MOUTH: What's the gag? What's the gag? Resnick, another one of your jokes? Go home, Grampa.

MAC: I'm MacDonald. Firebrand Lefty MacDonald. I useta pitch for Brooklyn—'fore the war.

MOUTH: Yeah? Which war? The Civil War? You don't look old enough to have spent the winter at Valley Forge. Come to think of it—was it really as cold as they say it was there?

MAC: They said I could come down and show you my stuff!

MOUTH: Comedians! Go home, Grampa.

MAC: I come all the way from Carterville to pitch. And I ain't aimin' to move until I do!

RESNICK: Go ahead, Mouth. Let him pitch a few in to Chavez.

MOUTH (*Mimicking falsetto*): Go ahead, Mouth. Go ahead, Mouth. An' who's gonna pick up the body when he finishes? Dad, will ya go home awready?

MAC: That Chavez out there?

RESNICK: Go out there and pitch him a few.

MOUTH: Who am I? What am I doin' here? The publicity man runs the team. One of Lincoln's seventy-five thousand volunteers is on the mound. I might as well go drown in the shower. So go ahead, Dad. Pitch. An' when you're finished we'll give yuh a nice rubdown with formaldehyde!

Mac picks up a glove and pounds it, a set look on his face. He tips his cap and turns to Mouth.

MAC: Mister, you just got yourself a boy!

He climbs out of the dugout and heads for the field.

MOUTH: A boy, he says! This comedy don't ever end!

RESNICK: He couldn't be any worse than the puppets you got pitchin' now!

In the background we hear the sound of a ball plopping against a catcher's mitt.

MOUTH: Is that my fault? I don't hire on this ball club. I manage what's hired. Why, ten years ago I wouldn't let a man on this ball club put oil on the bats! Today, I gotta use 'em as regulars.

RESNICK: Well, if you ask me—

MOUTH: I wouldn't ask you the time of day. Resnick, you're so crooked when you die they'll have to screw you into the ground!

RESNICK: I get crooked havin' to make up lies about you, you bigmouthed clunk! If you're a manager, I'm a locomotive!

MOUTH: Yeah? Well, listen, Resnick . . .

Mac comes back down into the dugout, takes off his cap.

MAC (*Modestly*): I struck him out. Three curves.

MOUTH (*With a brief look at him*): Very nice. Now go home. And another thing, Resnick—

MAC: I said I struck him out. Three pitched balls.

MOUTH: And I said that's very nice. Go home.

MAC: Where do I sign the contract?

MOUTH: What contract? What, what, what? Grampa, you're a grand old man. I love you. You're a credit to mankind—but go home.

MAC: Ain't I . . . ain't I goin' to get a chance to play?

MOUTH (*Incredulous*): Baseball? Are you kiddin'? Look, I humored yuh. I let you pitch to a real major-leaguer. Now go on and get outa my hair.

MAC: I struck him out.

MOUTH: Great. Real great. Goodbye.

Mac looks at him closely, sees that he's in earnest, looks down at the cap in his hands. Then he turns and goes out. Mouth turns to Resnick ready to pick up the barrage once again when Monk, with his catcher's mitt, and Chavez enter the dugout.

MONK: If I hadn't seen it with my own eyes, I wouldn't of believed it. I never seen a curve like it. It's inhuman! It's positively inhuman!

CHAVEZ: Honest, boss, I ain't never run across anything like him before. The ball sails in like a big balloon and looks like a football hangin' on a rubber band. You cut at it—and it ain't there! It just ain't there!

MOUTH: What are you characters talkin' about?

MONK: The old guy with the freak uniform.

CHAVEZ: MacDonald. This guy's got a curve ball he controls like it was a yo-yo!

MOUTH (*On his feet, his eyes wide*): That old gleep? That Methuselah in the costume? MacDonald? He's got a curve ball?

MONK: What a curve ball!

CHAVEZ: Hittin' at it is like tryin' to bat with a toothpick!

MOUTH (*Running out of the dugout*): Hey, MacDonald! Hey! Hey, Lefty! (*He stops, turns, runs back into the dugout, grabs the phone*) Get me Beasley's office! (*Champs at the bit, finally thrusts the phone at Resnick*) When he answers tell him to draw up a contract for MacDonald. Tell him he's as old as the earth, but if we can keep him alive for one month we'll have ourself a pitcher!

He runs out of the dugout once again and we fade out. Fade on again with a shot of the front porch of the Home for the Aged. Carol is serving fruit drinks out of a large pitcher to several old men. She carries over two glasses to the chess players, turns and sees the rocking chair that Mac usually sits in. She looks toward the door, then walks toward it and into the house. We cut to a shot of Mac's room in the semidarkness. He stands by the window looking out. There's a knock on the door.

MAC: Nobody to home. Go away.

CAROL: It's Carol Adams, Mr. MacDonald.

MAC: What yuh want?

CAROL: Time for your juice. May I come in?

MAC: Awright. Come on in.

She walks inside, sets the glass on a table.

CAROL: It's a beautiful day. I thought you'd be out on the porch. Lots of visitors, too. Today's Sunday, you know.

MAC: I know it's Sunday. And I know it's visitors' day. I ain't feeble-minded, nurse.

CAROL (*Softly*): What happened yesterday, Mr. MacDonald?

MAC: Nothin'.

CAROL: You don't want to tell me?

MAC: If I told yuh, yuh wouldn't believe it. Who could believe that a man who hasn't thrown a baseball in better'n forty years could go out an' strike a man out in three pitches? And then– and then, mind ya–get kicked out. Three curves and I had that boy swingin' and missin' and lookin' 'bout as dangerous as a melon ball.

CAROL: I'm sorry. Why don't you come out on the porch and–

MAC: Gettin' me on that porch an' havin' me face them three galoots alla time walkin' on their lower lips–why, it'd be easier pokin' hot butter in a wildcat's ear. I just ain't goin' out there. I kin just hear Peters now. (*And he imitates him*) Try out for the Brooklyn Nationals, did ya? An' what happened, Mr. MacDonald? What happened?

CAROL: It is visitors' day and–

MAC: I never get no visitors, anyhow. And what's more, I don't want none.

There's a tap at the door. Porter sticks his head in.

PORTER: You have visitors, Mr. MacDonald!

MAC: Visitors? Who'd be visitin' me?

PORTER: Let's see–one's name is Beasley. He's the general manager of the Brooklyn Nationals. And the other–rather a large man with a loud voice–

MAC: Mouth McGarry! They're here to see me?

PORTER: Said something about trying to find you after you left the ball field. And something else about a contract. I told them you'd be there in a half hour.

MAC: *A half hour?*

PORTER: With all of yesterday's excitement, and now this, I told them it'd be best if you took a little nap before you saw them.

MAC: Mr. Superintendent, get outa my way. I'm comin' through!

PORTER: Mr. MacDonald! You are not leaving this room for one half hour!

We cut abruptly to the outside porch door as before, as we see MacDonald storm out, followed by Porter and Carol, who is stifling a smile. Mac stomps off the porch, turns, faces them.

PORTER: Mr. MacDonald, you're absolutely incorrigible!

MAC (*Thunderous*): Pshaw! (*Then toward the two chess players*) To you too! *He stomps off. We dissolve to a close-up of a battery of flashbulbs going off intermittently. Dolly back for a cover shot of Mac signing a contract, then shaking hands with Beasley.*

REPORTER: May we ask you a few questions, Lefty?

MAC: Shoot.

REPORTER: Is it true that you have an unusual kind of curve ball?

BEASLEY (*Interrupts just as Mac is about to answer*): He most certainly has. Lefty MacDonald'll win twenty games—at least.

REPORTER: You don't think you're too old?

BEASLEY (*Again Mac's mouth is open as he's cut in on*): Absolutely not! He has the stamina of most men one half his age.

REPORTER: How old are you, Mr. MacDonald?

BEASLEY: He's over forty. Just leave it at that.

REPORTER: What's your full name?

Mac turns to Beasley expectantly.

BEASLEY: Go ahead. Answer him.

MAC: You been doin' pretty good. Ain't you gonna answer that one?

BEASLEY (*Smiles*): I . . . I don't recollect it.

MAC (*Witheringly*): He don't recollect it. (*Thrusts the contract at him*) Read it, ye cement head. You kin read, can't yuh? (*Points it out to him*) Right there on the dotted line–Maxwell MacDonald. (*He yanks the contract back*)

REPORTER: You realize you're rather an oddity in sports, don't you, Mr. MacDonald? I mean a man your age going actively into baseball after laying off so many years?

MAC: Oddity-shmoddity! I'm better'n I ever was. I got me a curve now that'll burn up the league. I gotta go back to the Home now an' pack my stuff.

Thank yous, etc., general bustle.

MOUTH (*Gets up rather pontifically*): Gentlemen, I'd like to say a few words. As manager of the Brooklyn Nationals . . . (*The room is emptying very fast*) I want to say that . . .

He looks around. Resnick lies on a couch, resting on an elbow, surveying him caustically–the only man left in the room.

RESNICK: Why don't you just jump out the window!

Mouth slams on his hat and stomps out of the room. We dissolve to Mac's room, crowded with the other old men watching him pack a suitcase on the bed. Men can be seen outside in the hall.

PETERS: How often do yuh have to pitch, generally?

MAC: Oh, mebbe once every three-four days.

GART: They feed yuh pretty good, Mac?

MAC: Good? Why, it's nothin' to eat steak at least once a day. (*Holds up two fingers*) This thick. Got to. Ball players need energy.

GART: Steak once a day. If I had my own teeth again–what a diet!

Mac has opened his bureau and is removing some shirts. He looks in the drawer, then toward Peters. He slowly removes the little horseshoe trophy.

MAC: Ahh . . . Peters, I was . . . ah . . . just borrowin' this the other day. Wanted to see how it'd look on my dresser.

PETERS (*Takes it, looks at Mac, his suitcase, then back to the trophy*): Funny thing. It never looked quite so small as it does tonight.

There's a silence as Mac's head goes down, then up as he speaks.

MAC: Wasn't so small that I didn't try stealin' it. That's–that's why I had it. Might's well admit it now. (*Turns away*) There was a time not so long ago that I figured that trophy was the only thing left that I could go after. I'm–I'm sorry, Peters.

PETERS: Shucks. Don't make no mind. But . . . ah . . . (*He looks around and they nod encouragement*)

GART (*Whispering loudly*): Go ahead. Give it to him now!

PETERS: Mac . . . ah . . . well . . . fact is–us fellers took up a little collection and we bought yuh a little somethin' as a goin'-away present. (*He holds out a scrapbook*) Didn't have no fancy wrappin' paper. So you'll just have to take her as she is. (*Hands it to him*)

GART: We figured you'd be needin' a new scrapbook now!

SLOANE (*Nods vigorously*): 'Specially now!

GART (*Whispering again*): Make a speech, Peters!

PETERS (*Looks around. They nod again*): Well . . . we just wanted yuh to know we were all behind yuh–every step. (*There's a pause and his words take on an earnestness*) I got kinda funny feelin's about your goin' back into the major leagues. Bein' famous again and all that. An' I figure all the rest of 'em kinda feel the same way. You're goin' out and doin' big things–somethin' we never do again. So . . . so you're kinda representin' us. Like a . . . a symbol, sort of. So every time you win a ball game, we'll kinda figure that . . . that it's us who won a ball game, too. So . . . "Bone" voyage . . . and . . . and good luck. (*Sniffs*) And don't ferget us old coots back here at the Home! (*Blows into a handkerchief very loudly*)

Mac looks around at the circle of faces, and we pan with his eyes to take in each one–smiling, warm, loyal–right down to the last two, the two old chess players. Then we take a slow dissolve out.

ACT THREE

We fade on with a film clip of a major-league baseball game. Super over it these headlines: "Aged Pitcher Signs with Brooklyn." Clear for "Variety"–"Flatbush Fetches Fossil Flinger." Clear for "You're Only As Old As You Feel, Says Maxwell MacDonald." Clear for Time magazine cover, his picture with caption "Old Man of the Year." Clear and hold clip a few seconds, then dissolve to an "On the Air" sign in a studio. Pan down for shot of an announcer on a sportscast.

ANNOUNCER: And that brings us, friends, to our sports spotlight—which in turn only naturally takes us to Brooklyn. The acquisition of Lefty Maxwell MacDonald by the Brooklyn Nationals has set the sports world tilt on its ear. The aged pitcher hasn't been used yet, but it doesn't seem to make much difference. Paid attendance at all Brooklyn games, at home and on the road, has been phenomenal, and what's more, for the first time this season, the Brooklyn baseball club has started winning games like a house afire. Most people buy tickets just to get a look at the venerable old hurler when he demonstrates his fantastic curve before each game. But so far, as we said, Manager Mouth McGarry has shown no inclination to actually start MacDonald in a game. Elsewhere on the sports scene . . .

We dissolve to a close-up of a stethoscope and dolly back for a cover of a hotel room. A doctor is examining Mac as Beasley, Resnick and Mouth look on, plus a few others.

MAC: That thing's cold, Doc.

DOCTOR: Just relax. I'm almost finished.

MAC: Every doggone day. I'm gettin' tired of you pushin' your thumb all over my back!

DOC: That's the Commissioner's orders. You get a physical checkup every day.

MAC: Pshaw! (*Points to Mouth*) I'm a darn sight healthier than he is.

MOUTH (*Who swallows a pill*): It's my stomach. Nerves, I guess.

RESNICK: Mr. McGarry isn't used to winning baseball games.

BEASLEY: It's the crowds that do it. You give any ball club a full rooting section, they're gonna win.

DOCTOR (*Folds up his stethoscope, puts it into the bag*): Yep. You're in good shape, Mr. MacDonald—with the exception of that shoulder.

MAC: Back on that again, huh?

DOCTOR: I frankly don't understand. It's the funniest-looking dislocation I've ever seen. And you're sure it doesn't bother you?

MAC: I don't like to chew my cabbage twice. I already told yuh— it don't hurt a particle! Not a particle.

DOCTOR (*Rising*): All right, then. You pass again. (*Puts on his hat*) See you tomorrow. (*He goes out*)

MAC: Well, McGarry? Do I start today?

MOUTH: Well, no. We're gonna hold you back a little longer.

MAC (*To Beasley*): You're payin' me a parcel of money to just throw five pitches 'fore each game and spend every mornin' havin' this horse doctor make me say "Aaah"!

BEASLEY (*Pats him tenderly*): Don't you worry, Mr. MacDonald. We're just concerned that you don't throw out your arm.

RESNICK: Now if you throw out your head, you automatically become a manager–like McGarry.

MOUTH: Beasley, I'm not gonna stand for this!

BEASLEY: Tell you what. Lefty, you go into your room and rest up a bit. We got a double-header tonight, you know. We want you to be fresh!

MAC (*Rising*): Fresh fer what? If you fellers don't use me soon I'm gonna mosey over to the Giants. Durocher knows a good thing when he sees it.

RESNICK: He married Laraine Day!

MAC: I think mebbe I *could* do with a little nap. Wake me in about an hour–O.K.?

BEASLEY: Sure thing. You take a nice nap.

MAC (*Stops by the door*): McGarry, don't forget!

MOUTH: Now look, MacDonald–oh . . . awright!

Mac smiles, goes out.

MOUTH: Can you beat that? I'm supposed to cut out his clippings and paste 'em in his scrapbook. It's an agreement he made me sign!

RESNICK: The right man for the right job.

MOUTH: Beasley, I'm–

BEASLEY: I know. I know. You're not gonna stand for it. We got a problem, Mouth–you know that?

MOUTH (*Nods*): *Don't* I know it.

BEASLEY: We're gonna have to use him one of these days. The fans demand it.

RESNICK: Why not? He's got a curve ball. We've seen it!

MOUTH: We've seen it for three minutes at a time. What happens when he's supposed to go nine innings? Whatta we do–rent a pulmotor and revive him in between innings? Right now he's a wonderful drawing card.

BEASLEY: And for some reason he makes the club win games.

RESNICK: Sure he does. They take a look at this old codger in a baseball uniform, and it makes 'em feel ashamed. They win in self-defense!

MOUTH: Which still don't tell us what we're gonna do about his actually startin' a game! I musta been nuts to even sign him up! But that curve ball!

RESNICK: Are you guys crazy? You've got yourself the best hunk of publicity since Babe Ruth. Let him just draw the crowd. Maybe stick him in as a reliefer every now and then. Do you guys know we're in fifth place now? A month ago we were so far in the cellar our roster included an infield, an outfield and some heating pipes! Quit worryin' about his collapsing on the mound. We just don't let him out on the mound that long!

BEASLEY: The fans are gonna demand it!

RESNICK: Just keep dangling him. Whet their appetites.

MOUTH: Is this guy a pitcher or a wiener! I tell you, Beasley—

There's a knock on the door.

MOUTH (*Roaring*): Go away.

The door opens. Pinches sticks his head in—a bespectacled little fast-talker.

PINCHES: I'm sorry to trouble you. We're looking for Mr. MacDonald.

MOUTH: Mr. MacDonald is taking a nap.

PINCHES: I made an appointment to see him. We're from the ad agency. I brought the photographer.

MAC (*Appears from the adjoining room*): Yeah, come on in.

Pinches opens the door and motions the photographer in. He follows him, smiling, nodding, into Mac's room.

PINCHES: Now, Mr. MacDonald. According to our agreement—

MAC: First, I wanna know just what I'm endorsin'. I ain't endorsin' anything I don't have a hankerin' for!

PINCHES (*Smiles broadly*): You'll . . . ah . . . have a hankering for these things, Mr. MacDonald. First— (*He pulls out a box of cereal*) First, a box of Zam–the breakfast meal of athletic heroes! Eat Zam–go wham! Try it.

MAC (*Dips his hand into the box, eats it*): Not bad.

Pinches produces a bat and baseball cap. He sticks the former in Mac's hand, the latter on his head.

PINCHES: All right, Mr. MacDonald . . . ah . . . wait just a moment. (*He goes over to him and turns the cereal box around, label to the front*) There we are. Now smile . . . ah . . . look toward the cereal! O.K.! (*The flash-bulbs go off*)

PINCHES (*Producing a bottle*): Now this here, Mr. MacDonald . . .

MAC: What's this?

PINCHES: It's called Hut-Leah. That's Health spelled backwards! Now in this picture–

MAC: What's it for?

PINCHES: You might call it a . . . a rejuvenator–a wonderfully healthful, vitamin-packed discovery that sends youth coursing through old veins.

MAC (*Hands it back to him*): When I want youth coursin' through my veins I take a nip of corn. I ain't gonna endorse this here thing. Now about the money–

PINCHES: Payable to the Carterville Home for the Aged. I've got a check made out.

MAC: Good.

PINCHES: You sure you don't want to try the . . . (*He points to the bottle*) Awfully good for the nerves, too!

MAC: Nerves! Pshaw! We don't got nerves on our ball club. (*He opens the door and they move into the other room*) No nerves at all.

He and Pinches stop, look from one to the other. We pan around from Beasley, methodically ripping a paper to shreds; to Mouth torturing a pencil, breaking it into pieces; and finally to Resnick, who drums a staccato on the table in a scene exactly as in the beginning of the play.

BEASLEY: Mr. Pinches, if you don't mind– (*Points to the door*)

PINCHES: We were just leaving. (*Turns, shakes Mac's hand*) A real pleasure, Mr. MacDonald. You'll be seeing the fruits of our labor in all the major magazines. Lefty MacDonald, star Brooklyn pitcher, eats Zam! And goes wham! (*And as Beasley propels him out the door*) You too can eat Zam and go– *The door closes behind him. Then the photographer, who is still in the room, smiles apologetically, opens it and follows Pinches out. Beasley slams the door, turns to Mac.*

BEASLEY: You're gonna need more than cereal for this one. Sit down.

MAC (*Sitting down*): You got troubles?

BEASLEY: We just got a telegram phoned in to us.

MAC: Pshaw, I got me a mess of telegrams in there. I got one from–

BEASLEY: This particular telegram is from the Commissioner.

MAC: Nice feller. I met him once–oh, 'bout twenty years ago. I come back fer a–

BEASLEY: He has said in effect that unless you've been hired as a regular member of the team, you're ineligible.

MAC: I don't under–

RESNICK (*Interrupting*): In other words, if you're just a publicity stunt, nothin' doin'.

MOUTH: Remember when Veeck hired that midget at St. Louis?

MAC: I ain't no midget!

BEASLEY: No, you're a sixty-seven-year-old man.

MAC: With a curve ball, remember–with a curve ball!

MOUTH (*Intent*): MacDonald, do you think you could start the first game tonight?

MAC: Start it and finish it–then go bicyclin'! I'm in the pink, McGarry!

MOUTH: Buddy, if you don't show up good, I'm the one who's gonna go bicyclin'!

MAC: What are yuh all worried about? You hired me. You seen my curve ball. I may not be as fast as I was, but there ain't a man in either league who can touch what I offer!

BEASLEY: The question is, how long can you keep offering?

MAC: You'll see tonight. (*Gives his shoulder a twitch*) Look at 'er! That ball'll have more hops than beer!

RESNICK: I'll phone the papers. We'll still be able to hit the sports editions. Well, Mac, get ready for headlines. Old MacDonald starts tonight!

We cut quickly to a large banner headline reading "Old MacDonald Starts Tonight." Cut to the "On the Air" sign, then pan down for a shot of the announcer.

ANNOUNCER: Well, sports fans, tonight's the night. Maxwell MacDonald—the oldest pitcher who's comeback was from way back—starts against a strong St. Louis team at Ebbets Field. The Commissioner's office verified a report that it had sent an ultimatum to Bertram Beasley, general manager of the Brooklyn Nationals, to indicate good faith in the MacDonald situation or release him. In other words, let him stop being a side show and show his side arm. Starting for St. Louis tonight will be . . .

He fades off. We cut to a film clip of Ebbets Field just before game time. Then cut to a shot of the Brooklyn dugout, a line of players sitting on the bench. Mouth paces back and forth. A trainer comes into the dugout.

TRAINER: Mouth, I can't find the rubbing liniment!

We cut to Mac finishing taking a long swig from a bottle. He puts the cap back on it.

MAC: Here, I got it.

TRAINER: You been drinkin' that stuff?

MAC: What'd yuh tink I was doin' with it—rubbing myself?

MOUTH: O.K., MacDonald. Go out and start warming up. And go slow. Go very easy. Save your strength. Don't get nervous. Above all, don't get nervous.

MAC: Check. See yuh.

He pounds the ball in a mitt and goes out toward the field. There's a tremendous roar from the crowd.

LOUD-SPEAKER: Number seven, MacDonald, pitching for Brooklyn!

We cut to a shot of Mouth.

MOUTH: Just my luck to have a damp night when the old man starts. He'll probably get pneumonia by the third inning.

TRAINER: Whattayuh mean a damp night?

MOUTH: Can't yuh feel it? The water's just drippin' off me.

The trainer looks down toward Mouth's feet as we pan with his eyes to one of Mouth's feet in the water bucket. Mouth looks down, sheepishly removes his foot, looks back at the bench full of players.

MOUTH: First guy who laughs gets fined fifty bucks!

We cut to a shot of Mac standing on the mound. The scene is staged exactly as a similar shot is televised on a screen of an actual game. The light shines down on him and only he is visible. Behind him is the giant scoreboard, appearing very large, as if shot by Zoomar.

We dolly in for a close-up of Mac's face as he rubs rosin on his hands. We hear the filtered voices that speak inside his mind.

CAROL'S VOICE; (*Filtered*): Mr. MacDonald, you're not a young man any more. You can't play baseball. Not any more!

MOUTH'S VOICE (*Filtered*): One of Lincoln's seventy-five thousand volunteers on the mound. So go ahead, Dad–pitch. And when you're finished, we'll give yuh a nice rubdown with formaldehyde!

BEASLEY (*Filtered*): You're a sixty-seven-year-old man.

RESNICK (*Filtered*): Old MacDonald starts tonight!

Mac looks down at the rosin bag and in a gesture of anger and with great effort flings it away. But at the end of the throw his arm remains stretched out. He's looking at it bugeyed. A strange expression on his face. He brings his arm in, tries twitching the shoulder. It doesn't twitch. He tries again, growing, frightened concern on his face.

MONK'S VOICE (*Off*): Couple more, Mac. Down to second on the last one. Let's go.

Mac looks at him, starts to shake his head "no" and realizes he must throw. He takes the ball, winds up and lets it go. Monk appears walking toward him.

MONK (*Handing him the ball*): What was that?

MAC (*Gulps*): Ahh, change of pace.

MONK: That didn't have no pace. That was a balloon ball with nothin'! Stick to curves, Mac. Stick to curves. Couple more like that last one, in the game, we'd have to push back the fences to Omaha City. Couple more. Let's go.

He goes back. Mac wets his lips and tries twitching his shoulder again—with the same result. He winds up, throws. Out comes Monk, very worried.

MONK: What's the matter, Mac?

CHAVEZ: What's the matter, Mac?

MOUTH: What's the matter, Mac?

MAC (*Looks around at them forlornly*): Curve's gone.

MONK: Gone?

CHAVEZ: The curve?

MOUTH: The curve's gone? Oh, no. Oh, no! Oh, no!

MAC: Lost the twitch. Can't curve nothin'. When I threw the rosin bag I musta tossed it back into shape. I'm . . . I'm sorry, Mouth.

MOUTH: He's sorry, Mouth.

MAC: Without that twitch I'm nothin'.

MOUTH: Without that twitch he's nothin'.

MAC: What'll I do?

MOUTH: Take two things. First a shower, then a powder. Me–I'll wait till midnight. Then I'll take poison. (*Turns, motions across the field*) Fletcher, come on in.

Mac slowly removes his glove, shoves it into his hip pocket. He looks up at the crowd, whose noise is thunderous, and starts slowly off the mound. We take a slow dissolve out. We fade on with a shot of the sign "Carterville Home for the Aged." Dissolve to a shot of Mac standing at the window in his bedroom. There's a knock on the door, a pause. The door opens. Carol enters.

CAROL: Welcome home, Mr. MacDonald. The night watchman saw you come in last night.

MAC: Didn't have no other place to go. I saw my room was empty, so . . . so I just . . . just moved on in.

CAROL: It's still your room.

MAC: Anybody . . . anybody see the game last night?

CAROL: We all watched it on television.

MAC (*Turns to her*): I wouldn't have minded if I'd lost. Wouldn't have hurt a particle if they shelled me right off the mound. But not to even be able to pitch a single ball! To flop before I even got started!

CAROL: We were all very proud of you.

MAC (*Incredulous*): Proud of me? Proud of me?

CAROL: Because you tried. You pushed the years away and tried doing something no one else has ever tried to do. You tried to get back some old glory. And you succeeded.

MAC: I made a jackass out of myself. I succeeded in doing that!

CAROL: Why don't you come outside? It's a beautiful morning. It's Sunday–visiting day.

MAC: Don't make me no mind. I never had no visitors. And I never will. And what's more I don't give a hoot! (*And suddenly his shoulders bend and he's very old*) Yes, I do. I always did want somebody to come see me. Now it'll be just like before-same porch, same old rockin' chair, same old spendin' the day watchin' everybody else have a good time. Last few months, made me a peck of money, don't even know how to spend it.

CAROL: You spent some of it. All of us appreciate the check. It was for a lot of money. It'll help the place a great deal.

MAC: Pshaw. An' I suppose Peters and Gart and Sloane an' everybody else is just waitin' out there to gimmee the horse laugh!

CAROL: Why don't you come out and see?

There's the sound of a brass band playing "For He's a Jolly Good Fellow." Carol opens the door. He walks out. We cut to a shot of the porch. Everyone's outside waiting for him. He appears at the door and there's a chorus of cheers. He steps outside. Peters grabs him, pounds his back. They crowd around him. Porter is seen scurrying back and forth. He finally breaks through the circle.

PORTER: Mr. MacDonald, two buses just came in from town. Loaded with people wanting to see you. I couldn't very well say no. It *is* visiting day. And there's a troop of boy scouts hiking this way. They'll be here after lunch. They want your autograph. And the Mayor of Carterville called–

PETERS: They'll all just have to wait! You know what today is, Mac? Horseshoe Tournament Day. (*Holds out the trophy*) And this here is on the block again!

Laughing, shouting, they head off, leaving Porter wringing his hands. He sees the chess players in their usual position. He goes over to them. They're unaware of him.

PORTER: Everybody's trying to get in here today. And I've got three dozen wires asking if we have accommodations for more men. I've got one here– (*Pulls a wire out*) –all the way from Kansas City. From a Mr. . . . let's see . . . Mouth McGarry. Wants a quiet room with southern exposure!

OLD MAN (*Looks across to his partner*): MacDonald's back. (*The other nods*) Your move.

We cut to the doctor's office as Carol enters.

DOCTOR: Quite a homecoming, huh?

CAROL: Just . . . wonderful!

DOC: Good. Well, now the excitement's over. It was fun while it lasted–but just between you and me, I'm glad we're back to normal!

And as he says this a horseshoe flies through the window, landing on the same shelf. The doctor rushes to the window.

DOC: What fool threw that?

VOICE (*Off*): MacDonald!

DOC (*Hands to head*): Oh, noooo! You mean–?

VOICE: Yep. Got his curve back!

We cut abruptly to a phone-booth door closing and MacDonald on the phone.

MAC: New York City? I wanna person-to-person talk with Leo Durocher. That's right. This is Firebrand Lefty MacDonald. . . . O.K. I'll wait.

And he settles back with a relaxed, happy look of "here we go again." We take a slow dissolve to blank.

AUTHOR'S COMMENTARY ON OLD MACDONALD HAD A CURVE

LIVE television, for the most part, has never been too successful in presenting comedy. Probably the most important reason for this is that laughter is something that should be shared. And it's technically difficult, if not impossible, to have a live audience present during the production of a television play to generate some spontaneous laughter and reaction to sight gags and a humorous story line. As a result, television drama has shied away from most comedy situations. It's for this reason that none of the well-known television writers are noted for a contribution of comedy to the live dramatic show.

Old MacDonald Had a Curve was one of three comedies I've written in an output of about one hundred scripts. I can't explain the reason for it, but it played as a funny piece when it was done and I think it still reads humorously. It was produced on the *Kraft Television Theatre* in August 1953, and directed by Harry Hermann. It starred Olin Howlin and Jack Warden. You'll note that its premise is a rather fantastic notion: an old man who can throw fabulous curves. But I guess its net effect is what might be called that "willing suspension of disbelief" when an audience or a reader is sufficiently jollied by a comic idea not to probe any deeper to find a legitimate reason for it. There was no attempt in *Old MacDonald* to document the whys and wherefores of the human anatomy that permit an old man to pitch curve balls. But for some reason the explanation doesn't seem at all necessary. Any more than it is obligatory to explain in any legitimate fashion how a baseball club like the "Brooklyn Nationals" can have such a dearth of talent as to necessitate the inclusion in the roster of an Old MacDonald. It also requires no little stretch of the imagination to accept the idea that a team will begin to win ball games on the strength of the appearance and spirit of an old fossil. But the writer, the cast, and the director approached this play with tongue in cheek, played it strictly for what it was—an excursion into fantasy—and it came out as a terribly funny commentary on the Great American Pastime.

Television consistently gets into trouble when it tries to simulate a sporting event or any large-scale physical action. In *Old MacDonald*, we had the problem of showing, at least inferentially, the inside of a baseball park, not to mention the ball players and the other accouterments of the National League. Harry Hermann staged this in such a way that the illusion was almost perfect. When Firebrand Lefty MacDonald walked down to the mound, though you couldn't see the stands, you never doubted for a moment that they were there and that there were about twenty thousand people cheering. When the ball players in Act III converged around the old man after he had been unable to reach home plate with his practice pitching, you accepted without question that this scene was played on an official-sized baseball diamond. Actually the trick utilized was simply to play this against a black backdrop. The effect was much like viewing an actual night ball game with close-ups instead of cover shots of the physical area.

I never met Olin Howlin, the lead, personally, because I wasn't on the scene when this production took place, but everyone connected with the show told me he was a wonderful man. His only problem the night of the show was extreme excitement, so that in a number of his lines he did some juxtaposing and ad libbing which resulted in the placing of Johnny Mize in the wrong league, Dizzy

Dean in the wrong position, and some rather well-established baseball records on the wrong dates and with the wrong people. But his performance was consistently good and very funny.

Old MacDonald is somewhat unique in the record of my writing. It was one of the few things I attempted with nothing but sheer entertainment in mind. I had no ax to grind and no issue to solve. I think it did show, even at this relatively early date, something of my later preoccupation with the age-youth problem, so obvious in *Patterns*. On occasion you get a glimmering of it in the dialogue of MacDonald himself, particularly when he tells the nurse that there's something tragic about winding up a life sitting on the front porch of an old men's home. "Just one more time . . . just one more time . . . I'd like to get cheered." There was no attempt, however, to inject this as a central thesis, to remind the audience overtly that if they may laugh at this old man for eighty per cent of the time, they must cry with him for the balance. The problem of aging without grace and perhaps without dignity was threaded in subtly and in a small enough measure not to affect the entertainment value of the piece at all.

Old MacDonald was fun to write. And I think it was fun to watch. It proved to me, and I think to others, that it's possible for live television to attempt a comic idea and get a laugh without a pratfall and without a pre-established set of funny characters. It indicated yet another dimension to be utilized in live television production, and it was a satisfying venture all the way through. I hope its reading will be no less satisfying.

REQUIEM FOR A HEAVYWEIGHT

CAST

MOUNTAIN MCCLINTOCK: *A fighter in his early to middle thirties. A battered hulk of what was once a big, muscular man. His speech is the slow, halting, inarticulate language of the nearpunchy. But through the wallowing, makeshift language of this relic are a human warmth and sensitivity that almost shine.*

MAISH: *The manager. A small ferretlike fight pilot who has a heart and feelings, but both come in second to an innate fear that governs him and his actions.*

ARMY: *An ex-fighter in his late forties. A scarred yet not unattractive little handler who is so honest and so fine that you look beyond the tissue and see a rewarding kind of guy.*

GRACE: *A social worker, in her early thirties, open-faced, pleasant. This is a terribly human dame who, prior to Mountain's entrance, was well able to disassociate her work from her emotions.*

FOX: *A manager.*

PARELLI: *A promoter.*

A BARTENDER

A DOCTOR

A BOY

HIS MOTHER

Various fighters, ex-fighters and others connected with the game.

ACT ONE

We open on a long angle shot looking down a bare cement corridor dimly lit by intermittent green-shaded 25-watt bulbs. This is the underbelly of a fight arena and from off stage comes the occasional roar of the crowd. On one far wall are visible a couple of fight posters announcing the cards for that night and the weeks to come. Two men stand close to one of the posters and talk in low voice. From the far end of the corridor appear Army and a fighter named Harlan "Mountain" McClintock, walking slowly toward the camera, the fighter leaning heavily on the arm of Army.

The two men pause under one of the lights and we get our first definitive view of the fighter's face. He has a bathrobe thrown loosely over his shoulders, and his body is a mass of red welts and skin abrasions. The bridge of his nose has a red crack down the middle of it. One eye is shut, the other is swollen almost to the same point, and on his cheek is a bleeding bruise. His chest is covered with sweat. Army is an ex-fighter, a small man, with long arms, in his late forties. He has thinning hair that reveals two thin scars that run down toward his cheeks on either side of his temple. Beyond that his face is open, kind of pleasant, rather intelligent.

ARMY: How about it, Mount? Can yuh make it? Make it okay?

The fighter nods, wets his lips as if to say something and then can't get it out. Over their shoulder we see Maish, the manager, coming down the corridor. A man steps out from the wall and detains him.

MAISH (*Calls out to Army*): Army, stay there with him a minute will you? I'll be right there. *The camera moves over for a close shot of Maish and the man.*

MAN: Two words, Maish. Cough up.

MAISH (*Furtive look toward Army and the fighter*): Will you relax? I'll get it. I'll get it. Tell him I'll get it. Tell him to phone me.

MAN: Mr. Henson's no collection agency.

MAISH: I know. I know. Tell him he'll get it.

With this the camera moves away, leaving them talking in low, unintelligible voices.

Army and the fighter take a few more steps down the corridor until they stand very close to the two men who stand near one of the posters. They cast a few disinterested glances at the fighter and then continue their conversation.

MAN #1: So I told him. And he said I gotta.

MAN #2: So what did he say?

MAN #1: He says I gotta.

MAN #2: Cut ice?

MAN #1 (*Shrugs*): Wid him? Illokadisguy. Itellimstraight, djaeverseeanyguywalkinaringwidabusted hand?

MAN #2: Whaddehsay? Cut ice?

MAN #1: Neh! IgottaputiminnestT'ursday.

At this point the camera pulls away from them so that we can no longer hear them, but we see them in pantomime as they continue talking only an arm's length or so away from the fighter who stands bleeding in front of them, but totally oblivious to him.

We cut to a shot of Maish and Army appearing again at the far end of the corridor. Army now has his arms full with a bucket, some towels, and a pair of gloves. He starts to continue down the corridor when Maish takes his arm, and with a nod toward the fighter still standing there—

MAISH: How is he?

ROD SERLING

This set (CBS-TV City, Hollywood) gave an illusion of space and depth relatively unknown in television. At least three major scenes from the play took place in this alley. I almost eliminated it in the original script for fear we wouldn't have room for it.

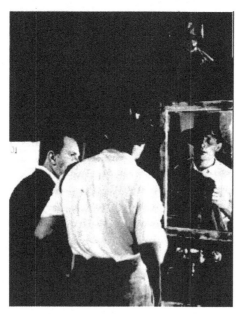

For me, this was one of the poignant and shattering scenes in the play—the moment when Mountain looks in the mirror and sees a clown. It is immediately after this that he turns on his manager and finds an anger and humiliation he has never before been able to articulate.

This was as close to a love scene as was played in the entire course of the play. Mountain has just spent the evening with Grace, the girl from the employment office. Something of the strange chemistry that links two human beings makes them completely atease with each other, and this is the first moment on the long road to the fighter's rehabilitation. I was scared to death of this scene because it required an underplaying and a subtlety I wasn't sure we could capture, but I think it was captured.

This was the scene in the bar played between Maish, the manager, and Army, the trainer and cut man. Keenan Wynn was great in this. He was a weak, vacillating, terribly frightened little man—but he was also a man with a conscience and a heart. You couldn't sympathize with this kind of s.o.b., but you could at least understand his problem: This was a moment in the play when the character of Army might possibly have been better played by a younger man and a tougher one. It was the moment when, sick with revulsion at what the manager is doing to the fighter, he turns on him and warns him to watch his step. The strength of Ed Wynn lay in his great heart and wonderful pathetic quality that was a composite of age and understanding. But at this juncture in the play it called for a kind of guttiness and toughness that Ed couldn't give it.

PATTERNS

Army gives Grace a railroad ticket so Mountain can get out of there. I love the dialogue here:

ARMY: Do you love him, miss?
GRACE: I don't know. (*A pause*) I feel so sorry for him I want to cry.
ARMY (*nods and smiles*): Then you tell him that. Tell him he's a sweet guy and you like him, but for the time being you don't come with a kiss. He's been chasing a ghost so long— I figure the next thing he's got a hunger for he ought to get. It's only fair. Thanks, miss. Thanks very much.

This was the opening shot of the play. The winning fighter comes down the ramp toward his dressing room. I don't know who the young fighter is, but he looks just like Bud Smith, a lightweight out of Cincinnati.

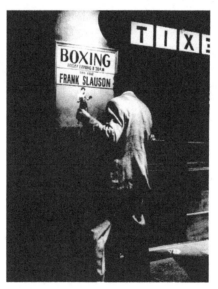

This was known as the "Alley Scene," and it occurs just a few hours after Mountain's last fight. This is a man who can't articulate, even to himself, how he feels. He knows a sense of loss and futility and in this scene he expresses it the only way he knows how. He hits out at his poster on the wall and almost breaks his hand. Originally it was Army who comes out to help him, but the producer and director felt that this scene should be played with Maish, the manager. What it did accomplish was to give Maish just a little bit more dimension and at least a semblance of compassion.

ARMY (*Shrugging*): This wasn't his night, that's for sure.
MAISH: You are so right.
Then the two men continue down the corridor. They approach McClintock from either side, each taking an arm, and help him move forward. They walk a few more feet and then stop by the door to the dressing room and usher him into it. A fighter and his manager are just coming by.
MANAGER: What hit him?
MAISH: Don't get impatient, Jock. That's a fast track out there.
(*Then he looks at the young fighter obviously ill at ease*) You ought to see the other guy. (*The manager hustles his fighter out, then Maish closes the door*)
MAISH: Not a mark on him.
Both he and Army help McClintock on to a high rubbing table. Army pours some water into the bucket from a dirty sink, brings the bucket over to the table. Maish takes a towel, dampens it and starts to wipe away the sweat and blood.
MAISH: Mountain, can you hear me okay? (*The fighter nods*) Give me some of that alum, will yuh, Army?
Army digs into his pockets and brings out a little jar. Maish dabs his finger in it and starts to apply it to the fighter's face.
ARMY: I don't think alum'll do it, Maish. I think that's going to take stitches.
MAISH (*Peers into the fighter's face more intently*): Yeah. They get wider and wider.

ARMY: The Doc's going to be coming in a minute anyway. He'll do it.

McClintock wets his lips and now he speaks for the first time. His voice is heavy and belabored and still short of breath.

MCCLINTOCK: Maish? Hey, Maish—

MAISH: Go easy. Go easy. We've got a lot of time.

MCCLINTOCK: Maish—too fast. Much too fast.

MAISH (*Nods*): Bum night, kid. Just a bum night all the way around. There'll be others.

MCCLINTOCK: Sure. Others.

McClintock moves a bandaged hand awkwardly down to his side and feels.

MCCLINTOCK: Check there, will yuh, Maish? By the belt. *Army hurriedly pulls the trousers down a quarter of an inch.*

ARMY: You've got a little rope burn down there. It'll be okay. Rubbed a sore there. It'll be okay.

MCCLINTOCK: Hurts.

Then he breathes deeply again and Maish goes back to dabbing water on his face.

The door opens and the doctor enters. He is a thin, vinegar-faced old man in his sixties with a single-breasted, old-fashioned suit with a vest, all the buttons buttoned. He carries a beaten-up black bag, which he tosses onto the foot of the rubbing table.

DOCTOR: Mountain, haven't you had enough yet?

MAISH: It's his eye, Doc.

DOCTOR: I know. Just as well, Maish. If he hadn't folded I wouldn't have let him out for number eight.

Maish nods but doesn't say anything. He pulls out the butt of a cigar from his pocket and lights it. The doctor squints, pushes his arm away.

DOCTOR: Let me breathe, will you?

He leans over the fighter and examines the eye, then pushes the face to the other side a little roughly and examines the other bruises and cuts. Then he snaps his fingers at Army, who picks up the bag and hands it to him.

DOCTOR: Where do you buy your cigars, Maish? I'll see that they condemn the store.

Then he reaches into the bag and takes out some gauze, a stick with cotton on the end of it, and a bottle of medicine. He starts to administer to the fighter.

ARMY: How much longer you got, Doc? You're out this week, ain't you?

DOCTOR: Let's see. This is Wednesday—I leave Friday.

MAISH (*Staring down at the fighter and obviously making small talk*): Vacation?

DOCTOR: Vacation? Retirement. I'm the one man in the fight business who walks away without a wobble. Thirty-eight years, Maish. Retirement.

ARMY (Clucks): Thirty-eight years.

DOCTOR (Administering to the fighter as he talks): Thirty-eight years. Wife says I oughta write a book, but who'd buy it?

MAISH: You've seen some good ones.

DOCTOR: Good ones and bad ones. Live ones and a couple of dead ones.

Then he straightens up, massages his back and points down with the stick toward McClintock.

DOCTOR: And almost dead ones. He's got no business in there, Maish. You hungry—is that it?

MAISH (*Picking up the fighter's hand and massaging it absently*): What do you mean, hungry? In 1948 he was number five. You can check that in *Ring Magazine*. I could show it to you, number five, and that was only in 1948.

DOCTOR (*Looks at him a little quizzically*): Only 1948? And this is 1956. And that means eight years ago. Too bad he isn't a machine, Maish. Too bad none of them are machines. (*Then he laughs softly*) I've seen a lot of them. Thirty-eight years. When I first come in they used to lay them out in front of me. They were human beings then. They were young men. Do you know what it's like now, Maish? Army? (*He leans back over McClintock and starts to work again*) Now it's like a guy who grades meat in a packing plant. They roll the carcasses down the line in front of him and he stamps them. Beef. Understand? (*He motions toward McClintock*) Just a hunk of something inanimate. That's what thirty-eight years has done. (*Then musingly*) Thirty-eight years. And suddenly I don't have a single patient with a first and last name. A set of scars. A blood type and a record—that's all my patients have. Look here, Maish, I want to show you something.

Maish leans over.

DOCTOR: Look at his pupil. See? Known as sclerotic damage. Look at the tissue there. Couple of good solid rights to that eye—and you can buy him a tin cup and some pencils. (*He straightens up again, puts his things back into the bag as he says*) Or maybe that won't have to happen. Maybe some night he'll bang his head on a bathroom door and bleed to death. Either way, Maish. It could happen either way. (*Then a long pause and a deep breath*) No more. This was it. Mountain and I will both retire this week.

Maish looks from the fighter to the doctor and his voice is strained.

MAISH: What do you mean?

DOCTOR: No more.

MAISH: He could rest up. I've got nothing scheduled for him—

DOCTOR (*Interrupting*): He can rest up for the rest of his life.

MAISH: What're you talking about? He's fourteen years in this business. Suddenly he gets a cut and we've got to put him out to pasture?

DOCTOR (*Turning to him*): Suddenly. It doesn't go fourteen years and then suddenly. And it's never one cut. It's fourteen years of cuts. (*He stretches, hoists up the bag*) Yep, write me a book. All about my gladiator friends. You too can become pathological in thirty-eight years of relatively easy lessons.

MAISH (*Interrupting*): Joker. Big joker.

Doctor walks over to the door, turns the knob, then looks back at Maish.

DOCTOR: Joker? (*He shakes his head, nods toward McClintock*) Who's laughing?

He walks out of the room and shuts the door. Army and Maish stare at each other, then both look toward McClintock. Army goes over and starts to cut away the bandages on his hands. Maish stands back a few feet, smoking his cigar thoughtfully. Finally McClintock sits up, closes his eyes, moves his mouth and touches his jaw gingerly.

MCCLINTOCK: Doc here?

ARMY: He left.

MCCLINTOCK: It hurts, Maish.

MAISH (*Turning his back*): I don't doubt it.

Then Mountain shakes his head, reacts with pain, touches the bandage on his eye.

MCCLINTOCK: Deep, huh, Maish?

MAISH: Enough. You could hide your wallet in there. Go lie down. Rest up a minute, and then take your shower.

McClintock pushes his feet around heavily so that they hang over the side. Then he balances himself with his hands. His head goes up and down and he breathes deeply.

MCCLINTOCK: I'm coming around now. Oh Lordy, I caught it tonight, Maish. I really did. What did I do wrong?

MAISH: You aged. That was the big trouble. You aged.

McClintock looks at him, frowns. He hies to get some thread of meaning out of the words but none comes.

MCCLINTOCK: What do you mean, Maish—I aged? Don't everybody age?

MAISH (*Nodding*): Yeah, everybody ages. Everybody grows old, kid. Go ahead. I think a shower'll do you good. Try not to get that bandage wet.

McClintock gets on his feet a little wobbly. He holds the table for support, then walks out of the room toward the shower. Army starts to pick up the dirty towels and put them in a big container alongside the door.

ARMY (*Without looking up*): What're you going to do, Maish?

MAISH (*Shrugging*): I dunno. Maybe I'll cut my throat.

ARMY: Somethin's wrong, isn't there?

MAISH: Where were you when the lights went out? I just lost a boy! Get with it, Army.

ARMY: Besides that—

MAISH: Besides that, nothing. Forget it. (*Then with a desperate attempt at a kind of composure*) I just gotta go huntin' and peckin' around, that's all. Find somebody else. Maybe try a lightweight this trip.

ARMY: I was just wondering—

MAISH: You wanna pull out, huh, Army? A million offers, huh?

ARMY: I didn't mean—

MAISH (*Interrupting*): Don't gimme a whole megillah. I know you're good, Army. You're the best cut man in the city. I know that. You probably could take your pick. I don't know why you haven't before.

ARMY (*With his head down*): Never mind about me. What about the Mountain?

MAISH (*Reacts a little guiltily*): I dunno. He'll find something.

ARMY: It's been fourteen years.

MAISH: Fourteen years what?

ARMY: Fourteen years fight. Then one night you get out of the ring—it's all over. And what've you got—

MAISH: You made a living, didn't you? You did all right. (*Then he chuckles*) Remember how I used to tout you? "The Hero of the Argonne." I even gave you the name. "Army." So don't complain, Army. You came out of it with a name, at least.

ARMY (*In a kind of wistful voice*): Still, a guy ought to have something to show for it besides the name.

At this moment the sound of the shower water is heard from offstage. Army looks up toward the shower.

ARMY: He was good, Maish.

MAISH (*Thoughtfully, turning toward the shower*): One of the best. He had everything that was needed. Hands, legs, brains. He could take a cannonball in his face and you could fix him up with an aspirin. He was good all right. Oh, brother, where am I ever gonna find one like him?

The camera pans over to the door leading to the shower. We get a shot of McClintock as he comes out from the waist up. He dries himself with a towel, then looks up.

MCCLINTOCK: Hey, Army. Bathrobe, huh?

The bathrobe is thrown to him and he puts it around him. Then we pull back for a cover shot as he walks back into the worn toward the table. He stands there and does a little hop-and-jump routine on the floor, loosening up—throwing his shoulders and head back, breathing deeply and moving his hands and feet.

MCCLINTOCK: Feel better, Maish. Lot better. Eye kind of feels funny, but I'll be okay now. Got a lot of spring yet, huh? (*He moves his feet around, shuffling ringlike. He shadowboxes a bit*) How about it, Army? Still there, huh?

Army nods, not able to say anything. He exchanges a look with Maish.

MAISH (*Finally*): Mountain, sit down, huh?

McClintock stops his dancing, looks from one to the other, goes over to the rubbing table and sits down.

MCCLINTOCK: Sure, Maish. Sure.

Then he waits expectantly. Maish starts to say something, then he looks at Army, who turns away. Then he wets his lips.

MAISH: The doctor looked you over.

MCCLINTOCK (*Grinning*): Yeah. I thought he was in here. I wasn't sure, though. (*He taps his head*) A little groggy yet, you know?

MAISH (*Nodding*): Yeah. Well, anyway, he looked you over good this time.

MCCLINTOCK: Yeah?

MAISH: He figures . . . he figures you've had it.

He turns away, coughs, takes out a cigar and lights it. McClintock stares at him for a long moment.

MCCLINTOCK: What did you say, Maish?

MAISH: The doctor says you've had it. No more. He says you've got to leave now.

MCCLINTOCK: Leave? Leave where?

MAISH (*Whirls around and shouts*): Army, lay it out for him, will yuh? Mountain, no more fights. You get it? This is where you get off. You leave.

There's another moment's pause. McClintock gets off the table, walks over to Maish, pokes at him with a forefinger.

MCCLINTOCK: Leave? Maish, that's . . . that's crazy.

MAISH (*Shrugs, turns away*): So it's crazy. Maybe I think it's crazy, but that's what the doctor says. Go fight the commission. (*Deliberately turning his back on McClintock*) Have you got everything all cleared up here, Army? (*Army nods*)

MCCLINTOCK: Maish—?

MAISH (*Without turning to him*): What do you want, Mountain?

MCCLINTOCK: What'll I do?

MAISH: What'll you do. I dunno. You do whatever you want to do. Anything you like. It's as easy as that.

MCCLINTOCK: I mean . . . I mean a guy's got to do something.

MAISH: So? A guy's got to do something. So you do something. Do anything you like.

MCCLINTOCK (*The words come out hard*): Maish, I don't know anything but fighting. You know, fourteen years pro. You know, Maish. I've been with you fourteen years.

MAISH: And before that?

MCCLINTOCK (*Smiles and shrugs*): Before that what? Who remembers?

ARMY: Why don't you go back home, kid? You talk about it enough. The green hills of Tennessee. Is that what you call it? Go back home. Go back to Tennessee. The hills are probably still green.

MCCLINTOCK: What's back there?

He takes a few steps toward the other two men and looks from one to the other as he talks.

MCCLINTOCK: What's back there? I haven't been back in all those years. I don't know anybody. Nobody'd know me. (*And then suddenly, as if struck by an afterthought*) Maish, we could try another state, maybe?

MAISH (*Shakes his head*): Now you're talking crazy. If you don't pass muster in New York State, you don't pass muster any place else. You know that.

MCCLINTOCK: Maybe some club fights. You know, unofficial.

MAISH: Where've you been? Those kind of club fights went out with John L. Sullivan.

Army nods, follows Maish to the door, then turns back toward McClintock.

ARMY: Want me to help you dress, Mountain?

MCCLINTOCK (*Shakes his head*): No. No, I can dress myself. (*Then he looks across at Maish*) Maish?

MAISH: Yeah?

MCCLINTOCK: I'm . . . I'm sorry about tonight. I'm sorry I lost.

We cut to a very tight close-up of Maish as his features work and then he has to turn his eyes away.

MAISH: That's okay, Mountain. Don't give it another thought.

He goes out and closes the door. Army sort of hangs back by the door.

ARMY (*Finally*): We can go over to the hotel later on and—and talk this out, make some plans.

McClintock nods and doesn't say anything. Then Army goes out the door. McClintock stands there numbly and motionless for a long moment. We cut to the corridor outside the dressing room. Maish is walking very slowly down the corridor. He stops abruptly.

MAISH (*Waves and hollers*): Hey, Foxy. Hey, Fox!

A figure ahead of Maish pauses, turns, walks back toward him. This is a little mousey guy in a jacket, with a face like a weasel.

FOX: Whadda yuh say, Maish? I just seen Slaughter on Tenth Avenue. Was there enough left to sew together?

MAISH: Break your heart, does it?

FOX: I got my own troubles. (*And then very confident*) You want to see the kid now, Maish? I got him right out here. You said you might be interested—

MAISH: I said I *might* be.

FOX: Maish, he's a real sweetie. Middleweight. A good, fast middleweight, but he's built like a tank and I can't get him matched on accounta the business.

MAISH: How is the business? Did you get that fixed up?

FOX: I was one year revoked. But you know that was a bum rap, Maish. To pinch a guy like me for fixing fights. It's to laugh. I swear, it's to laugh. I couldn't fix a parking ticket. But . . . ah . . . meanwhile I got no contract with the kid because I got no license to manage, so if he could just hook up with someone—you know—a real solid guy to handle him for a bit—

MAISH: Foxy, don't dress it up, will ya, pal? If he's here, put him on the block. Let's take a look at him. But don't choke me with publicity.

FOX: Maish, you're a doll baby. You're an ever-loving doll baby. (*He turns and shouts*) Bobby! Bobby, Mr. Loomis would like to look at ya.

At this moment a fighter walks down the ramp iwm out of the shadows and approaches them. He walks with a stiff gait of an old rooster and his face looks like the battle of the Marne.

FOX: Here he is, Maish. Bobby Menzey.

MAISH (*Looks him over with the practiced eye of a veteran*): So what's to tell, Foxy? I'd like to see him spar.

FOX: He'll spar, he'll spar. I'll get a boy lined up at the gym tomorrow.

MAISH: Tell me about him.

The fighter starts to say something. Maish holds up his hand and points to Fox.

MAISH: Let *him* talk.

FOX: Like I told you before, Maish, he's a sweetheart. He's fought mostly out west.

MAISH: What's his record?

FOX (*Wets his lips*): Like I say, he's fought mostly out west.

MAISH: Wins and losses. Lay them out. Is that hard?

FOX: Well . . . well, his record ain't so well known, Maish. He was fighting out west.

MAISH (*Suddenly reaching out and grabbing Fox by the vest, pulling him toward him*): What are you trying to pull off, Fox?

FOX (*With a worried look toward his fighter*): Go easy on the kid, Maish.

MAISH: Kid? I'd hate to have my hands in boiling water since he was a kid.

MAISH (*Turning to fighter*): What's your name?

FIGHTER: Menzey—Bobby Menzey. Maybe you heard of me.

MAISH: I heard about you yesterday. But the last time I saw you fight, your name wasn't Bobby Menzey.

The fighter gulps and starts to stammer.

FOX (*Hurriedly*): You've got him mixed up, Maish. Menzey. Bobby Menzey. M-e-n-z-e-y.

MAISH: Stop it! Correct me if I'm wrong. LaPlant, isn't it? In 1949 you were a lightweight—a real comer. Sixteen straight. Then you fought Red Johns in Syracuse. He knocked you out in the second round. Then you lost six or seven straight.

After that I saw you in Detroit. That was three, four years ago.

The fighter looks at Fox helplessly.

FOX (*With a huge smile*): You got me, Maish. You really got me. I had him change his name, but that don't prove nothing about his fighting.

MAISH: It doesn't, huh? It means you're trying to pass off a stumble bum on me as a comer. (*He grabs Menzey's face and turns it to the light*) Look at it. I know a bleeder when I see one. One punch and his face falls apart. And this is the sweetheart, huh? This guy will never live to see the day when he's anything else besides a poor, beat-up slob.

FIGHTER: What're you talkin' about? I'm as good as I ever was.

FOX: That's right. He's still got it, Maish. Would I try to put something over on you? (*He slaps him expansively on the arm*) Would I? A wise one like you? Think I'm crazy or something. It's to laugh, Maish. I swear it's to laugh. Go ahead, Bobby. Box around a little for him. Go ahead.

The fighter starts to shadowbox in front of them. Maish and Army exchange a look.

FOX: Who does he remind you of? Baer?

MAISH: Yeah, a big brown one with a ring in his nose.

FOX: Look, Maish—

MAISH: Knock it off. You'd better send him back to your factory. Right now.

FOX: Maish, give me a break, will ya?

MAISH: I've given you a break. I won't split your head. That's a break. I'll see you around, Fox.

Maish turns and walks past him. The Gghtei, suddenly seeing his shadow against a wall, begins to shadowbox.

FOX (*Pushing him*): Mud for brains! So stop already. No deal.

The camera picks up Maish as he staits up the ramp. The man steps out from the wall once again and stops him.

MAN: Hey, Loomis—

MAISH: I'll get it! I'll get it! What does Henson need, bail money? I told you I'd get it for you. Now lay off, will ya?

MAN: Mr. Henson would like to know *where* you're going to get it.

MAISH: Mr. Henson'll have to guess.

MAN: Mr. Henson will take it out of your skin, Loomis. Just remember that.

He walks up the ramp and disappears. Maish watches him go and the tight, set look on his face disintegrates and suddenly he is very frightened. But he recomposes his face when he sees Army walking toward him.

MAISH (*With a forced smile*): Come on, I'll buy you a drink.

ARMY (*Looks toward the ramp*): Fox showing off his wares? You work fast, Maish.

MAISH: People have to eat—or are you different?

ARMY: I'm not the one drumming up trade five minutes after I get the word.

MAISH: I'm drumming it up for you too, remember, boy scout! Fox has got a boy and he can't handle him. I've got no boy and I *can* handle him. That's simple stuff, Army. That's arithmetic. (*Then his shoulders sag*) What difference? He was a clinker. The worst.

ARMY: What now?

MAISH: I think I'll go shadowbox off a cliff. Come on, I need a drink.

ARMY (*Nods toward the dressing room*): I'll wait for the kid.

MAISH: Sure. (*He looks up toward the ceiling and grins*) The kid. That's what I call him too. The kid. I think that's where we goofed. As long as they wear trunks and gloves we think they're kids. They're old men. They're the oldest. I'll see you later on, Army.

He walks on up the ramp, pausing near the top to look at a poster which advertises the fight that night. On it is a picture of Mountain and his opponent and the words "main bout" are prominent. He takes a few steps farther and looks at another poster. This one shows two big clowns in a plug for a wrestling match. He takes a few steps closer to the poster and stares at it, taps it thoughtfully with his finger. We cut to a brief, tight close-up of Army noticing this. Then we cut to a long shot as Maish disappears up the ramp. We dissolve to a shot of a little hotel and adjoining bar as seen through its front window. We dissolve through the interior and get a cover shot of the entire place. This is about a twenty-foot-square, dingy little bistio frequented by people in the fight business—mostly ex-fighters and ring hangers-on. On the wall aie pictures of fighters going back to the 1800s. A championship belt is in a frame over the bar. Other than these the place has no pretensions. It is simply there to serve diink and make up for what is probably a loss in the hotel business alongside. At the far end of the room theie's a handful of fighters, obviously in nightly clatch. One Gghtei is holding sway with an excited blow-by-blow horn some monumental battle of years before. As we pan around the room we pick up part of his speech.

FIGHTER #1: So he comes in at me. (*He holds both his hands up*)

FIGHTER #2: Yeah, yeah. Go ahead.

FIGHTER #1: He comes at me. I sized him up. He throws a left, I duck. He throws another left, I duck. Then he throws another left.

FIGHTER #2: You duck.

FIGHTER #1: No, I don't duck. I take it right smack dab on the jaw. I'm down. Oh, man, am I down.

We pan past them at this moment for a shot of McClintock and Army as they enter. The bartender is a flat-nosed ex-pug who nods very biieEy at them as they sit on the stools.

BARTENDER: How're you, Mountain? Army?

ARMY: Two beers, huh, Charlie?

BARTENDER: Two beers.

He draws them and expertly shoots them down the bar one at a time. Army takes out some money—three one-dollar bills. He separates them and lays one on the counter.

BARTENDER: How'd you do, Mountain?

MCCLINTOCK: Not so good, Charlie. Almost went the route, though. Doc says I'm over the hill now.

BARTENDER (*Clucks*): That's too bad. (*Then philosophically*) So, now yuh can join the Wednesday-evening coffee clatch. (*He jerks with his thumb in the direction of the rear of the room, then with a long look at McClintock he takes out a bottle and says*) Have one on the house. This is the only one in the house that ain't watered.

He pours two healthy-sized glasses and shoves them in front of each of them, then walks back down the bar.

ARMY (*Turns to Mountain, holds up his glass*): To Mountain McClintock. A hundred and eleven fights.

MCCLINTOCK: He wasn't no good, but he never took a dive.

Army returns the laugh, staits to drink. He takes only the barest of sips, looking over the top of his glass at Mountain, a sad and knowing look on his face. At this moment Army sees the reflection of Maish in the mirror. He turns around.

ARMY: Hey, Maish. Here we are.

MAISH (*Walks over to them*): Let's get a booth.

MCCLINTOCK: How're you doing, Maish?

MAISH: I'll tell yuh when we get to the booth.

As they get away from the bar a drunk tipsily bangs into Maish, and McClintock rather firmly places him out of the way.

MCCLINTOCK: Watch it. That's my manager.

The three men go to the rear and sit in an empty booth.

MAISH (*Without any preliminaries. Obviously intent on getting this over*): What did you do with your dough, Mountain?

MCCLINTOCK: You mean—

MAISH (*Impatiently*): The dough for the fight. You got six hundred and thirty-three bucks, didn't you? Where is it?

MCCLINTOCK: It's mostly gone. I owed the hotel half of it, Maish.

MAISH (*Wets his lips*): What about the other half?

MCCLINTOCK (*Very slowly*): Well, I suppose I've got some of it . . .

MAISH (*Excited, blurts it out*): Look, don't get cute with me. This is Maish. I asked you a question now. Have you got any money at all?

McClintock reaches into his pants and pulls out a crumpled roll of bills. He lays them out one at a time on the table.

MCCLINTOCK: I've got some. Twenty, forty, fifty-five, fifty-six, fifty-seven, fifty-eight bucks, Maish. (*He collects it and shoves it over in a bunch to Maish*) Here.

MAISH: Fifty-eight bucks.

Maish picks it up and looks at it. He throws it back down on the table.

ARMY (*A little wisely*): What's the matter, Maish? You in hock?

MAISH (*Nods*): Heavy.

ARMY: How much?

MAISH: Three thousand dollars.

ARMY (*Whistles*): Three thousand dollars.

MCCLINTOCK (*Very worried*): Gee, Maish, that's a lot of money. How're we gonna get it?

MAISH: I don't know. But I haven't got much time.

ARMY: How did you get into that kind of a crack, Maish?

MAISH (*With side look at McClintock, his tone changes*): You don't know, huh? Mountain, when you were in the hospital last month with a bum hand—remember?

ARMY: That comes off the top. What're you givin' him?

MAISH: Sure. But I brought in a specialist, didn't I? And that came out of here. (*He pats his own pocket*) And the training camp. He wanted to go up to New Jersey, so he went up to New

Jersey. How much do you think that cost me a month? A lot more than my cut, I'll tell ya.

MCCLINTOCK: Gee, Maish, I didn't know that.

MAISH: I'm not complaining. I'm not complaining. But the money goes, you know. And one half of your take hasn't been much lately. It doesn't cover expenses, so I've been filling up the rest of it for you. Well now, we've got to pay the fiddler, kid. We're at the end of the line now.

MCCLINTOCK (*His face very concerned*): I've been thinkin', Maish, if I could get me a job—you know, something to tide us over—

MAISH (*Barely listening to him*): Sure. Sure. (*Then to Army*) Jake Green's got a lightweight he's touting. Maybe we could buy a piece. (*He looks up to the ceiling*) Yeah, we could buy a piece. With what? We could get his thumb. That I could afford.

MCCLINTOCK (*Very softly*): Get a new boy, Maish?

ARMY (*With a quick look at Maish*): Not for a while yet, Mountain—just an idea.

MCCLINTOCK: Oh. Oh. I see. (*He glances around the room, looking at the people, the tables and the pictures. Very quietly*) I remember the first night I come in here, Maish. I remember the guy's name even. Shipsky. Morty Shipsky. I knocked him out in the first round. And you and Army stood up on the bar and you shouted. You shouted, "Everybody take a drink on Harlan McClintock, the next champ." (*He looks from one to the other*) Remember? That was the night you give me the name "Mountain."

ARMY (*Quietly*): I remember.

MCCLINTOCK: Sure. You asked me where I was from and I told you. I told you I lived in Tennessee on a mountain. And that's when . . . that's when Maish here says, "That's what we'll call ya. We'll call ya Mountain." (*He looks around the room again*) How many nights we come in here, Maish? How many nights?

ARMY: A lot of 'em.

MCCLINTOCK: Couple of hundred, I guess? Couple of hundred nights. We could just sit and talk here by the hour about this fight or that fight, or some other fighter, or a fight we were gonna get. By the hour.

MAISH (*A little disjointedly*): It's the breaks, that's all. It's the breaks.

MCCLINTOCK: All of a sudden I—I'm sittin' here and it becomes different. Like . . . like right now even. I'm on the outside lookin' in. Like . . . I didn't belong with you guys any more.

Then suddenly his face becomes a mask as realization seems to flood into it, and he slowly rises to his feet.

ARMY: Look, Mountain—

MAISH: Why don't you sit down and have another drink? It's early.

MCCLINTOCK (*Shaking his head*): I think I'll just . . . I'll just take a walk. I'll see you later.

He turns to go and is suddenly aware of the little knot of men in the back of the room still talking about fights. He looks at them for a moment, almost winces, and then, to nobody in particular, says:

MCCLINTOCK: That's no way. That's no way at all.

ARMY: What did you say, Mountain?

MCCLINTOCK (*As if awakened suddenly*): Nothin'. Nothin', Army. I'll see you later.

McClintock turns and walks down the room to the door and goes out. The bartender comes over with a tray and places it on the table in front of Maish and Army.

BARTENDER: How about you, Army? You want something?

Army doesn't answer him. He is staring toward the door. Maish drops a coin on the tray and makes a motion with his head for the bartender to get lost. The bartender walks back toward the bar.

MAISH: Hey, Army.

ARMY (*Without looking at him*): What?

MAISH: Look at me when I'm talking to yuh, will yuh? I don't like talking to a guy's neck.

ARMY (*Reluctantly turns toward him*): How'd you lose the dough?

MAISH: How do you think?

ARMY: You bet against him, didn't you?

MAISH (*Not meeting his eyes*): Something like that.

ARMY: You don't side-step very good.

MAISH: You want it clearer, huh?

ARMY: A little bit.

MAISH: I said he wouldn't go four.

ARMY (*Smiles a crooked little smile*): Big disappointment, huh?

MAISH: There was another way? The minute they tell me he was matched against Gibbons I figure we should throw in the towel while he's signing the contract. Save wear and tear. Gibbons! Thirty-one fights and thirty-one wins. He's got a lit fuse in each hand. And they match him against the Mountain.

ARMY: They match him?

MAISH: Did I? I just go through the motions. Good fast brawl, they said. Couple of nice crowd-pleasers in a pier six. Harlan Mountain McClintock, ex-leading heavyweight contender. Ex is right. Very ex. Eight years ex. He's past prime, Army. I take what I can find—you know that. They say fight Gibbons, I say O.K. They say Marciano, I say bring on Marciano.

ARMY: You coulda tole 'em—

MAISH: Tell 'em, tell 'em, tell 'em. Tell 'em what? Tell 'em I've got a dead-weight has-been on my back? That he shouldn't fight any more? And then what do I do? Put in for a pension?

At this moment a man walks up to the table, nods briefly at Army, and then smiles broadly at Maish.

MAN: What's the good word, Maish?

MAISH (*Staring straight ahead*): Blow. That's a good word. I don't want any.

MAN: How do you know what I'm selling?

MAISH: So pitch. I'm busy.

MAN: Mr. Henson sent me.

Maish's hand hits the ash tray nervously and knocks it off the table. Maish bends down to pick it up and we cut to tight close-up of the man's foot on Maish's hand. Maish looks up horn the Eooi, his face dead-white.

MAN: Now you pitch. Tell me when Mr. Henson can expect his dough.

MAISH: Soon.

MAN: How soon is soon?

MAISH: Three weeks.

MAN: You said two, didn't you?

Maish bites his lips. The man's foot remains on his hand.

MAISH (*His voice a croak*): Two weeks.

The man lifts his foot, picks up the ash tray, sets it back on the table.

MAN: You dropped something, Mr. Loomis. I'll see you in two weeks.

He turns and walks away. Army stares across the table at Maish. Maish takes out a handkerchief and wipes his face, then reaches into his pocket for a half-smoked cigar. He pats around for a match.

MAISH: Got a match?

ARMY: You and a mouse. That's a match.

MAISH: Who am I, Atlas? These guys play for real, Army—you know that. This is no bank transaction. If I welsh, you can take a spoon, scoop what's left of me off the wall and put it in a cup. That's how serious they look on bets. And if they don't go to that trouble, they'll get my license so quick they'll blur the ink. I won't be able to sell peanuts at a fight, so I'm licked either way.

ARMY: Who told you to bet?

MAISH: Who told me I hadda eat?

ARMY: You picked the sport.

MAISH: This isn't a sport. If there was headroom, they'd hold them in sewers. So what do I do?

ARMY (*Very quietly*): What does the Mountain do?

MAISH: You tell me. That's this precious business of ours. He gives them a million dollars' worth of fighting for fourteen years, and then they're not interested in paying for the dump truck to cart 'im away. The sport. The sport and the precious crowd.

ARMY: *You* ever buy him a ticket back to Tennessee?

MAISH: Don't stick it on me. All I do is curry the horse. I'm one of the stable boys. I don't set up the rules. I get sucked in just like he does. (*He stares at the chair Mountain was sitting in*) He asks me . . . He sits there and he asks me, "What'll I do, Maish?" He asks *me* what he's gonna do. Like I was the Book of

Knowledge and I'm supposed to tell him. I don't know what to tell him. I'm so scared right now, Army, that—

ARMY: Stop it. You lost a bank roll and a meal ticket. But this poor beat-up kid—did you ever figure out what he lost tonight?

MAISH: You don't think I feel sorry for him? I don't want to hurt that kid, Army. I swear I don't want to hurt him. He thinks he's the only one that's got a memory. I got a memory too. I remember him like he was. Like the first day he comes into my office—all hands and feet and his mouth full of teeth and he talks like General Lee.

Maish shakes his head and pats in his pocket again for a match. Army lights his cigar.

ARMY: Take one on me. (*Long pause*) You talk about memories, Maish. Remember Christmas 1945? Right at this table. We had six bucks between us. Four of it you spent on a beefsteak and a new tie for him. Remember that, Maish?

MAISH (*Nods*): Sure. That horrible-lookin' tie. He wore it until there wasn't anything left of it.

ARMY: I remember a lot of times like that. That time in Scranton when that big Swede knocked him out. Remember? We couldn't get him back on his feet. They took him to a hospital that night. I remember waiting outside in the corridor with you. (*Maish nods*) You cried that night, Maish.

MAISH: All right, knock it off.

ARMY: Okay. But you hear me out now, Maish. I'm telling you this now. I'm telling you that I love this guy like he was of my flesh. And I figure if I don't watch for him and weep for him—now nobody else will, least of all you, for some reason. So be careful, Maish. That's what I'm telling you now. Be careful.

Army rises, leaves the table, goes across the room and out the door. Maish watches him for a moment and then rises after him. He starts to walk slowly toward the door. Dissolve to the alley outside the fight area. We see McClintock very slowly walking into the alley, aimlessly, without direction. Once in the center of the alley he leans against the wall, his back touching one of the torn fight posters. The crowd noise comes up momentarily loud and sharp. McClintock's head goes up. He slowly turns so that he is face to face with the picture of a boxer, with his hands up, on the poster. And then for no reason he starts to spar with the picture. First lightly, as if he knew it were a joke, then much more seriously, until pretty soon his hands flick out in short jabs, they hit the wall and they hurt. He suddenly draws back with his right as if to smash at the poster when suddenly a hand comes down on his shoulder. He stops. His head goes down. We pull back to see Maish standing near him.

MAISH: Mountain, take it easy.

MOUNTAIN (*Nods slowly, numbly*): Yeah. Yeah, Maish. Take it easy.

MAISH: The world didn't end tonight. Remember that. The world didn't end because you left the ring. It didn't end for you either.

MCCLINTOCK: Sure. Sure, Maish. Just . . . just stick around for a little, will ya? I could always depend on you, Maish. I always . . . I always needed to depend on you.

Maish nods slowly, pats his arm, but as he does so his eyes travel down the wall to another poster showing a big, stupid Arabian prince in a wrestling costume. And there is a big sign "wrestling" over the top of it. Maish's eyes slowly move from the poster to McClintock, who stares up at him hopefully like a pet dog desperately needing reassurance.

MAISH (*Wets his lips*): C'mon, let's get out of here.

The two men slowly walk away and down the alley. We take a slow fade to black.

ACT TWO

We dissolve to an anteroom of a small office with a sign on the door: "New Yoik State Employment Office." Sitting on a bench are McClintock and Army. McClintock appears nervous and fidgety. He is constantly running a finger through his collar, which is much too tight, as is his suit, shirt and everything else he wears. He looks helplessly at Army, who pats his arm reassuringly.

ARMY: You look fine. Don't worry. You look just great.

MCCLINTOCK (*In a whisper*): But what do I say, Army?

ARMY: What d'ya mean, what d'ya say? Just tell her you want a job, that's all. It's simple.

MCCLINTOCK: But what kind of a job?

ARMY: You don't have to worry about that. You just tell her the sort of thing you can do and it's up to them to find you one.

MCCLINTOCK: Army, in the past two days I've been thirty-five places already. Most of these jokers won't even let me in the door.

ARMY: It's different here. This place is official. They're here just to get people jobs. People like you that can't find them easy on their own.

At this moment a young woman appears at the door of the inner office.

GRACE: Mr. McClintock, please.

McClintock bolts to his feet, almost upsetting Army.

MCCLINTOCK: That's me! That's me!

GRACE (*Smiling*): In here, please, Mr. McClintock.

McClintock turns to Army and grabs his arm.

ARMY (*Firmly removing his fingers*): I'm right here at ringside, but I can't go in to fight for you. Go ahead.

McClintock, with another journey of his finger through his collar, walks hesitantly after the young woman. We pan with them into her office as the door closes. He turns around with a start at its closing.

GRACE: Sit down, Mr. McClintock. Right over here, please, near the desk.

MCCLINTOCK: Thanks. Thank you very much.

He sits down with another eye toward the door. They both start to speak together.

MCCLINTOCK: I was—

GRACE: Now, Mr. McClintock—

MCCLINTOCK: I was just wondering if . . . Oh, I beg your pardon.

GRACE: You were going to say?

MCCLINTOCK: I was just wondering if my friend could come in?

GRACE: Is he looking for employment too?

MCCLINTOCK: No. No, not exactly, but . . . well, he's kind of my handler.

GRACE: I beg your pardon?

MCCLINTOCK (*Wets his lips*): It's okay. He'll stay out there.

She looks at him and smiles, then glances at a sheet of paper.

GRACE: Harlan McClintock. Your age is—

MCCLINTOCK: Thirty-three.

She makes a little notation with a pencil.

GRACE: Place of birth?

MCCLINTOCK: Kenesaw, Tennessee.

GRACE: I see. Your education? (*She looks up at him*) Mr. McClintock, you left that blank here.

MCCLINTOCK: My education? You mean school?

GRACE: That's right.

MCCLINTOCK: Ninth grade.

GRACE: Then you left, is that it?

MCCLINTOCK (*Nodding*): Then I left.

GRACE: Now, field of interest.

MCCLINTOCK: I beg your pardon?

GRACE: Your field of interest. What do you like to do?

MCCLINTOCK: Most anything. I don't much care.

GRACE (*Looks down at his sheet and frowns slightly*): Past employment record, Mr. McClintock. You have nothing written down there. (*She looks up at him*) Who've been your past employers?

MCCLINTOCK: Well . . . you see . . . I really haven't had past employers—I mean, past employers like you mean down on that sheet. I've always been kind of on my own, except you might say I've been working for Maish.

GRACE: Maish?

MCCLINTOCK: You see, all I've been doing the past fourteen years is fightin'.

GRACE: Fighting.

MCCLINTOCK: That's right. You know, in the ring.

GRACE: You mean a prize fighter?

MCCLINTOCK (*Smiles*): That's right. Prize fighter.

GRACE: A professional prize fighter.

MCCLINTOCK (*Delightedly*): Yeah, that's it. You catch on. A professional prize fighter. Heavyweight.

Grace stares at him for a moment and we cut to a tight close-up of McClintock's face as he becomes conscious of her stare. He almost unconsciously puts one hand across his face to hide the scar tissue. He turns his face away ever so slightly. Grace notices this and turns away herself, and then looks down again at the paper.

GRACE: That sounds like interesting work, Mr. McClintock.

MCCLINTOCK (*Looking up at her*): Well, it's . . . it's a living. I don't want you to go to no trouble. Army says I should just tell you that . . . well, anything you got's jake with me. Dishwashing—anything.

She looks at him again for a long moment.

GRACE (*Kindly*): Let's see if we can't examine something else, Mr. McClintock—something you might like even more. How about factory work?

MCCLINTOCK (Shaking his head): I never worked in a factory. I wouldn't know anything about it.

GRACE: No sort of assembly-line work, blueprint reading, anything like that? (He shakes his head, she wets her lips) Anything in sales, Mr. McClintock? There's a lot of openings in that sort of thing now. Department-store work. Anything like that?

MCCLINTOCK (*Shaking his head*): I . . . I couldn't do anything like that. I couldn't sell nothin'. (*Then with a kind of lopsided grin*) With my face I'd scare away the customers.

He laughs lightly at this and when he looks up she is staring at him, not laughing with him at all. He becomes embarrassed now and half rises to his feet.

MCCLINTOCK: Look, Miss, I don't want to take up your time. (*And now in his hopelessness the words come out; he forgets his embarrassment*) The only reason I come is because Army said I should come. I've been answering all these ads like I told ya and I've been getting no place at all. Maish needs the dough real bad and I can't do nothin' for him any more, and I got to. I got to get some kind of a job. Don't make any difference what I do. Anything at all.

GRACE: Mr. McClintock—

MCCLINTOCK (*Unaware of her now*): A guy goes along fourteen years. All he does is fight. Once a week, twice a week, prelims, semifinals, finals. He don't know nothin' but that. All he can do is fight. Then they tell him no more. And what's he do? What's he supposed to do? What's he supposed to know how to do besides fight? They got poor Maish tied up by the ears and I got to do somethin' for him. (*He looks down at his hands. He pauses for a moment*)

GRACE (*Quietly*): Mr. McClintock, we handle a lot of placements here. I'm sure we can find you something—

MCCLINTOCK: I know you're going to do the best you can, but . . . (*He points to the paper on her desk*) I don't fit in any of the holes. I mean that question there. Why did you leave your last job? State reason.

GRACE: That's question nine. You see, Mr. McClintock—

MCCLINTOCK: I understand it but what do I write down? What do I write down that would make sense? I left my last job because I got hit so much that I was on my way to punchy land and I'd probably go blind. How would that read there?

GRACE (*Her eyes narrow*): Punchy land?

MCCLINTOCK: Sure. You fight so long and then you walk around on your heels listening to the bells. That's what happens to you. Doc looks at my eyes, says one or two more I might go blind.

GRACE (*Very softly*): I see.

MCCLINTOCK (*Getting excited again*): And that's not fair. It's a dirty break, that's all. In 1948 they ranked me number five. I'm not kidding ya. Number five. And that wasn't any easy year neither. There was Charles and Wolcott and Louis still around. And they had me up there at number five. Maish was sure that—

GRACE: Maish? Who's Maish, Mr. McClintock?

MCCLINTOCK: Maish is my manager. And where does it leave him? That's a nice thing to do to a guy who's kept you going for fourteen years. You stop cold on him. So it's a bum break. It ain't fair at all. (*He rises and turns his back to her, and he slowly subsides*) I'm . . . I'm real sorry, Miss. I didn't mean to blow up like that. You ought to kick me out of here. Honest, I'm real sorry.

GRACE (*Again quietly*): That's perfectly all right, Mr. McClintock. As long as you've got your address down here we'll contact you if anything comes up, and we'll—

She stops, staring across the worn at him—at the big shoulders that are slumped in front of her and the big hands down by his sides that clench and unclench. A certain softness shows in her face—a pitying look. She wets her lips and then forces a smile.

GRACE: Right after the war I did a lot of work with disabled veterans.

As soon as she has said this she is sorry. His head jerks up and he turns slowly toward her.

MCCLINTOCK: Yeah? Go on.

GRACE: I meant . . . I meant you'd be surprised the . . . the different kinds of openings that come up for—(*She struggles for a word*)

MCCLINTOCK: For cripples. For those kind of guys?

GRACE: I didn't mean just that. I meant for people who have special problems.

MCCLINTOCK: I've got no special problems. (*He takes a step toward her*) There wasn't no place on that question sheet of yours—but I was almost the heavyweight champion of the world. I'm a big ugly slob and I look like a freak, but I was almost the heavyweight champion of the world. I'd like to put that down some place on that paper. This isn't just a punk. This was a guy who was almost the heavyweight champion of the world!

He slams his fist on the desk, and then as quickly as the anger came it leaves. Very slowly he takes his hand from the desk. He looks at it biieHy, closes his eyes and turns away again. He looks down at his hand and feels of the bruise over his eye. He looks away from her. Grace is staring at him all the time.

GRACE: Did you hurt your hand, Mr. McClintock?

MCCLINTOCK (*Looks at his hand*): I guess I did. That's the . . . that's the thing of it. When you go for so long the hurt piles up and you don't even feel them. You get out of the ring and you go back to a dressing room and you look in the mirror. You look like somebody just ran over you with a tractor—but somehow it doesn't seem to hurt. There's always a reason for it. You know that . . . you know that you just took another step up. Then after the last one—when the wad's all shot and you're over the hill and there aren't going to be any more—then suddenly you do start to hurt. The punches you got fourteen years ago-even then. And when Maish and the Doc and Army—they were all standing around me that night and I heard somebody say, He's wound up. Then it hurts. Then it hurts like you've got to scream. Like now. It hurts now. Before, at least—before every little piece of skin they took off you—was part of the bill you had to pay. And then all of a sudden one night you have to throw all the fourteen years out into an alley and you know then that you've been paying that bill for nothing.

We cut to a very tight close-up of Grace's face as she comes around from behind her desk. She touches his arm tentatively.

GRACE: Mr. McClintock, I think . . . I think we can get you something you'll like. Just give us time.

MCCLINTOCK (*Looks at her*): Something I'll like? Do that, Miss. I don't want much. Just . . . the heavyweight championship of the world. That's all.

He stares at her and you can see in his face that he wants to say something—wants to apologize, wants to explain to her that this is a bitterness directed at no one, but it can't come out, it can't be articulated. He turns slowly and walks out of the room. She stands there watching him through the open door. We see Army rise. The two men exchange words and then they both leave. Grace slowly closes the door, goes back to her desk pensively. We take a slow fade-out on her face.

Fade on a shot of Maish's hotel room—night. In the semi-dark room Maish and Army play cards. Maish slaps down a card with tremendous vigor.

MAISH: Jack of Spades.

Army goes through a series of facial and body movements, shrugging left and right, opening and closing his mouth, drumming on the bridge of his nose with his fingers.

ARMY: That's good to know. That's very good to know.

He draws a card, throws it down. Maish draws another, he throws it down.

ARMY: Queen of Spades.

MAISH: That's what it looks like, doesn't it?

ARMY (*Nods*): That's good to know. That's very good to know. (*He goes through the series of motions again*) That's very good to know.

MAISH (*Looking up at him*): Army, would you not say that any more, please?

ARMY: Say what?

MAISH: "It's good to know. It's good to know. It's good to know." Everything is good to know with you.

Army grins, draws a card, throws it face down, lays out his hand, throws a single card across the table.

ARMY: I'll knock for two.

MAISH: You've got me. I've got a Jack and eight free. You've got me.

ARMY: That's good to know.

He ducks away jokingly. Maish rises and flings the cards at him across the table.

ARMY: C'mon, I'll play you another hand.

MAISH: Don't do me any favors. (*He rises and pats around his pockets*)

ARMY (*Pointing to an ash tray*): It's over here.

Maish walks across the room, takes a half-smoked cigar out of an ash tray, lights it.

ARMY: One inch shorter you'd be smoking your nose.

MAISH: So does it hurt you?

ARMY: Wanna watch television? There's a fight on.

MAISH: You don't get enough of that, huh?

ARMY: It's somethin' to do.

MAISH: If it's somethin' to do, go to a bar, will ya? I get my gut full of it nine, ten hours a day. I don't like it in my hotel room.

ARMY: Cards?

MAISH: How about ice skating? You bored, Army? (*He chomps nervously on the cigar*) What am I going to do?

ARMY (*Shrugging*): Ask 'em for another week.

MAISH: Ask 'em, ask 'em, ask 'em—do you think it'll cut ice with them? They want their money.

The phone rings and Maish nervously and quickly picks it up.

MAISH (*On the phone*): Hello . . . Yeah. (*A pause*) Well, when he gets in tell him I want to talk to him, will ya? No, I can't talk to you. I want to talk to Parelli himself. Thanks. (*He puts down the receiver and finds Army staring at him*) Well? You want to lodge a complaint? You look it.

ARMY: Parelli handles wrestling.

MAISH: Is that a secret?

ARMY: What do you want with a wrestling promoter?

MAISH: You got the longest nose in the business.

ARMY: You gonna answer, Maish?

MAISH (*With an enforced matter-of-factness*): For a kick, Army. We'll let the kid wrestle a few.

ARMY: Mountain?

MAISH: Why not? They pay good for that stuff, just like they pay actors or somethin'. I could work up a routine for him— ya know? We could make him something like—well, you know, like Gorgeous George and the Mad Baron. He'd be . . . he'd be Mountain McClintock the Mountaineer. We could dress him up in a coonskin hat and a . . . a . . . costume of some kind. And we could bill him as—(*He stops abruptly. He sees Army staring at him*) So what's wrong with it? It's money, ain't it?

ARMY: It's money, sure, but what kind of money is it, Maish?

MAISH: What difference does it make what kind of money it is?

ARMY: A guy like him don't take getting laughed at.

MAISH (*Whirls around at him*): What're you talking about—a guy like him? So what is he? A prima donna? All of a sudden he's sensitive! All of a sudden he's very fragile, like precious china or something. Since when does a guy like him get sensitive all of a sudden!

ARMY: Since when? Since we knowed him! That's since when. You never see things like that, Maish.

MAISH: Maybe I got no time. Ever look at it that way? Maybe I'm too busy stitching him up so he can show the next week. Maybe I'm too busy on my hands and knees pleading with a promoter to use him so we can get groceries. Maybe I've got no time to hold these poor sensitive boys on my lap.

ARMY: Hey, Maish—you stink.

MAISH: Sure I stink. I'm a crummy selfish louse—because for fourteen years I nurse along a pug, and instead of three square meals for my old age I got nothing but debts and a headache. You want to know who owes who? Okay. Just check the records. Look at the win-and-loss. The Mountain comes in at the short end. He owes me. I figure it's as simple as that. What do I ask of this guy? Stick on a costume and make a few people laugh a couple of minutes. Is that going to curdle his sensitive in-sides?

ARMY (*With a barely perceptible tremor in his voice*): He's only got one thing left, Maish—that's his pride. You don't want to job that off. (*Maish doesn't answer. Army walks over to him and grabs him*) Leave something, will you? You talk about him when he was number-five contender in *Ring Magazine*. You want to remember him that way. Leave it so that's the way he'll remember himself. Not a . . . not a clown. Not like somebody who takes a pie in the face so he can eat that day. He was a somebody, Maish. Let it go at that. Don't turn him into a geek.

Maish looks intensely at Army. He can't vocalize his frustration any more than he can put into words the sense of the truth that he gets from what Army has toïd him, and it is a truth that Maish cannot answer. Finally he Icicles at a table, upsetting a lamp.

MAISH: So I'm selling his soul on the street! So weep for him! So rip your clothes a little. So I may take an inch off his pride, but, by everything holy, I'll have a full gut to show for it. You can starve to death, wise guy.

He turns almost aimlessly, not knowing what to do, and finally goes out the door and slams it.

Dissolve out.

Fade on with a shot of the squared circle bar as in Act I. It is mid-evening and the place is only partially filled. At the far end of the room the same group of old fighters stand in a semicircle around one of the others. McClintock stands on the fringes, listening, and as the men talk he studies their faces. All of them are scarred, ring-battered, and there's a kind of sameness in each face.

FIGHTER #1: That was Keister. Willie Keister. Used to fight out of Philly. Lightweight.

FIGHTER #2: He wasn't never no lightweight. He always fought middle. I remember him good.

FIGHTER # 1: Middleweight, your bleeding ears. He never weighed more than 135 pounds in his life.

This talk continues underneath as the camera moves away to take in a shot of the bar and the archway that adjoins the lobby of the little hotel. From out of the lobby we see Grace enter the bar. She looks around.

BARTENDER: Sorry, Miss, unescorted ladies ain't permitted.

GRACE: I was looking for Mr. McClintock. The man at the desk said he'd be in here.
BARTENDER: McClintock? The Mountain, you mean. That's him.
(*He points down toward the end of the room*)
GRACE: Thank you.
She walks very slowly toward the group of men in the rear and when she gets close we can then pick up what they are saying.
FIGHTER #1: So it's round four. He comes out real slow like he always does.
FIGHTER #2: Yeah. He always did come out slow.
FIGHTER #1: He jabs a couple of times. Remember how he used to do that? From way up high on the shoulder. You could hardly see it coming.
FIGHTER #2: You hardly ever could.
FIGHTER #1: He touches me a couple of times up on the forehead. I back off. He keeps coming after me. I want him to lead. Now this is a guy you got to let lead because he's the best counter-puncher in the business.
FIGHTER #2: Yeah. He can always counter-punch. Man could that boy counter-punch! I remember one time in Chicago—
FIGHTER #3: Go ahead, Steve. Go ahead.
FIGHTER #1: So we keep sparring like that right on through the round. He don't hurt me, I don't hurt him.
He continues to speak underneath as McClintock turns and sees Grace. He reacts, leaves the group and walks hurriedly over to her.
MCCLINTOCK: Miss Grace, what're you doing here?
GRACE: Well, I—
She is suddenly conscious of the rest of the men looking at her and McClintock sees this too. He takes her arm.
MCCLINTOCK: Let's go over here and sit down.
He takes her to a booth and they sit down. The men move away, chuckling, with an occasional glance at them.

GRACE: A friend of mine and I had dinner over at McCleary's. It isn't very far from here. She got a headache and went on home, and I—

MCCLINTOCK: Yeah?

GRACE: And I remembered your giving me your hotel and—

MCCLINTOCK: It was real nice of you to look me up.

She looks around the room and smiles a little embarrassedly.

GRACE: You know, I've never been around here before.

MOUNTAIN (*Nods*): No change. If you're here once, you've seen it all.

GRACE (*Smiles*): Atmosphere.

MCCLINTOCK: Yeah, you might call it atmosphere.

She looks over his shoulder at the men in the back of the room. One fighter is going through the motions of a battle. Grace looks questioningly, at him and then at McClintock.

MCCLINTOCK: That? That goes on all the time around here. Maish says this part of the room is the graveyard. And these guys spend their time dying in here. Fighting their lives away inside their heads. That's what Maish says.

GRACE: That's . . . that's kind of sad.

MCCLINTOCK: I suppose it is.

GRACE (*With a smile, leans toward him*): I've got a confession to make. I didn't eat at McCleary's. I ate at home. I came on purpose. I asked for you at your hotel. I've been thinking about you alot, Mr. McClintock. (*There is a long pause*) I was just wondering—

MCCLINTOCK: Yeah? Go ahead.

GRACE: I was just wondering if you ever thought of working with children. (*There's a long pause*)

MCCLINTOCK: What?

GRACE: Work with children. Like a summer camp. You know, in athletics.

MCCLINTOCK: I—I never give it much thought.

GRACE: Do you like children?

MCCLINTOCK: Children? Well, I haven't had much to do with kids, but I've always liked them. (*Then thoughtfully, going over it in his mind*) Yeah, I like kids a lot. You were thinking of a summer camp or something—

GRACE: That's right. That sort of thing. In a month or so there'll be a lot of openings. I was thinking, well, perhaps you ought to give that some thought.

MCCLINTOCK (*His hand goes to his face*): But they'd have to see me and listen to me talk and—

GRACE: Why not? You've got to begin some place. You've got to give it a try.

MCCLINTOCK: Sure, I'm going to have to. (*Then he stares at her intently*) Why did you come here tonight?

GRACE (*Looking away*): I've been thinking about you. I want to help—if I can.

Then, as if to dispel the seriousness of the mood, she cocks her head, grins very girl-like.

GRACE: How about it, Mr. McClintock—could I have a beer?

MCCLINTOCK: A beer? You mean here?

GRACE: I kind of like it here.

MCCLINTOCK (*Grinning at her*): Why, sure. (*He stands up and calls to the bartender, who is passing*) Hey, Charlie! Two beers, huh?

The bartender acknowledges with a wave, goes back toward the bar. McClintock sits down again and looks across the table at her.

GRACE (*Pointing to the jukebox*): How about music?

MCCLINTOCK: What?

GRACE: Don't you like to listen to music when you drink beer?

MCCLINTOCK: Music? Why . . . I never even gave it much thought. Sure. Sure we can play music.

He rises, fishes in his pocket, takes out a coin, puts it into the jukebox. We cut to a tight close-up of Fighter #2 across the room—a toothless, terribly ugly little man.

FIGHTER #2 (*Smiling*): Hey, Mountain, play "My Heart Tells Me." *There's laughter at this. McClintock quickly turns his face away, shoves a coin into the slot, indiscriminately punches a few buttons, then returns to the booth. The bartender brings over two bottles of beer, sets them down in hont of them.*

MCCLINTOCK: How about a glass, Charlie, for the lady?

BARTENDER (*Over his shoulder as he heads back to the bar*): Fancy-Shmancey.

There's another moment's pause.

GRACE: Pretty.

MCCLINTOCK (*Listens for a moment*): Yeah. Yeah, it is kind of pretty. Them are violins.

GRACE (*Smiles*): Beautiful.

MCCLINTOCK: I never paid much attention to music before. I never had much time.

GRACE: What's that?

MCCLINTOCK: Music. Just plain old music. (*He looks away thoughtfully for a moment*) The only music I know by heart really is the National Anthem, because they play it before every fight. The National Anthem. (*Grace smiles at this*) Oh, yeah—there was Smiley Collins, too.

GRACE: Who's Smiley Collins?

MCCLINTOCK: He was a fighter. He used to play a violin. (*A pause*) That's funny, ain't it? He was a fighter but he used to play a violin.

As McClintock talks we can see him losing himseli in the conversation and in the sheer delight of having a girl across from him.

GRACE: He used to play the violin? Seriously?

MCCLINTOCK: Real serious. Oh, I don't know nothin' about his violin playing, but oh, man, did that boy have a right hand! Like dynamite. He could knock down a wall with it.

GRACE: What about his violin?

MCCLINTOCK (*Interrupting her, not even hearing her*): I remember his last fight. He fought a guy by the name of Willie Floyd. Floyd had twenty pounds on him.

At this moment the bartender brings a glass, puts it down in front of Grace, then walks away. McClintock picks up her bottle and pours the beer for her.

GRACE (*Smiling*): Thanks.

MCCLINTOCK: They don't have many ladies here—that's the reason he forgets to put glasses out. (*He holds up his bottle to her glass*) Drink hearty. That's what Maish always says. Drink hearty.

GRACE (*Smiles again*): Drink hearty. Drink hearty, Mr. McClintock.

The two of them drink. His eyes never leave her face. She notices this, smiles again.

GRACE: You think a lot of Maish, don't you?

MCCLINTOCK: He's number one. They don't come like him.

GRACE: He was your . . . manager.

MCCLINTOCK (*Nodding*): Yeah, for fourteen years. He's been a real great friend, not just a manager. In the old days . . . in the old days when I was just getting started, Maish would stake me to everything from clothes to chow. He's a real great guy. (*Then he stops abruptly and stares at her*) Why ain't you married?

GRACE (*Laughs*): Should I be?

MCCLINTOCK (*Nods*): You're pretty. Not just pretty. You're beautiful.

GRACE: Thank you.

MCCLINTOCK: Pretty as a young colt. That's what my old man used to say.

GRACE: Your father?

MCCLINTOCK (*Nods*): Yeah. A girl's as pretty as a young colt, so he used to tell me.

GRACE (*Very interested*): Go ahead, Mountain.

MCCLINTOCK: About my father? Big guy. Nice old guy too. I remember once—I fought a guy named Jazzo. Elmer Jazzo. And he looked just like my old man. Spittin' image. And in the first round I didn't even want to hit him. Then in round two I shut my eyes and I—

GRACE (*Interrupts*): Mountain . . .

MCCLINTOCK (*Looks at her*): Yeah?

GRACE: There isn't much else, is there—besides fighting?

MCCLINTOCK (*Very thoughtfully looks away*): No. No, there isn't, I guess. I'm . . . I'm sorry.

GRACE: Don't be. It's just that there is so much more for you that you'll be able to find now.

They look at each other and both smile. The music is playing and they are both aware of it suddenly.

GRACE: Hey, Mountain—

MCCLINTOCK: Yeah?

GRACE: Them are violins.

They both laugh. The camera pulls away from them as they start to talk, lost in an awareness of each other and in the pleasantness of being together. We continue a slow dolly away from them, and then a slow fade-out to black. We fade on with a shot of the alley outside the arena. Grace and McClintock walk slowly away from the door, toward the street.

MCCLINTOCK (*Kicks a can out of the way*) A garden, ain't it?

GRACE: Where are the flowers?

MCCLINTOCK (*Flicking his ear*): Right here. (*Grace smiles a little forcedly*)

GRACE: It's late, Mountain. I've got to go home.

MCCLINTOCK: I'll get you a cab. (*She starts to walk away*) Grace . . . (*She turns to him*) I . . . I've had a good time.

GRACE: I have too.

MCCLINTOCK: You know when we came out of the bar I heard Charlie say that I had a pretty date.

GRACE (*Smiling*): Thank Charlie for me.

MCCLINTOCK: It wasn't just that he thought you were pretty; he said that I had a date. It's like with the music; I don't even think I ever had a real date in all this time. A real one. Not somebody I liked. Somebody I wanted to be with.

GRACE: I think that's a compliment.

MCCLINTOCK: One time . . . one time Army had a girl friend living in St. Louis. She had a friend. Army fixed me up. We were supposed to meet after the fight. These two girls were waitin' for us outside. This girl that I was supposed to go with—she takes one look at me and she . . . she—

GRACE: She what, Mountain?

MCCLINTOCK: She turned around and she ran away. She looked at my face and she turned around and ran away. (*Grace instinctively touches his arm and holds it tightly*) That shouldn't have hurt. I should have been used to it. I know what I look like. I know what I sound like, too. But it . . . it did hurt. I didn't want it to happen again, so I never let it happen.

Cut to a tight close-up of Grace as she stares at him and she wonderingly shakes her head, feeling that acme of tenderness a woman can feel for a man.

GRACE (*Softly*): The cab, Mountain. It's late.

MCCLINTOCK: Sure.

The two start walking again toward the opening of the alley.

GRACE: Remember to think about what I told you. I think you'd like working with children.

MCCLINTOCK: I'll think about it. I'll think about it a lot. Don't build me up none, Miss Grace. Don't say I'm anything special. (*A pause*) Tell 'em . . . tell 'em I fought a hundred and eleven fights. Tell 'em I never took a dive. I'm proud of that.

Grace looks at him intently for a moment and there's a continuing softness on hex face.

GRACE (*Whispers*): Sure you are, Mountain. You must be very proud.

She quickly kisses him on the side of his face, studies him for a moment and hurriedly walks away from him. He stands there touching his face, looking after her. We take a slow dissolve out to a shot of Maish's hotel room, the same night. The door opens, McClintock enters. In the room are Maish, Army and a fat man who has been sitting in a corner of the room. The fat man rises.

MAISH: It's about time. Army was lookin' for ya. Somebody said you left the bar with a girl.

MCCLINTOCK (*Grins broadly*): I want to tell you all about it, Maish. No kiddin', she's a wonderful girl. Her name is—

MAISH: Tell me later. We've got business to attend to here.

MCCLINTOCK (*Filled to overflowing*): Army, it's the girl from the employment office. Miss Grace.

ARMY: Pretty kid.

MCCLINTOCK: Beautiful. Beautiful girl.

PARELLI: How about it, Maish? I ain't got all night.

MAISH: Right away. Mountain, I'd like you to meet somebody. This is Mr. Parelli. Mr. Parelli promotes wrestling matches at Mathew's Arena.

MCCLINTOCK: I'm gladda know you.

PARELLI: Likewise. So get with it, Maish.

MAISH: We've got ourselves a nice deal here, kid. Want to tell him, Mr. Parelli?

PARELLI: There isn't much to tell. Maish here thinks you might be a good draw. Your name's pretty well known. I've seen you fight a couple of times myself. (*McClintock smiles*) Yeah, I think I can line you up with some matches. I think it might be worth both our while.

MCCLINTOCK (*His smile fades somewhat*): Maish didn't tell ya. I'm not supposed to fight any more. I don't think I can get my license back.

Parelli looks at Maish questioningly and Maish forces a smile.

MAISH: We're not talking about boxing now, kid. This is for wrestling. I told ya Mr. Parelli promotes wrestling matches.

MCCLINTOCK: Wrestling matches? I don't know how to wrestle.

PARELLI (*Laughs*): You don't have to know how. Couple hours and you can learn the holds. There's really only two big things you've got to learn in my business, kid. That's how to fake, make it look real, and that's how to land without hurting yourself. That's about it.

MCCLINTOCK: I don't get it.

MAISH: What do you mean you don't get it? He's laying it out for you. And listen to what else, Mountain. I've got a funny idea. We'll dress you up in a coonskin hat, see, and you're going to be billed as the Mountaineer. How about that, huh? Just like old times. Even buy you some kind of a big long squirrel gun or something.

There's a long, dead silence as McClintock turns away.

MAISH: Well?

PARELLI: I don't think he goes for it, Maish.

MAISH: What're you talkin' about, he don't go for it? Mountain, what've you got to say?

MCCLINTOCK: I'd lose you a fortune, Maish. I can't wrestle. I don't think I could win a match.

Parelli laughs.

MAISH: What do you mean, win a match? These are all set up, kid. One night you win, the next night the other guy wins.

PARELLI: It depends on who plays the heavy.

MCCLINTOCK: A tank job.

MAISH: Will you talk sense? This is an entirely different thing. Everybody knows there's a fix on in these things. It's a part of the game.

MCCLINTOCK: I never took a dive for anybody. A hundred and eleven fights. I never took one single dive.

PARELLI: It's like Maish says. These aren't exactly dives . . . (*Then there's a long pause*) Well, look, I'll tell you what. You guys talk it over. Give me a call, Maish, by tomorrow. I've got to know by tomorrow.

MAISH: You get the contracts ready. We'll be ready to sign in the morning.

PARELLI: Sure. Nice meeting you, Mountain.

McClintock nods. Parelli goes out. There is the offstage sound of the door closing. McClintoclc stares at Maish. Maish averts his glance.

MAISH (*With his back to Mountain*): I figure you owe it to me. (*Then a pause*) What do you figure?

MCCLINTOCK (*Nods*): I guess I do.

MAISH: So there's nothing more to it, then.

McClintock turns. His face shows an anguish we haven't seen before.

MCCLINTOCK: But, Maish, I was almost heavyweight champion of the world.

Maish turns, walks over to him and grabs him tightly. His voice is fierce and intent.

MAISH: Then you remember just that. When I stick you in a silly costume you just remember you were almost heavyweight champion of the world. And I'll remember I was the guy who managed you. We'll do this one with our eyes closed.

Then he releases him, breathing a little heavily.

MAISH: Army, take him home.

He turns his back to them. Army walks over to McClintock.

MCCLINTOCK: Never mind, Army. I'll go home by myself. (*Mountain exits*)

MAISH: He's upset—that's all. He just don't know.

ARMY: He knows. Believe me, he knows.

MAISH: But he'll come around.

ARMY: Sure he will. You'll fix it that way. You gotta knack, Maish. You violin him to death. And if that don't work, squeeze a little. Back him up. Twist it up a little for him. What a knack you got.

He turns to go. Maish's voice is soft, pleading.

MAISH: Army, stick, will ya?

ARMY: Stick?

MAISH: Help me with him. Just stay alongside.

ARMY (*Understanding now*): Partners again, huh? If he sees me, he'll move faster—that the idea?

MAISH: He'll want both of us. It'll help him, Army—a lousy one-night stand.

ARMY: Stop it! You break him into a dummy harness once, he'll stay with it. (*Pounds his fists silently*) It ain't enough I gotta watch him go down all these years. Now you want me in the pit. I gotta officiate at the burial.

MAISH: It don't have to be that way.

And now desperately groping for the words and for the first time we're listening to the mind of this man. Army grabs him by the lapels and holds on to him very tightly.

ARMY: This is a slob to you, Maish. This is a hunk. This is a dead-weight—has-been. This is a cross you got to bear? I'll tell you what he is, Maish, this boy. This is a decent man. This is a man with a heart. This is somebody flesh and blood, now, Maish. You can't sell this on the market by the pound, because if you do, if you do, you'll rot in hell for it. You understand me, Maish—you'll rot! (*He cries uncontrollably, and then stops*)

MAISH: Please, Army, for him at least. Don't leave him alone.

ARMY: Of course not. I can't leave him alone. He'll do it for you even if I'm not there. So I'll *be* there. (*A pause*) Why is it, Maish—tell me, why is it so many people have to feed off one guy's misery? Tell me, Maish—doesn't it . . . doesn't it make you want to die?

Fade out.

ACT THREE

Fade on with a tight close-up of a suit of buckskin, the coonskin hat, an old relic of a muzzle-loading long-tom rifle, a powder horn and a few other accouterments. Then we pull back for a cover shot of the room. It is a small dressing room very similar to the one in Act I. Parelli is looking over the costume and chuckling softly through his cigar. He picks up one of the legs of the trousers, examines it, laughs again, tosses it aside, then starts toward the door as it opens. Maish enters.

PARELLI (*Nodding*): Looks good. Where is he?

MAISH: He's coming.

PARELLI: The guy at the gym says he don't have those holds down at all. Didn't understand them.

MAISH: He will. Give him a little while.

PARELLI: He knows just what to do, doesn't he?

MAISH: Yeah. He's all zeroed in.

PARELLI: And this is important. When the other guy gets a lock on him or any kind of a hold, have him look in pain, you understand? That's important. He's got to look as if he's giving up the ghost. (*Then with a grimace*) Pain, you understand, Maish. Real pain. Torture. Agony.

MAISH (*Sardonically*): He'll die out there for ya. (*Then he looks out toward the open door*) How's the house?

PARELLI: The usual. Not good, not bad. They want action. It don't have to be good action but it's got to be action. So tell your boy to move around.

MAISH: I told you he knows all about it.
PARELLI: Okay.
He starts to walk by him and Maish pinches his sleeve with two fingers.
MAISH: The dough, Parelli.
PARELLI: It'll be waiting for you after the fight. I don't know how you talked me into an advance. Most people can't.
MAISH (*With a grin*): With me it's an art.
PARELLI: It must be. (*He looks at his watch*) He better get here soon. (*Then with a grin*) It's going to take him a long time to get into that outfit.
MAISH: He'll be right along. I just talked to him.
PARELLI: Okay. I'll see you later.
He goes out of the room and closes the door. Maish walks over to the table the costume is on. He picks up the pieces one by one and looks at them. He has a dull, emotionless look on his face. When he gets to the gun he picks it up, and the door opens. Army enters.
ARMY: What's the season—grouse? What you huntin', Maish?
MAISH: Right now I'm huntin' a wrestler named McClintock. Have you seen him?
ARMY (*Shakes his head*): Not since last night.
MAISH (*Slams a fist against his palm*): He's late.
ARMY: That's good to know.
Army kicks the door shut and walks over to Maish. He looks down at the paraphernalia.
MAISH (*Staring at him*): Enough to make a fuss over? (*He points to the clothes*) Is it, Army?
ARMY (*Shrugging*): I don't have to wear it.
MAISH: If you did, it would break your heart, huh?
At this moment there's the sound of the crowd from up above and both men look up and then look at each other.
MAISH: Army.
ARMY: Go.
MAISH: You know me, Army.

ARMY: You bet I do.

MAISH: I don't mean just that way. I mean you know me inside. You know how I hate this. You know how it keeps me from sleeping. You know how it eats away my stomach, Army.

At this moment McClintock enters. He smiles at Army.

MCCLINTOCK: I looked for ya. I was afraid you wasn't gonna come.

MAISH: He's here. You better get into this thing.

MCCLINTOCK: Sure, Maish. Sure.

Then suddenly his eyes fall on the coonskin cap and costume and the gun leaning against the wall. His face goes numb. He walks over to them, lifts them up one piece at a time, stares at them.

MAISH (*Wets his lips, forces a smile*): Ain't that a lark, kid? It's gonna kill 'em. Gonna knock 'em dead.

McClintock nods dumbly.

MAISH (*Continuing hurriedly*): You know you take it off when you get in. You walk around the ring a couple of times and you take it off. You don't have to wear it very long. (*His words tumble out in a torrent*) And underneath you wear Long Johns and it isn't until after the bout you've got to put the stuff back on—(*He stops abruptly as McClintock turns to him*)

MCCLINTOCK: Clown.

MAISH (*Points to Army*): He called it that. You're taking it from him. Can't you think a thought for yourself?

MCCLINTOCK (*Shakes his head*): He called it that but I call it that too. (*He nods toward the hallway*) And everybody out there will call it that too. Clown.

He puts the flat of both hands on the table, and bends his head far down so that his face cannot be seen.

MCCLINTOCK: Maish, *don't make me!*

Cut to a very tight close-up of Maish. What we see on his features is a look of pain—a kind of sudden, personal agony—and then he composes his features almost one by one and his voice comes out loud again and shrill, along with a laugh.

MAISH: What do you mean, don't make you? What am I, your father? Don't make you. You don't do nothin' you don't want to do. If you don't think you owe it to me. Okay.

There's a knock on the door.

MAISH: Yeah?

The door opens and Parelli is standing there. Behind him is a photographer.

PARELLI (*Grins into the room*): How about a couple of pictures, Maish? We ain't had any with the costume yet.

MCCLINTOCK (*His head goes up*): Pictures?

PARELLI: Part of the build-up, kid. One picture is worth a million words. That's what the Greeks say. (*Then to photographer*) How about it? You want 'em in here or out in the hall?

PHOTOGRAPHER: Out in the hall. I've got more room.

There's a long pause. Parelli waits expectantly.

PARELLI: So? What's he waiting for—a valet? Let's hurry it up.

He goes out, closing the door. McClintock rises, looks quickly at Army and then at Maish, then turns back to the table and picks up the coonskin hat, puts it on his head. Then he puts his arms into the coat and slowly puts it on. Maish turns away. We are looking from close-up at him and at his face and features as they work, and a little of the agony returns. Over his shoulder we see McClintock buttoning the jacket, then he takes the gun, looks at it. McClintock goes to the door, stops, with his hand on the knob, stands there motionless, his eyes closed.

VOICE: McClintock's on next. Let's go!

MCCLINTOCK (*Almost a whisper*): Tell 'em to go away, Maish.

MAISH: What're you talking about?

There's a loud knock on the door and this time Parelli's voice.

PARELLI: What's going on in there? What're you trying to pull off here, Maish? Get your boy out there. Photographer's waitin' for him and his match is on.

MAISH (*Raises his voice but it still comes out weakly*): He'll . . . he'll be right out, Parelli. He'll be right there. (*Then he turns to McClintock*) Mountain, you cross me now and I'm dead. Understand? I'm dead.

McClintock shakes his head back and forth, back and forth.

MCCLINTOCK: Can't. Can't, Maish. Can't.

MAISH (*Grabs him and holds him tightly by the shirt front*): You got a debt, mister. You owe me.

MCCLINTOCK: Maish . . .

MAISH: I mean it, Mountain. I've got my whole life on the line now. I can't afford to let you cross me.

McClintock shakes his head.

MAISH (*His voice desperate*): I swear I'll beat you to a pulp myself! I wouldn't have been in this jam if it weren't for you.

MCCLINTOCK (*Looks up*): Maish, I'll dp anything you want, but—

MAISH: But it bothers you too much. Well, it didn't bother you last week to stand up in a ring with your hands down at your sides and let Gibbons beat you to a pulp. That didn't bother you a bit! It didn't bother you that I had every nickel in the world tossed on a table to say that you wouldn't go three!

There's a long, long pause as McClintock's face shows a gradual understanding, and Maish on the other hand looks like a man whose tongue has suddenly got red-hot in his mouth.

MCCLINTOCK: Maish . . . Maish, you bet against me.

Maish doesn't answer him and there's another pause. McClintock takes a step toward him.

MCCLINTOCK: Maish, why'd you bet against me?

MAISH: Would it make any difference, Mountain, if I hocked my left foot to bet on you—would it have made any difference? You're not a winner any more, Mountain. And that means there's only one thing left—make a little off the losing.

McClintock takes another step toward him, and Maish, whose back has been to him, turns to face him. McClintock stares at him and his lips tremble.

MCCLINTOCK (*Finally*): You fink! You dirty fink, you, Maish! Dirty, lousy fink!

Maish's face goes white but he doesn't say anything.

MCCLINTOCK: And because I wouldn't go down—because I stood up and took it for ya, I've got to pay for it like this. (*He pulls at the costume*) Like this, Maish, huh?

He turns and walks away from him, shaking his head, trying to articulate, desperate to let something that he feels now come out without quite knowing how to let it come out.

MCCLINTOCK: In all the dirty, crummy fourteen years I fought for you I never felt ashamed. Not of a round, not of a minute. (*He turns to Maish, looks down, then across at Maish*) But now all of a sudden you make me feel ashamed. You understand, Maish? You make me feel ashamed. I'd have gone into any ring barehanded against a guy with a cleaver—and that wouldn't have hurt me near as much as this.

ARMY: Mountain, listen to me . . .

McClintock, suddenly unable to control himself any more, raises his hand and with the flat of it smashes Army across the face. Army falls backward against a table and then on his hands and knees. Maish starts toward him.

ARMY (*Raises his head*): Get away, Maish. Get away.

Very slowly Army rises to his feet, rubs his jaw briefly, looks at McClintock.

MCCLINTOCK (*In a whisper*): Army . . . Army, for the love of God—

ARMY: That's all right, kid. I rated it. I shouldn't have been here. I had no reason to be here. I had it coming. (*He turns accusingly toward Maish*) Go on, kid, go on and leave. Take what precious little you've got left and get out of here.

McClintock turns slowly and walks out of the room. After a few moments' pause Army turns and goes to the door, looks down the corridor and says:

ARMY: Good night, Mountain.

From down the hall at this moment comes Parelli—shouting, fuming, sweating. He arrives at the door almost too excited to speak.

PARELLI: He's walkin' out! The boy's walkin' out! What's with this? What's with it?

Parelli walks over to Maish, sticks his finger in his chest and prods him.

PARELLI: You know what I'm gonna do to you for this, don't you? (*Maish keeps his head down. Parelli shouts*) I'm gonna see to it that you don't get a license to walk a dog from now on. You don't think I will? You don't think I will, Maish? Well, let me tell ya—

The camera moves back over to Army, still standing by the door.

ARMY (*Very quietly*): Goodbye, Mountain.

Dissolve to the bar. Dolly down through it until we reach the rear and a group of men talking fight talk, all of them living in a little round-by-round dream world. McClintock stands a few feet away from the fringes, staring at them and listening. Finally one of them says loudly enough to be heard:

FIGHTER #1: That wasn't his name, Stevie. His name was Hacker. Charles Hacker. And he never fought Louis. (*Then he looks up over the cwwd and sees McClintock*) How about that, Mountain? You know him. Hacker. Charles Hacker. He never fought Louis, did he?

The crowd turns and stares toward McClintock, who takes a step toward them.

MCCLINTOCK: No, he never fought Louis. He fought me, though.

FIGHTER #2: No kiddin', Mountain. No kiddin'? How'd you do?

McClintock takes another step and the men make way for him until he is standing almost in their midst.

MCCLINTOCK: It went three rounds. He was always strong in the beginning.

FIGHTER #2: Yeah, yeah. He was always strong.

MCCLINTOCK: He come in at me and he don't box none. He never did.

Then he stops abruptly and he stares around the circle of faces. We pan, with his eyes, to take in a shot of each face, and then end up on a tight close-up of his own as he suddenly, slowly, shakes his head.

MCCLINTOCK: I . . . I don't remember it. I'm sorry but I don't remember it.

He turns, walks away from them and goes over to the bar.

MCCLINTOCK: Give me a beer, will you?

BARTENDER: Sure, Mountain. Comin' up.

The camera pulls away from the shot of Mountain sitting at the bar until he is framed in the window. It continues to pull away until we pick up a shot of Army across the street staring toward the window. Then we see Grace approaching him.

ARMY (*Turning to her*): I'm over here, Miss.

GRACE (*Approaching him*): You're . . . you're Army?

ARMY: That's right. Thanks for coming.

GRACE: Tell me what happened.

ARMY: What happened is that he walked out of a match. But I want to make sure he *keeps* walking. I didn't want him to stop at that graveyard over there.

GRACE: How can I help?

ARMY: You can help him by not conning him. He's been conned by experts. He's riddled. He'll listen to you. When he gets out of there head him toward Grand Central Station and give him this. (*He takes out an envelope and hands it to Grace*)

GRACE: What's that?

ARMY: That's a train ticket to Kenesaw, Tennessee.

GRACE (*Studies the envelope for a moment*): Is that home?

ARMY (*Very quietly*): It was once. Maybe it'll be again. (*Then there is a long pause*) Do you love him, Miss?

GRACE: I don't know. I feel so sorry for him, though, I want to cry.

ARMY (*Touches her arm gently*): You tell him that, Miss. Tell him you think he's a decent guy, and you like him. But tell him, for the time being, you don't come with a kiss. He's been chasing a ghost too long now, and the next thing he's got a hunger for he oughta get. It's only fair. Thanks very much, Miss. (*Then there is a long pause*) You're a brick.

He walks away, and as he does so Mountain comes out of the bar. Grace walks across the street to him. The camera stays with Army looking at the two of them over his shoulder. We can see them talking but can't hear them. Then we see Grace hand Mountain the envelope. He takes it in his hands, they exchange a few more unintelligible words, and then Mountain starts to walk away. Grace turns, starts across the street and then stops. Cut to close shot of Grace as she whirls around. Cut to very tight close-up of McClintock's face in the lamplight of the street—the broken nose, the misshapen ears, scar tissues, bruises that never healed and never will any more, the battered ugliness that is a legacy of the profession.

GRACE: Mountain!

Mountain stops, turns to her. Grace runs over to him and very lightly kisses him. Mountain reaches up and touches his face wonderingly.

MOUNTAIN: Thanks for that. (*Hesitantly, terribly unsure, he kisses her black*) Thanks for not running away.

GRACE: When you get home, when you get settled, write me and tell me what's happened.

MOUNTAIN: When I get home? (*He looks down at the ticket*) I'll go there, but . . . I don't know if it's home any more.

GRACE: Go find out. You look for it, Mountain. Because wherever home is, it's not over there. (*She points toward the bar. Then she hands him a slip of paper*) It's my home address, Mountain. Write me.

He very tentatively takes the paper and then slowly shakes his head. He crumples it in his fist. She grabs his hand and guides it into his pocket.

GRACE: Goodbye, Mountain.

He turns and walks slowly away. Grace watches him for a moment and then starts to cross the street toward the camera. Halfway across the street her head goes down and her hands are at her side. She blinks her eyes and very quietly begins to cry.

Dissolve out on her face to cover shot of the dressing room in semidarkness. Maish sits alone by the rubbing table. The only light comes from the bulbs out in the hall. Army appears at the door, peers inside, sees Maish and enters.

ARMY: You gonna stay here all night?

MAISH: That's a thought.

ARMY: Fox is out there with some other guys.

MAISH: It comes, I figured.

ARMY: If it comes, it comes. Get it over with, Maish.

Maish studies Army intently.

MAISH: Hey, Army, what are you going to do?

ARMY (*Smiles*): Tomorrow I'll be for hire. You know, Maish—you said so yourself—I'm the best cut man in the business. And after I patch up my millionth cut, maybe somebody'll give me a gold watch.

MAISH: You're needed, aren't you?

ARMY (*Nods*): A little bit. C'mon, take your lickin' and let's get out of here.

The two men walk out into the hall. Fox and two other men are waiting.

FOX: Maish . . .

Maish stops dead in his tracks, staring straight ahead. Fox comes up behind him.

FOX: This ain't a payoff, Maish. Relax.

MAISH: You here to give me a medal? (*Looks at the other two men*) It must be heavy.

FOX: We're here to give you a proposition. This is Mr. Arnold.

A heavy-set man comes up alongside. He is the same man we saw in the bar.

MAISH: Mr. Arnold and I have met. You work for Henson?

MAN: Yeah.

FOX: Here's the proposition, Maish. It's a sweetie, a real sweetie. *With this he propels the other man to the front and into the light. He is a young fighter in his late teens. At a first, sudden glance there is a striking resemblance between this boy and Mountain—as Mountain must have appeared very early in the game.*

MAISH (*Looking at him briefly*): What's he want—a haircut?

FOX: Mr. Henson would like him managed. Managed good.

MAN: Groomed—that's the word.

MAISH: Why me? That's the question.

FOX: He wants a nice dependable guy with know-how, Maish, and you're it. Some guy who knows his business—and who'll go along.

MAISH: I know my business.

MAN: And you'll go along.

MAISH: I've got a choice, huh?

MAN: Yeah, you've got a choice. You take this kid and make a fighter out of him, or the Commissioner gets a phone call that a certain manager's been making bets.

FOX: That's against the law, Maish.

MAISH: Is that a fact?

FOX (*Seriously*): You know it is. Parimutuels at race or harness tracks—that's the only place betting is permitted. They'd take away your license, Maish. It wouldn't be just a suspension, Maish—it'd be permanent.

Maish takes a step closer to the young fighter and studies his face in the light.

MAISH: Where're you from, kid?

FOX (*Interjects*): It's an amazing coincidence. It really is, Maish. He's from Kentucky. You could call him Mountain.

FIGHTER: Who's Mountain?

MAISH (*His lip trembles perceptibly*): He was a good, fast kid. All hands and feet with his mouth full of teeth and he talked like General Lee. Like you do—like you look. You better go back there and work in a drugstore. (*He turns away*)

FIGHTER: To hell with the drugstore. I want to be a fighter.

Maish studies him very intently for a moment, looking him up and down.

MAISH: You want to be a fighter? All right, check this. There's eight champions in this business. Everybody else is an also-ran. There's the good and the bad in it. The good's great, the bad stinks; so we'll give it a whirl. (*There's a long pause*) Army, you're needed.

Army, who has been standing by the door, sighs resignedly, joins Maish, and the two of them walk down the corridor with the young fighter in the middle.

We lap-dissolve to a film clip of a train and a section of a car. McClintock sits across from a woman and a little boy.

BOY (*Suddenly leaning over to Mountain*): Hiya.

MCCLINTOCK (*Looks down in surprise*): Hiya.

The boy picks up one of McClintock's hands and examines it.

BOY: You're a fighter, aren't you?

MCCLINTOCK: Yeah, I was a fighter.

BOY: I can tell by your ears. You got big ears.

There is a long pause, and very slowly Mountain grins.

MOUNTAIN: Yeah, cauliflower ears.

The boy returns his grin and we can see Mountain relaxing for the first time.

BOY: How do you get ears like that? I'd like ears like that.

WOMAN: Jeffey, don't be rude.

MCCLINTOCK: That's all right, Ma'am.

The boy goes over to sit next to McClintock.

BOY (*Suddenly assuming a fight position*): Like this? This the way you do it?

MCCLINTOCK (*Straightening the boy's hands*): No, you hold your right down, keep that left up, hunch your shoulder like this. Okay. Now lead. No, no, no—with the left, and don't drop your right. Okay, now lead again. (*The boy does all this, delighted*)

WOMAN: I hope he's not bothering you.

MCCLINTOCK: Not a bit, Ma'am. I like it.

WOMAN: Where are you heading for?

There is a long pause. McClintock reaches into his pocket and takes out the slip of paper that Grace had given him, unfolds it and smoothes it out.

MCCLINTOCK: Home. I'm heading for home. I don't know for how long, 'cause I . . . 'cause I'll probably be taking a job one of these days soon. Work with kids like Jeffey here.

BOY (*Impatiently*): C'mon, Champ. Let's you and me spar.

MCCLINTOCK: Okay, Champ. Now lead again. That's right. Right from the shoulder. Okay, now cross with the right. No, no, no—don't drop your left. That's right.

The camera starts to pull away very slowly from them until their voices cannot be heard and all we can see is the pantomime of Mountain McClintock and the little boy fighting the Mountain's greatest fight. We take a very slow dissolve to the film clip of the train as it disappears into the night. Fade out.

AUTHOR'S COMMENTARY ON REQUIEM FOR A HEAVYWEIGHT

TELEVISION shares one thing in common with motion pictures: its reluctance to tackle some areas of drama that are too specialized in terms of audience approach. One such dramatic background is the field of prize fighting. Hollywood makes no bones about its reluctance to take on what A.J. Leibling refers to as the "Sweet Science." Box-office receipts over the years tell an expressive, if depressing, story of how limited in appeal is the art of fisticuffs in terms of the drama. With very few exceptions, most prize-fight pictures lose money. Television holds much the same opinion. Television plays based on prize fighting are rarely successful, and within television's limited physical framework any attempt to simulate professional fighting always looks stagy and sometimes ludicrous. Beyond the physical limitations is the fact that most prize-fight stories follow a familiar line, and it is rarely that you find one possessing a fresh point of view, a different set of characters, or an unusual premise. Seemingly soldered onto stories of the fight game as permanent fixtures are the crooked manager, the girl who wants the guy to quit before he gets punchy, the unscrupulous promoter who sells fighters at the market place by the bleeding pound, and a whole line of equally unpalatable sub-humans whose stench must necessarily be part of the atmosphere.

When I first began noting down the early beginnings of *Requiem*, I had one basic idea. This was to slant a story of the fight game from a fighter's point of view. I wanted to analyze a human being who fought for a living but who was nonetheless a human being. I wanted a guy who would act, react, feel and think without sounding like the stereotyped, cauliflower-eared, punchy human wreck who has now become so familiar that he is funny. I wanted the dull, slow, painfully halting speech to elicit sympathy and understanding, but not a laugh. I've always liked fighting and fighters. As a nineteen-year-old paratrooper fighting at 118 pounds (a weight class known in those days as "Catchweight"), I had several fights of my own, and I know a broken nose when I feel one. I'd been trained in the Army by an ex-pro who had had sixty-eight fights of his own, and I had a reasonably good working knowledge of some of the ins and outs of the profession.

So *Requiem* was born. It was a story of a fighter that began in the brief moment after his last fight. Its basic premise was that every man can and must search for his own personal dignity. I thought there was particular poignance in having an ex-fighter begin this kind of quest because his background provided him with the least possible chance. Mountain McClintock represents the average fighter, the also-ran; he is one of the vast army who never become champions and who are lost to memory as one by one they fall by the ringside. What seems to give this idea the stature of tragedy is that the business of prize fighting never allows an alternate preparation for another field of endeavor. To be a fighter you have to live as a fighter. Everything you do, every action you take, every moment you live is part of and preparation for the next fight on the schedule. And when your career is finished, the profession discards you. In terms of society it discards a freak, a man able only to live by his fists and his instincts, and too often a battered hulk covered with the unhealing scars that are the legacy of his trade. So this was to be the story of Mountain McClintock, who walks into a world that is unfamiliar and foreign to him.

There are times in a career of a writer when a single performance in a play can add such a fantastic dimension and moving quality that the role appears to have been molded into the actor's shape.

This was the case when Jack Palance played Mountain McClintock. His interpretation left nothing to be desired. His was the slow, halting speech of the overfought and the outfought fighter who'd had too many fights for too many years. His was the incoherent, inarticulate yearning and hunger to belong to something he didn't understand. Here was the heart-rending picture of a misfit battered into a shapeless ugliness and yet possessing a simplicity, a humility and the kind of beauty that comes with decency. All this Jack Palance gave to Mountain McClintock. As of this writing he has been given a number of awards for his gift, and this brief tip of the hat is my own public acknowledgment of his contributions.

I think there were good moments in *Requiem* and some near-great ones. My favorites are the ones in which Mountain goes to the employment office and is interviewed by the compassionate case worker, and the curtain of the scene, when the girl (beautifully played by Kim Hunter) tells Mountain not to worry, just to give them time because they'll come up with something that he'll like. I feel that here was one of the most effective moments in the play. Mountain looks at her with that strange, intense look and says he doesn't want much—just the heavyweight championship of the world! The will-o'-the-wisp, the errant Erewhon in each man's life too high to reach, too far to grasp. For Mountain McClintock it was a title and the respect that went with it. Unfortunately, one of the tenderest moments in this play can only be suggested in the reading and really not properly experienced. This was the scene in the bar when the girl goes to Mountain and for one of the few times in his life the ex-fighter responds to someone else's gentleness and care. Ralph Nelson, who directed the play so well, outlined the scene carefully, choosing a perfect musical score to underlie the playing. This score, a composition called "The Seine," provided a beautiful obbligato to the words of the scene. (I have to point with pride to the scene in the dressing room when Mountain is bulldozed and conned into turning wrestler. Face to face with manager Maish, he realizes for the first time how he is being used and how the last shred of dignity that he clutches is being sold down the river. The confrontation sequence between the two men is, I think, a helluva powerful piece of writing.)

Unfortunately, the final act of *Requiem* is the weakest. I think the train sequence with the little boy spelled out the finish too blithely and too patly. The play should have ended when Mountain leaves Grace and heads for the railroad station. To have carried it a step beyond this was unnecessary and diluting. I had always had qualms about this scene but was willing to let it go in the hope it would play better than it read. Unhappily, it was as anticlimactic as I feared.

The only other really weak element in terms of the writing of *Requiem* was the constant inclusion (practically by the ears) of the hoods who pop in and out of dark shadows and provide a sort of menacing counterpoint. In *Requiem*'s initial conception there were really no hoods. The manager's motives stem from his fear of being exposed because of his betting, and consequently having his license revoked. There was no threat of the physical violence with which we ultimately did play it. Personally, I felt that this was lily-gilding and a little cheapening, a manufactured menace that had no real reason to be there. It probably clarified the character of Maish, however, in that it gave the audience a definite physical clue to the man's fears and weaknesses. The character of the girl, Grace, probably could have been better drawn. She's quite understandable, I think, up to a point, but I imagine an audience should be told more explicitly why she felt a compulsion to go to the saloon to help a broken-down fighter. Her compassion was not misplaced when Mountain came to her, but it's a moot question as to whether or not compassion in itself could have made her feel obligated to walk into a saloon crowded with pugs to follow through on what is really just another unemployment case.

There was another moment in the playing of *Requiem* that perhaps cannot be perceived in the reading. This was in the final act, when Grace takes the train ticket from Army and then gives it to Mountain, telling him that home is not in the saloon, the graveyard where punchy wreckages fight their lives away inside their heads. Ralph Nelson gave this a beautiful touch by playing that scene shooting from inside the saloon through the window to the alley outside. We didn't hear the voices of Mountain or Grace—we just looked at them, and on mike at the time was the tawdry, stupid, wandering prattle of a punch-drunk fighter that played constantly under the scene as we watched Mountain make a decision out in an alley. Unquestionably every script must gain something from its visual performance. But *Requiem* was luckier than most. It had the benefit of creative direction and superb acting performances—and how much do you pay for this on the market? There just isn't any price tag big enough.

Patterns seemed always to obscure everything else I had done, and I was desperate to change this situation. *Requiem* turned out to be exactly the right play to do this. Its enthusiastic reception when it was produced—and, later, the Emmy awards it received—proved to a lot of people that *Patterns* was not a happy accident. And, most important, it was proof to *me*.

ABOUT THE AUTHOR

ROD SERLING *was born in Syracuse, New York, on Christmas Day, 1924. He grew up in Binghamton, New York, graduating from Binghamton Central High School and enlisting in the Army on the same day, January 26, 1943. He served three years in the Army paratroopers—two of them in the Pacific—and came back to attend Antioch College in Yellow Springs, Ohio, graduating with a B.A. in 1950. He holds an unofficial record for produced television plays—over a hundred in eight years of writing for the medium. His awards include two Emmys for best original teleplay writing, 1955 and 1956, for* Patterns *and* Requiem for a Heavyweight; *two Sylvania awards for the same years; the first Peabody award ever given a writer in the seventeen-year history of the award; a Christopher award for the motion-picture version of* Patterns; *the 1956 Writers Guild award for best hour or more teleplay writing—*Requiem for a Heavyweight. *He's married, has two daughters—Jody, five, and Nan, two—and lives in Westport, Connecticut.*

Made in the USA
Las Vegas, NV
10 May 2024